ONCE UPON A STAGE

ONCE
UPON A STAGE

The Merry World
of Vaudeville

by Charles and Louise Samuels

ILLUSTRATED WITH PHOTOGRAPHS

DODD, MEAD & COMPANY
New York

ISBN: 0-396-07030-2
Library of Congress Catalog Card Number: 74-11502

Printed in the United States of America
by The Cornwall Press, Cornwall, N.Y.

For our children
Joan Katherine and Robert

Acknowledgments

Basic research for this book was done at the Library of Performing Arts with the cooperation of Paul Myers, Curator of the Theatre Collection, and his staff. We found the files of *Variety, Theatre Magazine,* and other theatrical publications invaluable, along with thousands of newspaper and magazine clippings in the Locke Collection and additional sources there. Also helpful were such standard reference works as *Current Biography, Oxford Companion to the Theatre,* Mark Sullivan's *Our Times,* and Daniel Blum's *A Pictorial History of the American Stage 1900 to 1950.* Other works consulted include Douglas Gilbert's classic study of Vaudeville's early days, *American Vaudeville; Show Biz,* by Abel Green and Joe E. Laurie; Laurie's *Own Vaudeville;* and *Variety's Cavalcade of Music,* compiled by Julian Mattfield.

Rich material, but not always accurate, was found in the life stories of vaudeville stars and other show people. Among the best were *Some of These Days,* by Sophie Tucker in collaboration with Dorothy Giles; *Clowning Through Life,* by

Eddie Foy and Alvin F. Harlow; *Weber and Fields,* by Felix Isman; *Much Ado About Me,* by Fred Allen; *My Wild and Wonderful World of Slapstick,* by Buster Keaton and Charles Samuels; *Goodness Had Nothing to Do with It,* by Mae West; *Will Rogers,* by Donald Day; *Castles in the Air,* by Irene Castle; *I Love Her, That's Why,* by George Burns with Jane Ardmore; *A Hell of a Life,* by Harry Richman and Richard Gehman; *Oscar Hammerstein I,* by Vincent Sheean; *F.F. Proctor, Vaudeville Pioneer,* by William Moulton Marston; *To a Lonely Boy,* by Arthur Hopkins; *The Merry Partners, the Age and Stage of Harrigan and Hart,* by Ely Kahn; *W.C. Fields, His Follies and Fortunes,* by Robert Lewis Taylor; *Ziegfeld Follies,* by Marjorie Farnsworth; *The Spice of Variety,* edited by Abel Green; *Max Gordon Presents Max Gordon,* by Max Gordon and Lewis Funke; *They All Sang,* by Edward Marks and A.J. Liebling; *Fanfare,* by Richard Maney; *The Great Comedians Talk about Comedy,* by Larry Wilder: *American Vaudeville as Ritual,* by A.F. McLean; *So Far, So Good,* by Elsie Janis; *The Bennett Playbill,* by Joan Bennett.

Also enlightening were books by Brooks Atkinson, John Mason Brown, Percy Hammond, and other critics, plus *Mirror for Gotham,* by Bayrd Still, *The Gangs of New York,* by Herbert Asbury, and *The Great Mouthpiece,* by Gene Fowler.

Contents

1. Beginnings   1

2. The Singing Women   50

3. Legends   90

4. Bring on the Clowns   115

5. "The Asylum Had to Keep Him"   148

6. Minstrels and Musicians   191

7. The Making of Times Square   220

8. Showcase for Stars   247

   Index   269

CHAPTER ONE

Beginnings

THE VERY SHORT OLD FELLOW standing on the corner of Fifty-seventh Street and Sixth Avenue had the shoulders of a blacksmith and stood as straight as a king. Though it was one of those unbearably hot New York afternoons, he looked cool and impeccable in his black derby and heavy woolen suit. For years on the vaudeville stage he had worn a derby much too large for him, with baggy pants and a coat so long that it reached almost to the floor.

What really made Jimmy Savo unmistakable were his huge, childishly impish black eyes. When a passerby recognized him and stopped, the eyes seemed to grow even larger and his mouth curled upward. Then Savo would roll his eyes in delight, bow low, lift his derby high and present a lollipop, saying, "An Oscar for you, my friend."

Children also got lollipops. They were enchanted by his little pantomime, though they'd never heard of Jimmy Savo. Their elders who read that Jimmy had a gangrenous leg amputated were delighted to see him doing a bit of his old routine. Savo, once a Bronx shanty child, had started in vaudeville billed as "a miniature strong man and juggler of everything from a feather to a piano." As a pantomimist many rated him second only to Charlie Chaplin.

Harland Dixon, the two-a-day's greatest eccentric dancer, also had troubles with his legs late in life. He had been among the most dedicated workers in show business, and spent hours each day perfecting inventive new routines.

But now, in his early eighties, the great hoofer limped and carried a cane. A friend who met him at the Lambs Club couldn't help exclaiming, "It sure must be rough on you not working."

"What are you talking about?" demanded Dixon. "I work all the time."

"How can you dance if you can't walk without a cane?"

Harland led him to an empty room. "Put out that chair for me in the center of the floor and I'll show you."

The friend complied. Harland Dixon sat down on the chair, put his cane aside, and stamped out a wild, rhythmic tattoo on the floor.

"I do this out in Queens where I live. I demonstrate all kinds of steps this way at affairs of the Elks, Knights of Columbus, American Legion post dances, and parties of any other fraternal, community, or charity group that asks me. My feet haven't gone back on me even if my legs have."

Like Savo, Dixon was doing—for nothing or for peanuts —the old vaudeville stuff which had once earned him $1000 a week.

❖   ❖   ❖

In the early fifties Buster Keaton, who had learned his trade as a child in vaudeville, was lying in a California hospital desperately ill; his life was despaired of. One day his agent came in waving a contract at Buster. "Do you want to lie here until you croak, Buster? Or would you prefer to get up and work as technical director on the Buster Keaton story that Paramount just bought. Donald O'Connor is going to play you."

In practically no time, Keaton got dressed, checked out of the hospital, and was on the way to the studio to start his new job. He worked and prospered for many years after.

These three stories tell something about the spirit all big-time vaudeville headliners and standard acts shared. Except for poverty-stricken childhoods and brilliant talent, they had little else in common. Above all, they were individualists, creative artists who were unique and unforgettable.

One thing is certain: no big-timer ever quit before he had to. In spite of its death in 1932, a victim of the Depression and the competition of talking pictures and radio, vaudeville's greatest and most adaptable stars had become big-name attractions in Hollywood, on the air, in Broadway musicals, and in night clubs.

But the others all dreamed of the day when big-time vaudeville would be revived. Such former great headliners as Georgie Jessel and Lou Holtz made costly attempts to bring it back to life. Each failure was another cruel disappointment to the hundreds of acts not able to adapt to the new forms of entertainment. While waiting for the resurrection of vaudeville, many had bought bars and small hotels and whenever they got the chance they kept their talent fresh and ready by performing in shows they staged themselves.

The big names who were making several times more than their highest vaudeville salary said they missed the warmth and feeling of closeness with the audience that they'd enjoyed at the two-a-day theatres.

Radio proved the coldest medium since it rarely had a studio audience. Those who succeeded in pictures quickly discovered that in Hollywood they were not allowed to select their material. The director decided not only what they were to do, but how. It was utterly unlike vaudeville where the artist could express himself exactly as he wished with the audience as his only judge.

Working in the huge movie cathedrals was no fun either. Georgie Burns complained that orchestra pits were so wide he couldn't even see the people in the front row. The stages themselves were so vast that the star felt shrunken, all but lost. About the biggest of these, The Roxy in New York, Joe Frisco warned his fellow artists, "Don't be caught on the Roxy Stage without bread and water!" Eddie Leonard, vaudeville's great minstrel, was told he could have only ten minutes to do his stuff at another cathedral. His manager moaned, "My God! It takes Eddie Leonard ten minutes just to bow!" When the manager of the Fox in Brooklyn kept cutting the time of his headliner, George Jessel, Georgie revenged himself by telling the audience about it, instead of doing his act.

All vaudevillians, even the acrobats and animal trainers, were called artists. During the half century from about 1875 to 1925 that variety shows or vaudeville reigned as America's favorite entertainment, there were 25,000 artists working part- or full-time in 4000 theatres ranging from lodge halls and converted barns to marble palaces. They played one-night stands in villages, split weeks in small towns, and spent whole weeks in cities. On the big time they played two shows a day, on the small time three or more.

These theatres were the massive training field where the novice trouper learned his business, measured his talents, discovered his limitations. In no other branch of show business—except possibly the ballet—were the apprentice years more arduous. The young vaudevillian had to learn to do everything by himself, all by himself.

They had no teachers or schools. And all but a handful were born and grew up in slum neighborhoods. They came from broken, overcrowded tenement homes hounded by poverty, drunkenness, or worse. A great many were orphans. The overwhelming majority of them began as child street entertainers, dancing on corners, singing in the backrooms of bars, serenading in backyards for housewives who threw down pennies wrapped in scraps of newspaper. They competed at amateur night shows in dusty 'd theatres where the grand prize was usually $5. If the second prize was a silver watch, the kid who won it immediately sold it back to the manager for a dollar. They played at house parties, weddings, and silver anniversaries for whatever they could get. They were wild with joy when they found a singing job at a nickleodeon for $12 a week. While they sang, colored slides to illustrate the number would be projected on a bedsheet used as a screen. They went on at the end of each show—their warbling was expected to discourage patrons from staying for a second showing of the flickering movies.

On being booked into real theatres, the young vaude-villians had to discover by themselves how to dress, walk on the stage, talk to the audience with precisely the right mixture of humility and pride, find the right songs and material, and judge how to use these and their talents most effectively. Every audience was different and the kid actors learned how to sense the mood of the crowd out front and, if necessary, change their whole approach. Sick or well, happy or miserable, hungry or not, they had to come out smiling and charm that audience on the spot.

The whole business was an endless elimination contest. Troupers who survived had to roll with the punches and duck the haymakers, top the hecklers out front, and turn the crowd to laughing at *them*.

Beside the audience—Oscar Hammerstein II once called it the "big black giant"—there were bad-tempered, dictatorial house managers who took delight in cutting your material, hounding you, doing everything possible to break your spirit.

One house manager might send a bad report on your work to the circuit's central booking office—and that could result in cancellation of your entire route.

Charm the "big black giant" the artist must, no matter who the folks out front were. Tough miners, farm families, millworkers, or city wise guys—somehow he had to contrive to make them fall in love with him at first sight, laugh at his jokes, gasp at his hoofing and acrobatics. As singers or dancers the girls had to make them all sigh and go dreamy over their looks, songs, and fast stepping.

It took about ten years for most of the successful artists to make the long, bruising trip from street corner clowning and amateur nights to the big time. Once they made it most of them stayed there.

And one of the finest tributes to these performers was paid by Arthur Hopkins in his memoir *To a Lonely Boy*. Like many other outstanding theatrical figures Hopkins had gotten his training in vaudeville before becoming one of Broadway's leading producers. He started as a press agent for a vaudeville theatre, became a booker, then produced one-act plays for the two-a-day. He said he had never realized how much genuine art there was in vaudeville until he came in contact with the artificialities of the legitimate theatre.

The vaudeville actor created. The legitimate actor strutted. Vaudeville was a severe test. The actor had but little time to establish his character. His act had to hold from the first. Vaudeville audiences became quickly restless. The actor was allowed no credit for previous performances. It meant nothing to a Tuesday night audience that his act had gone well on Monday night and the reviews were good. This was Tuesday night and a different audience. It had to be done all over again. Letdown, the curse of the legitimate theatre, was unknown to him. He always did his best. He had to. He could not recline on an established success and a run-of-the-play contract. He could not afford to be bored. Even if his act had been played for years it had to remain fresh to him. That was why he was welcomed again and again by audiences who had seen him many times. Seeing was always a new experience. He knew he could not get his effect by trying, but by being. If he tried too hard, he lost his audience. His only safety was in submerging himself completely in the character.

Brooks Atkinson, the most perceptive stage critic of his time, wrote that vaudeville was "A brilliant form of stage entertainment that expressed skill, personality, and ideas . . . and presented some of the most talented actors of all time."

When one considers the slum background of these charmers who had run wild in sad, sordid streets as little boys and girls and sometimes had to steal to eat, one understands why they never let down once they'd made it. They were people who had escaped a dark hell and entered a heaven alive and gay with light. It was their pleasure and pride to project warmth, laughter, and elation. And what they gave out across the footlights worked like magic. To the folks out front it was as though they too had triumphed over their troubles and sorrows and were up there singing like angels, dancing like wizards, cracking jokes that lifted the roof, performing feats of magic, mind-reading, tightwire walking, bareback riding, juggling, ventriloquism, acrobatics. Vaudeville drew on all of the other performing arts and presented opera singers, ballet dancers, circus stars, sports champions, minstrels, serious musicians as well as pianists who stood on their heads as they played, Swiss bell-ringers, troupes of midgets from Germany, tumblers from Japan, tabloid Wild West shows, and the great stars of the legitimate theatre. It featured horses that could count, female impersonators, trained seals and skating bears, monologists, harmonica players, xylophonists, fire-eaters, unicyclists, and everything else that was new, startling, or sensational—and best of all, unbelievable.

For half a century vaudeville's children introduced and made popular most of the hit songs, some that are now perennial favorites. Vaudevillians also wrote their share of those hits, patriotic, topical, religious, comic. They were first to sing the sentimental numbers about mothers, the girl left behind, and the charm of a humble childhood home as being better than all of the world's gold. Later on they ushered in the age of syncopation, jazz, and the wilder and ever wilder music of the twenties.

They set the whole country singing to the music of piano, mandolin, and guitar. Everywhere one could hear the sweet and melancholy, happy, snappy, and gay music first heard in vaudeville: at house parties, on porches, at picnics, in saloons, with or without musical accompaniment. Those songs remained among the most treasured youthful memories of the three generations who sang, fell in love, and had the best times of their lives while singing or listening to vaudeville's music.

Vaudeville also set the youth of the land to dancing everything from the waltz to those wild, whirling twenties steps.

Vaudeville did not, of course, originate in the United States. The word vaudeville is derived from the French *vau-de-vire,* which is believed to have been first used in the fifteenth century to describe the drinking songs written by Olivier Basselin, a millowner in the Valley of the Vire and Virène, in Normandy. These were sung by the *Compagnons Gallois,* or boon companions, after the day's work was done.

But vaudeville didn't start in the fifteenth century either. Under other names or no name at all, most of the specialties of variety entertainment were being performed before recorded history. Will Durant, the distinguished historian, points out in his massive *Story of Civilization:*

Probably long before he thought of carving objects or building tombs, man found pleasure in rhythm, and began to develop the crying and warbling, the prancing and preening of the animal into song and dance. . . . He sang before he learned to talk, and danced as early as he sang. . . . He developed it from primordial simplicity to a complexity unrivaled in civilization and varied it into a thousand forms. . . . From the dance, we may believe, came instrumental music and the drama.

In jungle settlements there were special people who danced and chanted prayers to the music of drums, flutes, and stringed instruments in order to propitiate the gods who would bless their harvests and put to rout their enemies.

Magicians, acrobats, contortionists and mountebanks, dancers, singers, and musicians entertained in the courts of early Oriental potentates.

Mimicry and animal acts were developed in ancient Rome. Both were enormously popular, partly because of the city's large polyglot population who knew only a few Latin words. Exotic beasts for the animal acts were trained in the zoological gardens of the emperors and wealthy citizens.

The animals learned "skilful exploits or merry pranks": apes were taught to ride dogs, drive chariots, or act in plays; bulls let boys ride on their backs; sea lions were conditioned to bark in answer to their individual names; elephants danced to cymbals struck by other elephants or they walked a rope or sat down to table or wrote Greek or Latin letters.

The art of magic, or conjuring, was known in Egypt before Biblical days. There is a reference in Exodus to magicians who tried to imitate the miracles of Moses—

these "may have been feats of manual dexterity without mechanical apparatus." Such magicians, like those in Greece and Rome, dazzled their audiences with optical illusions. So did the antics of the jugglers. Just as old is the conjuror's ability to eat fire, read minds, and cause both people and objects to disappear mysteriously.

The vaudeville arts have been practiced the world over in all ages since by wandering minstrels, gypsies, fiddlers, singers with voices that enchanted all who heard them, on country roads, in city squares. They brought the beauty of far-off places to bazaars, fairs, and festivals. In England, the first indoor variety shows were seen at the old roadside inns whose owners became famous for their hospitality.

These entertainments proved so popular that the innkeepers were encouraged to acquire the property next door and install a stage plus tables and chairs where their patrons could sit, eating and drinking, while listening to the show. Usually a passageway led right to the inn. Victorian times brought the gilt and satin theatres called music halls as their replacements.

But in both England and France, numerous restrictions, including licensing laws, delayed managers of variety shows from building or leasing theatres to compete with the established legitimate showhouses.

In the United States vaudeville also had a long and difficult struggle before it won public approval. Unfortunately the word itself was first used to describe the entertainment in the country's most sinister dives, those on the waterfront of our seaports and in honkytonks on the Old Frontier. Here patrons were fed rotgut whiskey (sometimes knockout drops also), got cheated at rigged gambling games, and were robbed by the house floosies with the connivance of waiters and bartenders. And most of the shows that took to the road during the decades when these sucker traps ran wide open had card sharps, thieves, and sluggers along for something more than the ride.

From Colonial times fiery preachers and their flocks made war on every kind of entertainment. They never stopped warning their congregations that they'd burn in hell forever if they set foot inside a theatre, a circus tent, or attended any other sort of show.

Despite these exhortations, there was a growing audience for every sort of traveling attraction, from dog-and-pony exhibits to medicine shows to circuses. These early performers offered joy, gaiety, color, excitement, and laughter—clowns were never hesitant about risking their necks to get a laugh.

P. T. Barnum, who entered show business in 1835, tried to win over the Puritans by calling his congress of freaks, fakes, monstrosities, and exotic animals a museum, an educational exhibit.

Other showmen tried to appear equally respectable. One circus owner whose outfit was touring through Ohio advertised "the chaste behavior of the entire company" and vowed there would be "no females in tights." But one clergyman denounced this show as "calculated to amuse the giddy and excite the laughter of fools."

The growth of entertainment after the Civil War caused the clergy to increase their exhortations. In 1867 Reverend Frederic Denison, historian of Westerly, Rhode Island, declared:

Various wandering companies, bands, troupes, mostly comic and vulgarly theatrical, are often flaunting their handbills on the streets and inducing vulgar crowds to attend on their mimicries. Usually the characters of the actors comport with the scenes. Such coarse buffoonery, set off by stale songs and monkey dances, only degrades and corrupts the spectators.

A mild example of the kind of song that offended him went like this:

> *Well, I went home one night,*
> *As drunk as I can be.*
> *I seen a head on a piillow*
> *Where my head ought to be.*
>
> *Come here, my little wife,*
> *And explain this thing to me.*
> *How come this head on the pillow*
> *Where my head ought to be?*
>
> *Ah now, my dear husband,*
> *I'll explain this thing to thee,*
> *It's nothing but a cabbage head*
> *That your parents sent to me.*
>
> *Well, I've travelled this world over*
> *A hundred miles or more*
> *But a moustache on a cabbage*
> *I never seen before.*

Casanova-like capers and the theft of everything in sight were attributed to the troupers by hotel men, storekeepers, and farmers with buxom young daughters. Sometimes pregnant girls blamed a thespian, even when the boy on the next farm was responsible. Publishers of small town newspapers were gypped so often that they demanded cash in advance and charged higher rates for all theatrical advertising.

When it was announced that a troupe was on its way to give a show, word was passed to housewives: "Take in your linens—the players are coming." To this advice was often added: "Take in your clotheslines too. Their managers are with them."

In many towns boarding housekeepers kept signs in their windows declaring "No dogs or actors allowed." Suckers who had bought cure-alls from medicine shows that did nothing to ease their pains and aches resented being fooled and cheated for the rest of their lives. All traveling shows were blamed for what every other kind of troupe had done.

The worst offenders of all were the circuses—even though circus performers personally maintained the highest moral and ethical standards. Yet with the circuses traveled con-men, sneak thieves, card sharps, pickpockets, and professional burglars. All of them paid the circus owners for various season privileges, including the right to strip clotheslines and burglarize local houses while the show was on. One thousand dollars a season was the average price of a ticket-selling booth in a good location. Ticket sellers didn't receive wages—they made their living shortchanging the customers.

Weight guessers patted a mark's hips and sides before making his guess to find out which pocket the man's wallet was in. Sideshow talkers (often mistakenly called barkers) also helped the pickpockets. While telling the crowd of the wonders of his exhibit, the talker gravely warned that there were pickpockets following the show despite the management's vigilance. He cautioned them to be careful. Many in the crowd would feel for their wallets, thus tipping off the dips who were eagerly watching.

Ahead of the circus would be a fixer, elegantly dressed in a silk hat and swallow-tail coat, and with an unctous, suave manner, who carried a thick wad of banknotes. His job was to bribe the sheriff or chief of police in each town not to interfere with the swindling. If there was an incorruptible official in charge, the fixer sent word back to the troupe to lay off crooked work there.

Hell often broke loose, however, when the outraged local citizens took matters into their own hands. They would descend on the show armed with clubs and knives, sometimes guns. As a boy acrobat with a wagon-show, Fred Stone saw more than half of his company arrested and jailed for several weeks. Two narrowly escaped lynching. That fight had started because the show-owner's daughter refused to pay a laundry bill.

As teen-agers, Weber and Fields had to run for their lives when townspeople in a lonely whistle-stop (David City, Nebraska) raided their circus, battered the roustabouts and performers, and burned down the main tent. An elephant flailed away at the local citizens with a tent-pole and sent them screaming with terror back to Main Street. This furious scrap had started when roustabouts beat up a David City man for complaining that he'd been cheated out of $20 by the show's three-card monte dealer.

Until quite a few years after the Civil War, variety shows remained raw, vulgar, and rowdy—an entertainment for rascals and bummies, male and female. It was not until 1881 in New York that Tony Pastor, a merry little minstrel, presented the first clean vaudeville show ever seen in the

United States. Tony never called it vaudeville; he felt the word was French and unmanly, or "too sissified." When his experiment made money, shrewd managers all over the country rushed to imitate him. One of their problems had been attracting audiences to matinees. Most men worked in the afternoons and respectable women shunned such places.

Pastor's achievement was making his variety shows entertainments for the whole family. He publicized a no-drinking no-smoking policy with no vulgarity or rough talk permitted on the stage. He also promised that mashers who attempted to approach women in the audience would be promptly ejected.

But what really brought the ladies to his matinees was his offer of door prizes to the first twenty-five women who appeared and purchased tickets for an afternoon performance.

James Ford, one of the era's most intuitive journalists, years later wrote, "The most important moment in the development of the theatre in the country was that in which Tony Pastor first gave away his coal, flour and dress patterns to secure the patronage of respectable women."

Ford also recalled that the art of "feeding" by the straight man was developed at Pastor's. A straight man or woman builds up the comic partner's jokes by listening in fascination, asking questions, and repeating the funny one's lines to give them increased importance.

The more successful showmen who followed Tony's example and put on clean shows made millions of dollars. They quickly grasped the fact that such family entertainment could be booked into a whole chain of theatres, multiplying their profits over and over again.

But like pioneers in so many other fields, Tony Pastor ended up almost broke.

*   *   *

Antonio Pastor was born in New York's Greenwich Village in 1837. His father was Spanish, his mother American. At six he made his debut singing in a church for a temperance society. Shortly afterward he was featured at Barnum's Museum as an "infant sensation." When he joined a circus that was going on the road he was still a child. He demonstrated his versatility by excelling as a tumbler, performing as a bareback rider and ringmaster, plus singing and playing an instrument in the minstrel show, at the time a feature of every circus. But like all contemporary child circus performers, Tony was assigned menial and dirty jobs, such as sweeping up, emptying slops, and washing out the clothes of the adult performers.

Pastor loved being a minstrel and a master of ceremonies. At 24 he was doing both jobs as well as writing many songs in his own Music Hall on Broadway, in downtown Manhattan. When business declined, he moved to another spot and, after some years, to a third location on Broadway.

The shows he put on in his first music halls were neither better nor worse than those on the Bowery. The air was thick with tobacco smoke, and the fumes of the cheap whiskey sold at the bar in the hall reached everywhere. The same kind of crowd was out front at the tables, howling at leg displays, and off-color jokes. Later on Pastor preferred not to discuss his early efforts as a showman.

The small theatre where vaudeville was made respectable

occupied a corner of Tammany Hall, on Fourteenth Street near Third Avenue. Since no copyright laws existed then, showmen pirated the Gilbert and Sullivan comic operettas with sensational box office results. These had become so familiar to theatregoers that some managers were even succeeding with travesties of them.

So Tony tried to play it safe when he opened his "Tony Pastor's New Fourteenth Street Theatre" with a burlesque version of *The Pirates of Penzance*. This acquainted New York with the matchless blonde beauty, Lillian Russell. "Airy-fairy" Lillian was born in Clinton, Ohio, and at the moment was living in Brooklyn. She was introduced by Pastor as "the beautiful English ballad singer whom I've imported at great trouble and expense. Ladies and gentlemen, I give you a vision of loveliness with a voice of gold, Miss Lillian Russell."

Lil, who became the darling of the age and its supreme symbol of feminine beauty and serenity, attracted attention but not enough to keep the show running for very long.

It was on October 24, 1881, that Tony presented the show which was to make theatrical history. He shut up the barroom. Smoking was forbidden. Most important of all, suggestive jokes and gestures were banned. A sign backstage announced that any performer guilty of vulgarity, obscenity, or irreverence would be fired on the spot. Tony, a deeply religious Catholic, had a shrine backstage where he prayed every night.

The headliner on that first clean show was Ella Wesner, a male impersonator who sang English ditties and did a monologue. With her on the bill were the French Twin Sisters, a girl instrumentalist, Dan Collyer—a character comic—and a knockabout comedy team. Tony himself sang, danced, and acted as master of ceremonies. The talented acts were delighted to play clean vaudeville; the less gifted ones were not. Without suggestive dancing, obscene gestures, and gamey stories they were sunk and knew it.

Though the show was well-received, it took time to convince New York's respectable housewives that they would be safe from mashers at Pastor's. Mashers—men who approached women on the street and tried to lure them to saloons—had been receiving much notoriety from the newspapers for some time and every nervous old maid (an old maid then being any unmarried girl of 21 or more) carried an extra hatpin to defend herself if approached by one of these scoundrels. The dailies warned that if a decent girl let down her guard she was likely to be drugged, seduced, and would wake up either in a brothel or on a boat heading for the white slave marts of South America. Such bounders were said to be everywhere: on the streets, in parks, on the buses, and especially in theatres.

At Tony's "Ladies Matinees" the valuable door prizes given to the first twenty-five women patrons included whole hams, bags of flour, and sacks of potatoes. But the women started coming to the matinees in droves only after he advertised silk dresses among the gifts.

"That really got 'em," said Pastor, "no woman in this world can resist getting a silk dress free."

Tony loved children and he gave them a Christmas party every year at his theatre. He needed such extra box-office lures. Because his theatre was small, he had to charge fifty cents for matinees and $1.00 at night for the best seats. Even the best acts got little money in the eighties and nineties and Tony could put on eight acts for $250 a week.

For years his variety shows were the best in the country. All the great acts of the day—The Four Cohans, Weber and Fields, Sam Bernard, The Three Keatons among others— appeared regularly at Pastor's. Nat Goodwin, later America's favorite light comedian, then an elocutionist, made his New York debut there. Lillian Russell kept returning to sing and thrill audiences with her hefty figure, facial beauty, plus gorgeous costumes and jewels. *The Old Homestead,* a heartwarming play that Denman Thompson wrote and later starred in for over twenty years, grew out of a one-act sketch which had been a hit at Pastor's.

Pastor was as big an attraction as any of his headliners. The short, paunchy, jolly man had merry black eyes and moustaches that would have aroused the envy of a Hungarian hussar. He wore tall boots, a high hat, and a long black coat. He was always at the theatre and came to know his regular patrons by name. Tony would greet them at the door and inquire about their children.

Actors loved Tony. They didn't resent his offering them a cut salary when he knew they needed work or were between engagements. His handouts to old timers down on their luck—he gave them work when he could—more than made up for his shrewdness they thought.

More than anything else, Pastor enjoyed being a performer. That may be why he never attempted to start a chain, though he saw other managers who followed his lead in producing clean vaudeville getting rich by expanding their holdings.

Each summer when he closed his theatre, Pastor would

sign up a company and go barnstorming with his "Tony Pastor's Minstrels." He claimed he knew fifteen hundred songs and would sing any of them on request. The hundreds of numbers he had written included patriotic songs plus ballads praising home, mother, and the simple life. One told the story of the wandering son who had not had time to write but in the end came home to die. He also wrote topical numbers, songs about Edison's latest invention, and the newest fads. One of these was credited with helping Abram Hewitt, a businessman, win an election for Mayor of New York. The big lines at the end were: "What's the matter with Hewitt?" to which the listeners would reply with a thundering: "He's all right."

After the turn of the century things started to fall apart for the much-loved Tony Pastor. The neighborhood deteriorated and his carriage-trade customers began to patronize Hammerstein's Victoria uptown. Two nearby vaudeville houses got other customers away from him because they charged only ten to thirty cents. A third neighborhood house, the Union Square Theatre, was taken over by the growing Keith Circuit which repainted and refurbished it and dressed its ushers and doormen in resplendent military uniforms. Actors' salaries also had gone so high that it now cost Pastor $2500 a week to stage a show—ten times what it had been when he opened his theatre.

In 1908, Tony's tiny theatre closed because he was unable to pay the rent. That summer, a New York *Times* reporter found him in his office at the empty showhouse. Even the old billboards and autographed photos of the great acts that had worked for him were gone.

Pastor explained that he came there every day to read

his mail and the newspapers. The reporter wrote, "Tony could not stop haunting the theatre that had been his life." His tribute to Pastor's sixty years in show business, published on August 6, 1908, covered a whole page.

Nine days later the merry old minstrel died. He left an estate of less than $9000.

With one exception the managers who made millions of dollars out of vaudeville were those who started with one theatre and expanded into a circuit of many. The exception was Oscar Hammerstein who owned the Victoria, the theatre on Times Square which supplanted Pastor's as the showcase of the big time.

Success as a vaudeville manager usually was achieved by tough-minded men who combined a gift for organization with a flair for putting on weekly shows that built, act by act, in excitement and entertainment value, plus an instinct for hiring and training aides who turned into first-rate showmen.

It was not easy to stage, week after week, eight or nine-act bills that pleased vaudeville fans. The minor acts, of course, went on first; there was an intermission; and the headliner came on next to last with an animal or athletic turn concluding the show. Between acts requiring a large stage there had to be turns that could work in "one" which was the narrow space in front of a curtain depicting a street scene. This gave the stage hands time to arrange the props behind the curtain. Acts that flopped at the opening performance of the week on Monday afternoon could be cancelled on the spot. The house manager simply removed the act's photographs from the displays in the lobby and had an assistant hand them to the crestfallen artists in their

dressing room before the next show. Far more difficult sometimes was finding a substitute act that was better. When a
bill did not play well the manager had to change the running order of the acts. Invariably that enraged the artists
who considered the switch to an earlier spot degrading.

The artists who developed box-office draw were among
the biggest headaches of vaudeville managers, large and
small. They considered accepting a cut in pay, inferior billing, or second-rate dressing rooms professional suicide. Mae
West and Joe Frisco were among the headliners who stayed
unemployed for years rather than agree to a pay slice.

Rare indeed was the star of the two-a-day who gave the
moguls of vaudeville credit for building up the circuits
that could guarantee him forty weeks of solid booking year
after year. They knew that they would be dropped cold the
moment they lost their following.

The managers, for their part, united every time the artists threatened to strike. If one manager wanted an unim-
portant act kicked out of vaudeville the others agreed not
to book the turn. Headliners who could fill their theatres
were treated the opposite, like so many temperamental opera
stars, and got away with murder. While uniting against the
actors the managers never stopped fighting among themselves
and were forever bringing legal action against one another,
or theratening to. In other words, they acted exactly like
power-hungry businessmen in more mundane trades.

There were exceptional showmen in the group who were
not tough or tricky with the actors: Percy Williams, John
Considine, and Marcus Loew were three. Loew had been
a furrier until he was 35, then got into vaudeville management after running a string of nickleodeons. He became

king of the small time, owned hundreds of vaudeville theatres, and also built movie cathedrals while organizing the
Hollywood gold mine called Metro-Goldwyn-Mayer.

The remarkable Percy Williams was the son of a Brooklyn physician and started in show business as an actor with
a third-rate traveling troupe. While on the road Percy noticed little wagon shows that used entertainers to attract
crowds to whom they sold elixirs, Indian tonics, and other
cure-alls were cleaning up.

So Williams organized a wagon show of his own and made
money peddling a "liver bag" which he guaranteed would
cure rheumatism. His father had sold such bags to his own
patients. Made of flannel, they were stuffed with herbs and
strapped across the liver and were welcomed by so many
rheumatics in hick towns that soon Williams was able to
put on a free traveling tent show with a whole company
of singers, dancers, minstrels, and musicians.

His success with the liver bags encouraged Williams to
market an electric rheumatism belt. The belt's batteries
packed a walloping shock that would make the most rheumatic man straighten up—at least for a time. He put this
on the road from a wagon show, with his spiel preceded by
blackface entertainers who sang, danced, and told funny
stories.

According to one vaudeville historian, Williams had a front
man working a few days ahead of his troupe. This fellow's instructions were to pick out the most rheumatic person in each
town and give him or her a belt free of charge. The lucky man
or woman was asked only to walk to the wagon when it
arrived. On seeing their crippled neighbor walking as straight
as George Washington himself, the belts sold to other arthritic

sufferers as fast as they could be handed out. Williams rapidly organized other wagon shows, with as many as sixty at one time coining money for him.

In the late nineties, Williams built a Brooklyn beach resort he hoped would put Coney Island in the shade. But mosquitoes ultimately defeated him. Winters he dabbled in small theatre ventures and opened a beer-hall. And in 1902 he opened the Brooklyn Orpheum, the best-appointed and most beautiful showhouse for big-time vaudeville in the country. During the next few years, Williams built or acquired eleven more handsome theatres. In 1912, he sold his chain to the Keith Circuit for $5,250,000.

When Percy Williams died in 1923 he left to the artists of the theatre his beautiful estate in East Islip, Long Island. He had told his lawyer, "The actors helped me make my money. Why shouldn't I give it back to them? I want them to enjoy my home after I'm gone." For over fifty years artists down on their luck have been able to spend their declining years in luxurious surroundings.

None of the other vaudeville managers felt that much gratitude toward their artists. Most of them were salty characters with larcenous backgrounds. Among the most colorful were the three who started their vaudeville circuits on the West Coast: John Considine, Martin Beck, and Alexander Pantages.

Considine may have been the only pioneer vaudevile manager who went to college. He was born in Chicago of respectable Irish parents and left for Seattle just before the Klondike Gold Rush. He began his career running a resort that was not respectable.

The Comique was a box-house. It was called that because

besides the usual honky-tonk attractions it had partitioned-off boxes on the balcony that overlooked the dance floor. Each box could be curtained off so a patron and the house girl of his choice could enjoy privacy as they sipped champagne and made love on the bed in the rear of the box. During the Gold Rush years, Considine and his brother George made a fortune in Seattle, which was then the great embarkation port, on the patronage of the Rushers trade and that of sailors of all races. Outside they hung a sign reading: "They're beautiful. Come in and pick one out."

Despite his profession, Considine, as a good Catholic and family man, was highly esteemed in that roaring Northwestern seaport. He was a soft touch for anyone in need and his word was his bond. Thousands of Seattle people stood by Considine when he went on trial for the murder of William Meredith, the city's police chief, a known grafter. The boxhouse owner's story was that Meredith had tried to shake him down for an excessive payoff. On being refused, the chief charged that Considine had ruined Mamie Jenkins, a 17-year-old contortionist in the Comique's show. A gun battle followed in which Meredith was killed. When Considine was acquitted, most of Seattle cheered.

In 1902, Considine bought an interest in Edison's Unique Theatre and acquired a few others as well. Then, with the backing of Big Tim Sullivan, the New York politician, he rapidly built the Sullivan and Considine Circuit with vaudeville theatres all over the West and as far East as Louisville, Kentucky. Considine is said never to have forgotten a friend or a favor, and a contract with his circuit was the only one you could borrow money on. Considine never cancelled an act.

Not so trustworthy was Considine's Seattle rival, Alexander Pantages, who built up a circuit that made him a multimillionaire, without taking time out to learn to read or write.

He was born in Greece in 1871 and christened Pericles which he then changed to Alexander after hearing about Alexander the Great's conquest of the world. His early life would have killed any ordinary man. At seven he was being worked and starved to death on a rotting Greek freighter, and he spent the rest of his childhood slaving on other ships that took him to all parts of the Orient. In his teen years he worked a donkey-engine in the malaria-ridden jungles of Panama where the French were making their disastrous attempt to build a canal. Pantages had not much more luck as a young man in his twenties on the West Coast. In Seattle he was a shoeshine boy, in San Francisco a waiter and a professional prizefighter.

But when the Klondike gold rush started Pantages had $1000 saved up. He bought a ticket to Alaska yet he lost all but seven dollars of his bankroll the first day out to professional gamblers. Hundreds of other adventurers died on the way from the blood-chilling cold and other privations, but the hardy little Greek managed to reach Dawson and get into the action. He worked as a waiter and later a bartender.

After seeing drunken miners spill gold dust on the sawdust-covered floor he took on the job of sweeping up nights after the place closed. He made extra money pimping for his sweetheart, Klondike Kate, the most popular prostitute–entertainer. He also talked Kate into loaning him all of her money. With this he opened his own music hall. When a gold strike was made in Nome, the Greek went there, leaving Kate flat broke. In Nome he opened his first theatre, selling tickets for

$12.50 each. He was prospering until the pickings got lean around Nome and the gold miners, his best customers, began leaving town in droves. Pantages joined them.

In Seattle in 1902 he opened a combination shoeshine parlor and fruit store next to Considine's theatre. Soon Pantages has his own tiny theatre across the street and the battle was on, intensifying as both spread out acquiring theatres. They played all sorts of tricks on each other to win away the acts that were box-office. If one learned that the other had a big act coming in, he would contrive to meet the artists and have his truckers move their props and scenery to *his* theatre, and vice versa. If the act protested, it would be offered a bigger salary. Pantages got into such a rage with one musical group that refused to switch that he threatened to burn their instruments.

Another trick the Greek played on the artists was to book an Eastern act for fourteen weeks though he really had thirty-two weeks open. The fourteen weeks always ended on the West Coast. Pantages would give the act a few days to realize they might have to pay their fare and other expenses to get back East, then would offer them the remaining eighteen weeks at a salary cut of 25 percent. They usually took it.

A shrewd showman, Pantages sometimes booked notorious people who had become front page news. When Ed Morrell, a member of the Evans–Sontag gang of train robbers, came out of prison after sixteen years in solitary confinement in San Quentin, Pantages signed him to a contract. Morrel, who claimed no other human being had ever survived that long in a dungeon, was a hit. He described how he had clung to life and sanity by imagining himself free and holding conversations with dear friends and relatives on the outside. Audiences liked the act, possibly because it proved what we all like to believe: that one's mind can triumph over anything.

Far more daring was Pantages's booking of Fatty Arbuckle the movie comedian who had been falsely accused in 1921 of killing Virginia Rappe, an extra. Arbuckle's studio had been so intimidated by the flood of anti-Arbuckle mail that it barred him from the screen for life and burned all of his films after calling back those in circulation. After being tried three times, Arbuckle was acquitted but the public's attitude failed to change. In 1924, Pantages gave Arbuckle his comeback chance and did good business with him as a headliner.

When he was well on in years, Pantages was sued for a fortune by his old flame, Klondike Kate. Later he was also accused of trying to seduce an aspiring young actress in his office, and was acquitted only after weeks of scandalous publicity.

The feud with Considine ended happily when the Greek showman's daughter, Carmen, married John Considine, Jr., in the best Romeo and Juliet tradition.

Martin Beck, the Pacific Coast showman who built the Orpheum Circuit, was a Czech who came to the United States as an actor in a German musical troupe. His tempestuous personality was almost as interesting as his spectacular career.

An outgoing man, Beck was quite secretive about his age and exact birthplace. He did admit the day was August 31. Men close to him suspected this confession occurred because Martin, an impulsively generous fellow himself, did not wish to deprive any of his admirers of the pleasure of giving him a birthday present each year. Beck said his father was a trader which, of course, could mean anything from a dealer in precious jewels to an old rags and bones peddler. He claimed he had been a tough boy, quick with his fists, and difficult at school, yet brilliant. His first disillusionment came after he won a gold medal. When he tried to sell it to a pawnbroker, he was told it was worthless. Beck said he had graduated from a dramatic school and then joined a troupe that toured South America before coming to the United States. It went broke and was stranded in Chicago.

Beck always claimed that he had mastered six languages in his youth. His competitors said that he spoke twelve, since Martin could bewilder all comers with double-talk in each. Nevertheless his linguistic ability got him nowhere at first in the Windy City. To avoid starving, he tried all sorts of ill-paid jobs, including door-to-door peddling of crayon drawings. He was overjoyed when he got a chance to work as a $12-a-week waiter in a beer hall, grandly named the Royal Music Hall. Tips were plentiful but he got none from Martin Downey, an actor playing there. When Beck brought a martini in a soda pop bottle, Downey gave the greenhorn a kick, something he began to regret when Beck started booking acts into his first vaudeville house. If Martin Downey ever played the Orpheum Circuit, it must have been under an assumed name.

During the 1893 World's Fair Beck, still a teenager, was a waiter at Engel's, the city's busiest beer and music hall. His efficiency at hauling the brew got his pay increased to $20 a week and tips fell to him in a silver shower. Later he helped manage the hall, worked as a part-time bartender, and booked the entertainment. He soon had enough money to buy a beer joint of his own, and put in a show featuring a comedian, two soubrettes, and a piano player.

At first he charged no admission. But when the show began drawing so many customers that they drank up all the beer on hand each night, he imposed a small admission charge. The difficulty for Beck in managing his bar was that it was located across town, miles away from Engels, where he still kept his job.

Having observed how much money light-fingered bartenders and disloyal waiters steal, he raced back and forth across Chicago several times a day to check on both places, using a bicycle to save carfare. For all of his hard work, the depression of 1897 put him out of business but this disaster led to Beck's big chance.

Unable to find anything worthwhile in Chicago, he agreed to manage the touring Schiller Vaudeville, which was headed for San Francisco. There he got a better job running the vaudeville entertainment at Gustave Walters' Orpheum, a Saloon Concert Hall. Soon afterwards, Morris Meyerfield and Dan Mitchell, whom Walters owed $50,000 for liquor, took it over. They knew nothing about show business and kept Beck on because they liked the way he was handling the entertainment end.

In 1899 this Orpheum became the first house in the great Orpheum Circuit which was to dominate the big time west of Chicago as long as there was a big time. Beck organized a corporation with Meyerfield as president, himself as vice-president and general manager, and ran the whole show.

A terrific salesman, Beck visited one Western city after another. In each he called on the leading businessmen and talked them into backing a local Orpheum. He promised to build a beautiful theatre that would present the finest of entertainment and add to the community's prestige and culture.

In addition to their financial assistance there were other advantages gained in lining up these important businessmen. They helped him select the right site plus a trustworthy contractor and aided him to obtain quickly the needed building permits, and to cope with labor problems and graft-hungry politicians.

Later, in association with Kohl and Castle, who ran a string of theatres in the Chicago area that included the attractive Majestic, Beck organized the Western Vaudeville Managers Association (WMVA). Until then his circuit and theirs had booked their acts through Keith's United Booking Offices. After the WMVA was in operation Beck was able to control the booking of all big-time vaudeville west of Chicago.

In 1905, he moved his headquarters and the WVMA to New York.

Showman Beck had the idea that larger audiences would be attracted to his vaudeville theatres if what was called high-brow entertainment were added to the usual assortment of comedians, woman singers, acrobats, song-and-dance teams, jugglers, and all the rest. Beck was the first big-time manager to hire 15-man orchestras for his houses. He was scornful when associates predicted that ballet, opera singers, and Broadway's dramatic stars in first-rate one-act plays would be unappreciated by two-a-day fans. He declared, "Well, let's educate them."

His greatest booking achievement was signing Sarah Bernhardt. He had to pay the world's most famous performer the record-breaking salary of $7000 a week. It was a tremendous achievement and gave vaudeville a prestige it had never enjoyed before.

Martin Beck, who brought a great deal of beauty and prestige to the big time, was the sort of eccentric businessman who on occasions drove both his colleagues and his rivals all but witless. Yet each time when he seemed just about to ruin himself with some whim or bit of stubbornness, his shrewd side would assert itself and save him.

He had a sense of humor, but never when the joke was on him. In restaurants and other public places, Beck would shout insults to his subordinates and associates but was outraged when they responded less than graciously.

To a good many vaudevillians, Beck seemed the ideal showman, having both a genius for organization and a true passion for offering first-rate entertainment in ideal surroundings. Despite his easily aroused temper he was extremely generous to his business associates and aides and enabled a good many of them to become wealthy.

Martin Beck was a rarity among the big-time moguls since he was a scholar of sorts, a collector of art and rare books, an opera lover, and a linguist whose six languages were German, Hungarian, Portuguese, French, Italian, and English. Other managers were always complaining that his knowledge of languages gave him a big advantage on his frequent trips to Europe to sign new headline attractions.

Beck was also an oddity among scholars, being a prankster, a braggart, an early aviation enthusiast, a demon pinochle player, and a jubilant 60-mile-an-hour racer of motor cars at a time when that was really scorching it up. He did not always keep his car on the road. Once he knocked over a telephone pole; on another wild ride he flattened a barn.

Martin Beck was shaped like a pouter pigeon whose bulge had slipped down to his waist. He was five-eight but his corpulence made him look shorter. Beck's face also was like a bird's, with its large beak and sleepy, close-set eyes. He wore pince-nez glasses and for years parted his hair in the middle. One of his boasts concerned his ability to work eighteen hours at a stretch without tiring. His associates were impressed until they discovered that every day he sneaked off to a secret hide-away in a hotel for a rubdown and several hours sleep.

Beck's interest in women was inexhaustible. It may have had something to do with his being physically unattractive. He would turn around and watch every woman who passed by, regardless of looks, shape, size, or age. It was a strange com-pulsion for a powerful figure in a profession that attracted more beauties than the royal courts of Europe ever saw.

The gifted performer, Joe Laurie, Jr., remembered being in Beck's office when Martin bawled out three acrobats who had just arrived from Europe for signing a year's contract with his circuit for $175 a week. He told them they couldn't eat de-cently, clothe themselves properly, and pay traveling expenses on so small a salary. He ordered another contract written. It called for a salary of $350. Hundreds of artists were grateful to Beck for such kindnesses. Though scores of others considered themselves victims of his unpredictable outbursts of rage.

There was no such division of opinion among artists about the hated B. F. Keith and E. F. Albee, the two New Englan-ders whose circuit in the end controlled all of the country's big time and much of the small time vaudeville. Except for their origin and the fact that both had been circus grifters, they didn't seem to have much in common.

Keith, who was ten years older than Ed Albee, looked and often behaved like an underpaid grocery clerk. Albee seemed to be the brain and spark-plug of the team, taking all the adventurous steps, making all the big moves.

Some of the men who had made deals with Keith and Albee said that was a delusion. Among the showmen who were im-pressed by both partners was R. H. Burnside, a canny Scot, who was Charles Dillingham's right-hand man for years. After prolonged negotiations to sell them Dillingham's Hippodrome in Cleveland, Burnside, who prided himself on his craftiness, said: "I'll take on either of those fellows alone, but deliver me from sitting betwen them. They act like conjurers. I came out only with my eye-teeth. But they got my watch, my shirt, and my pants."

Benjamin Franklin Keith was born on a farm at Hillsboro Bridge, New Hampshire, in 1847 and didn't get into variety entertainment until he was in his mid-thirties. He had run away with a circus at 14, been a mess-boy on a coastal steamer for two years, then went back to the circus. His new job was selling a phony blood tester which he bought for a dime and sold for a dollar, and more when he could get it. The tester was a small round glass bowl, partly filled with water and red dye, with a closed spout at the top. When the mark held the tester, the heat of his hand quickly made the water rise up into the spout. Keith said this proved the mark had high blood pressure and that if he owned a tester he could check up on his blood pressure every day, saving endless doctor's fees.

Keith was in his thirties and married with one child in 1883 when he quit the circus and (with a partner) opened "Keith's Museum" in Boston, next to the old Adams House. This was in a store that was 35 feet deep, 18 feet wide in front but only 6 feet wide in the rear. Keith started with a single exhibit: "Baby Alice," a prematurely born, two-week-old black baby who weighed only a pound and a half. In his pitch, Keith claimed Alice was so small that she could fit inside of a milk bottle. But Baby Alice grew so fast that in no time she was no longer box office and Keith's partner walked out in disgust.

B. F. quickly found another. This second partner had a very short bankroll judging from the exhibits he financed: monkeys, exotic birds of strange plumage, relics from the Greely Expedition to the Arctic. In the front of his store-theatre Keith installed an orchestrion, a barrel organ that produced the music of an orchestra.

John Royal, an early aide who became a manager of the Keith theatres in Cleveland and, decades later, an NBC vice-president, always marveled at Keith's showmanship in putting on a dancing chicken act. The chicks were induced to do a gavotte by heating the metal plate on the bottom of their their cage. But so little revenue came in that Keith's new partner soon withdrew.

There are conflicting accounts of the precise date Ed Albee joined this shoddy show. But almost from the moment he did, the money started to roll in. Albee was always willing to let the older Keith take the bows as long as he did not interfere too much with the actual operations, the acquisition of other theatres, and the building of new ones. In 1904, more than twenty years after Albee had become his general manager, Keith gave an interview to the Boston *Herald* that filled two solid pages in its Sunday magazine section but scarcely mentioned Albee. Keith also managed to overlook Tony Pastor in the long *Herald* piece, claiming: "The first real presentation of vaudeville was given in a room above my museum. It had a seating capacity of 123, and the stage was two and a half feet high. The actors, performing on this, could touch the ceiling with their fingertips."

Edward Franklin Albee was born in 1857 of an old and

wealthy family in Machias, Maine, a barren, windswept coastal village where his father owned a shipyard. During the American Revolution Albee's great grandfather, Nathan Albee, had distinguished himself in a 1775 sea battle with the British fought off Machias.

The Albee family was shocked when Ed, at 17, joined a circus as a laborer. His arrogance and airs of superiority soon offended the other roustabouts and, to keep him in his place, they had him assigned to the most back-breaking job on the lot—raising the center pole of the big tent.

Albee surprised them by taking it in his stride.

The same overbearing manner plus his willingness to work hard, together with Albee's gift for fast talk, soon got him promoted to cashier in what was called the outside ticket booth. This was set up on the road from town and was the first booth the customers saw. There were short-change artists in the other booths but the outside one was the biggest money-maker. Tickets bought there cost ten cents extra because they entitled buyers to enter the tent at once, without waiting on line, to get the best seats and visit the menagerie and freaks before the rush started. The real money came from short-changing. Albee quickly mastered the tricks of palming coins and folding over dollar bills so the mark counted one bill twice, while being hustled along by the capper behind him. If the mark managed to get back and complain, Albee's regal bearing and bored manner often discouraged him. If not, and he looked like real trouble, Albee would deftly deposit the demanded amount in a corner of his counter without being seen, then point to it disdainfully. "It was waiting for you all the time, my friend." Turning to the man behind him, he'd say, "How many do you want?"

Ed also proved very persuasive when it was necessary to cope with sheriffs waving writs of seizure for unpaid bills. He was a circus executive when, after seven years, he quit; he had decided he wanted a show of his own.

Ed was 26 when he first saw Keith's pitiful little museum, and walked in. Without asking for a job, he went to work, moving things around and performing other chores with Keith's three employees.

When someone asked Keith who the new man was, Keith said "I dunno." Albee, of course, was hired and proved to be such a brilliant showman that he was shortly afterwards made manager.

His first suggestion was to throw out the smelly old stuffed animals and replace them with beautiful wax models which he offered as "Living Statues."

His next idea put the struggling firm in the money. Gilbert and Sullivan's *The Mikado* was doing a big business at $1.50 top at the Holly Theatre down the street. Albee convinced Keith that they could clean up at their tiny theatre with the same show at twenty-five cents a ticket. "We'll do a short version of it and do four shows a day," he said.

Albee, at very little expense, transformed the front of their store theatre into a "Japanese Garden," putting in bamboo matting, low tables, temple bells, and screens. He added a touch of class by hiring a couple of pretty, vaguely Oriental girls dressed in kimonos to serve tea to the patrons.

When the show was ready, Albee himself went out into the street to harangue passersby, including many on their way to the Holly. "Why pay $1.50 to see *The Mikado* at the Holly when you can see the very same show at our theatre for only twenty-five cents?"

The four shows played to packed houses, making so much money that they were able to send another Mikado company on the road. This troupe also earned a solid profit and the team was on its way.

The first real Keith vaudeville theatre was the Bijou in Boston, a once magnificent house that was falling into ruin. They did most of the refurbishing themselves with heavy help from Mrs. Keith.

B. F. Keith, whose name later became a symbol for elegance and class entertainment in show business, was a fussing, fretting, fix-it-yourself man. He walked around the Bijou in overalls, carrying hammer and nails with which he repaired chairs, and boarded up broken places in the walls. Mrs. Keith saved the wages of a charwoman by scrubbing the floors and dusting the seats herself. Like the wives of theatrical managers in other cities, she also ran a boarding house for actors on the bill, calling it "The New York Hotel."

As a fervent Catholic, Mrs. Keith had the respect of Boston's priests and bishops. It was financing from the church that got the Keith organization started and kept it going all through its early years. However it was always the glib Albee, an Episcopalian, who made the sales talk that got the backing.

Mrs. Keith and the Catholic church were blamed for the sign backstage at all Keith theatres that read:

> Don't say 'slob' or 'son-of-a-gun' or 'hully gee' on this stage unless you want to be cancelled preemptorily. Do not address anyone in the audience in any manner. . . . If you have not the ability to entertain Mr. Keith's audience without risk of offending them, do the best you can. Lack of talent will be less censured than would be an insult to a patron. . . . If you are guilty of uttering anything sacrilegious or even suggestive,

you will be immediately closed and will never again be allowed to appear in a theatre where Mr. Keith is in authority.

Minor acts complained repeatedly that while headliners were forgiven for breaking the rule, the less important turns found that if they tried it, they would be barred for life. It also angered them that when sexiness was presented as art, the firm encouraged its flaunting—as with "living statues" acts in which men and women posed as figures in classic sculptures, with a layer of white powder or paint over them, and very little else.

When the headline act of Annette Kellerman, the shapely Australian aquatic star, flopped, Albee ordered mirrors set up all around the stage. Miss Kellerman appeared in a daring bathing suit.

"Don't you know," he demanded of the house manager, "that what we are selling here is backsides, and that a hundred backsides are better than one?"

They ran continuous shows at the Bijou, starting at eleven in the morning and ending at ten P.M. They charged ten cents for all seats at first, then raised it to a quarter. At this house as at Pastor's, the Four Cohans, Weber and Fields, and other popular acts worked for little money. It was also at the Bijou that young George M. Cohan had a run-in with Mr. Keith because the family act hadn't got the top billing Keith had promised. Keith said the sign painter had made a mistake but when young Georgie asked him to have it changed, Keith refused.

"I'll tell you this," Cohan declared, "no member of my family will ever again appear in a theatre with which you have any connection."

And no Cohan ever did.

Keith and Albee in 1887 acquired the Gaiety Museum in Providence as their second theatre. Then, with the help of their Catholic church backers, they built a million dollar showhouse in Philadelphia. Albee got half of the Main Line to attend the opening, making it a gala occasion.

There were other acquisitions to their chain from time to time. But it was not until 1893 that Keith invaded New York and took over the Union Square Theatre. Albee, who did not always tell his older, more cautious partner how much he was spending until a project was complete, invested a fortune renovating the theatre which he hoped would lure away Tony Pastor's carriage trade. The ushers were dressed in Turkish costumes while other employees had glittering military uniforms and attendants in the ladies' rooms wore frilly aprons and lace caps.

That same year Albee invested another million in building his ideal theatre, the Colonial, in Boston. Much of this money he spent for art works in the lobby and on the decor.

To publicize its opening he brought senators, cabinet officers, and other political notables on special trains from Washington. He also invited society figures, stars of the opera, and other front page characters, with all expenses paid.

Before the performance the illustrious free-loaders were taken for a tour of the theatre from the gallery to the spic-and-span cellar. As his final touch, Ed had installed a red carpet in front of the coal bins. For years Albee said that this red carpet, which cost $80, was his greatest pride as a showman.

As the partners expanded, they were deeply irked because one Frederick Proctor, a fellow New Englander, had established vaudeville theatres before they did, first in Providence, then in New York.

Proctor was born in Dexter, Maine, in 1852. His first job was as an errand boy in a Boston department store. In his spare time he became such an expert gymnast that a professional who saw him working out suggested that they team up in an acrobatic act and they played a few dates billed "Levantine Brothers." After they split up, Proctor, who was adept at foot juggling, continued working as a single. Foot juggling requires that a performer, lying on his back, juggle all sorts of objects with his feet: heavy balls, chairs, barrels.

What such dumb acts always needed was a flash finish to get them off to applause. Proctor thought up a dazzler. He painted the objects he kicked and revolved in brilliant colors. Then he cemented on them bits of colored glass. Under the spotlight the barrels, chairs, and balls glittered like a thousand jewels. He billed himself:

WORLD'S WONDER, F. F. LEVANTINE, EQUILIBRIST
IN HIS NEW AND MARVELOUS ENTERTAINMENT

Proctor appeared everywhere in this country and abroad, in vaudeville theatres, fairs, and circuses.

For years audiences applauded his act. But F. F. was less popular with his fellow performers since he was not only thrifty but a teetotaler as well. Every chance he got, he lectured the other acts on the evils of drink and the pitfalls of spending one's money on anything but bare necessities. Whatever kind of show he was with, Proctor also tried to buy the candy, balloon, or popcorn concession. Before and after doing his turn, he would rush out into the crowd with his wares.

Even the circus freaks looked down on this as unseemly activity for a fellow artist.

Proctor was 27 when he invested his savings in a rundown theatre in Albany, New York, called the Green Street. He changed its name to "Levantine's Novelty Theatre" and the first novelty planned was to have no bar and to ban smoking. This was in 1880 before Pastor had tried it. But the former operator warned Proctor that his high ideals would ruin him, since the house's profit came from the sale of cigars, strong waters, and beer. Proctor kept the bar.

Proctor hired a helper, but did much hard work himself getting the theatre in shape. Like Mr. Keith, he repaired the chairs and plugged holes in the walls and like Mrs. Keith he scrubbed floors, dusted, demolished cobwebs, and swept.

When his theatre was ready, he had handbills printed and distributed them himself on the street. They declared:

In Our Temple of Fun We Do All To Please
You Can Smoke Your Cigar and Drink at Your Ease

Unexhausted by all his hard work and hard thinking, Proctor appeared on that first bill, doing his foot juggling routine. He opened with a seventy-five cent top, but soon switched to a 10–20–30 cent policy, with continuous shows.

In the next nine years, Proctor and a partner, Henry Jacobs, acquired dozens of 10–20–30 cent vaudeville theatres, in upstate New York, Connecticut, Brooklyn, Wilmington, Delaware and Lancaster, Pennsylvania.

Somewhere along the line, the theatres became F. F. Proctor's instead of F. F. Levantine's. Proctor boasted in ads that he was running America's largest chain of low-priced vaudeville houses. He enraged B. F. Keith by also claiming to be the originator of continuous vaudeville. They argued about it in print for years. Actors who played continuous vaudeville said it was like two men fighting to be recognized as the importer of Chinese torture.

In 1889, Proctor and Jacobs dissolved their partnership. Each took half of the profitable theatres and sold the others. That same year Proctor built the first of his four New York theatres. At one time, under his continuous vaudeville policy, Proctor sometimes had as many as twenty acts on a bill. The entertainment began at eleven o'clock in the morning and the final curtain came down at eleven P.M. His advertisements read:

After Breakfast, Go to Proctor's
After Proctor's, Go to Bed

This solved many problems for mothers who would make up lunch boxes for their kids, drop them both at Proctor's, have as many hours as they wanted for leisurely shopping, and then pick up their youngsters at the theatre. When they couldn't locate their children in the crowd, the management sent out posses of ushers to find them.

The old foot juggler's official biography, *F. F. Proctor, Vaudeville Pioneer,* asserts that in 1906 "few of his contemporaries could deny he was king of vaudeville." And in 1929 Proctor sold his eleven theatres to RKO for between sixteen to eighteen million dollars.

But in the years from 1913 to the end of the big time, there was only one king of vaudeville and his name was Edward Franklin Albee. Ed was a real slugging champion. His partner Keith was the only one safe from his devious tricks and frontal assaults, and Keith was in virtual retirement for years before he died in 1914. But Albee took on everyone else: the rival vaudeville pioneers, owners of legitimate theatre chains, actors' unions, agents. He lost a few battles, but in the end was supreme.

In 1900 he made the move that provoked the first of the actors' strikes and also started him on the road to dictatorship over all the country's big time and its small time as well. In that year, he organized the Vaudeville Managers Protective Association (VMPA). The membership included most of the men who owned or controlled the big-time circuits. This established, among other provisions, the managers' right to deduct five percent of the salaries paid all acts. Such a stipulation was to pay for the expense of maintaining their booking offices, regardless of whether the artists were already paying agents five to ten percent of their pay.

On June 1, 1900, a group of vaudeville performers reacted by organizing a union of their own. They called it the White Rats. In a short while they had lined up several hundred other artists. They all were outraged by the five percent deduction—which they recognized as a kickback, a fee extracted by their employers for giving them work.

From the time the system of booking acts for a series of engagements at different theatres began, the vaudevillians had been, they said, the juiciest pigeons in show business, the victims of every sort of graft and chiseling practice by these very managers, their managers' employees, and the actors' own agents. At their meeting they compiled a bill of complaints almost as long as the Old Testament. Certain unscrupulous agents and the managers' bookers often conspired to cut into the acts' pay, sometimes by as much as half. Performers would be told their salary was only $250 a week but on the manager's books it might be $500. If the act discovered this and appealed to the manager, he got stalled. If he became difficult, he might find that his schedule had been "rearranged" and he now had expensive layoffs and sleeper jumps. Or that he had been blacklisted.

The system also set up the artists as the victims of grafting stagehands who would refuse to move their props in or out without tips. Orchestra leaders and their men got into the habit of expecting gratuities. Stage doormen and everyone else backstage took additional bites out of the vaudevillian's pay. They could louse up an act in a dozen ways: putting the props in the wrong place, pulling up the curtain or letting it down at the wrong time, not delivering messages or telephone calls.

Whenever the performer went to a manager with a complaint or a demand for a raise, he was told that he was being paid more than the actors in every other branch of show business. That was true. But they were outraged because in addition to the money they were gypped out of and that was paid to backstage grafters, they had to carry all their own expenses. The managers provided only the theatre, the house staff, the orchestra, a few standard props, and drops (curtains) showing a street, a park, a room, and an office. The performers paid for everything else—the material, their supporting actors, song arrangements, costumes, special props or drops, traveling expenses, living expenses, and freight charges.

The newly organized White Rats asked the Vaudeville Managers Protective Association for a hearing on these and other complaints. When they were ignored they went on strike. Performers reported "sick" and did not go on at several Eastern theatres, including Keith's Union Square.

On hearing the news, Ed Albee, who never lacked courage,

went directly to the headquarters of the White Rats. He found there several of the artists who had reported "sick" to the Union Square's house manager.

"You fellows don't look sick to me," he said.

They explained that what had made them ill was the news that the new VMPA had decided to deduct five percent of their salaries—just for booking them.

They expected Ed Albee to shower them with abuse. He threw them completely off guard by being conciliatory. He insisted that Keith and he had from the start been against the five percent deduction, but had been outvoted. Some of the performers ddin't believe him and asked whether they could see Mr. Keith.

"Of course," Albee replied.

A few days later a delegation called on B. F. Keith at his Holland House suite. Keith was relaxed and friendly but reserved. Some in the group had worked in Keith theatres for years but had never seen him before. He told them he had indeed opposed the five percent deduction clause. They could depend on both Albee and him to try to have it eliminated from the contracts of the other circuits and independent theatres throughout the country. But he called to their attention the fact that the VMPA had two branches, Eastern managers and Western managers. The two were scheduled to meet in three weeks. Keith promised that if the strike was called off he would do everything he could to get the other managers from coast to coast to drop the five percent deduction. Meanwhile he'd have that clause eliminated from all of the contracts written by his booking office.

"That would mean we have won, Mr. Keith?" one artist asked.

"Of course, my boy," said Keith.

The actors said that they would call off the strike if he would tell the press what he had just said to them; Keith said he would. The next day on the front page of the New York *Evening Journal* there appeared a story headlined WHITE RATS WIN!

The strike was called off, the artists went back to work. But they'd won nothing. The bamboozlers from Boston had wanted and needed time. There was no meeting of the VMPA in three weeks or three months. The five percent clause was not eliminated from the Keith contracts or any others.

Albee had used the time gained to tempt artists with two-year contracts which included the five percent clause. He knew which actors were broke—and got them. He knew which actors scared easily—and got them. Soon he had the White Rats quarreling among themselves and accusing each other of double-crossing.

The actors had lost.

An incident six years later proves that Albee could be just as ruthless and devious with managers who gave him trouble. That year, 1906, Ed pulled another coup by organizing the United Booking Offices (UBO) which was to pool the booking of talent. There were a few holdouts, but it was the defiance of S. Z. Poli, another New England manager, that angered him most. Poli had paid his initial fee with a check. Then, changing his mind, he had cancelled the check.

Albee retaliated by writing letters to the important banks in every town in which Poli had a theatre. The letters said that the Keith Circuit was planning to build a magnificent theatre in these towns, and requested the bank's advice about location and financing. The letters made it clear that, regrettable though it was, the established vaudeville theatres in the community would probably be driven out of business.

The banks lost no time in withdrawing all credit and calling back all outstanding loans to Mr. Poli's circuit. Poli himself lost no time in getting another check to Albee's new UBO offices.

The most interesting of all Albee's master strokes was made during his battle with Martin Beck for possession of the New York Palace which Beck had defiantly built in the heart of Ed's ever-growing empire. But that story later.

CHAPTER TWO

The Singing Women

THE GREAT GLOWING WONDER of the big time was its women singers. Even when their voices lacked power, they were able to project them into every remote corner of the theatre. They overwhelmed you with their eagerness to please and their ability to make you feel they were singing directly and only to you.

There were scores of these enchantresses, all headliners. Each was in some way different from the others and many had a special song that best expressed her personality. This was always played as the artist's name came up on the signs on each side of the stage.

"Some of These Days" announced the entrance of Sophie Tucker; "Waiting for the Robert E. Lee" was for Ruth Roye; "M-I-S-S-I-S-S-I-P-P-I" signalled Frances White, who lisped; and Louise Dresser walked on to the strains of "My Gal Sal." Irene Franklin's identification song was "Redhead"; Fritzi Scheff's was "Kiss Me Again."

When one of your favorite woman singers was on you became convinced of one thing: she was immortal. You could not imagine her dying, ill, being hurt, discouraged, dented, or tarnished. When you heard of a misfortune or indignity she had suffered you felt sick and outraged.

These singing singles, as they were sometimes called, held a following everywhere they played year after year. Headliners by right of conquest, they accepted second billing only when there was a booking emergency. Then their billing read, "Special Added Attraction" or "Held Over for Another Week by Popular Request."

As a teenager starting her career, the singing woman usually traveled with her mother, an elder sister, or a girl partner. If alone, there was always an older woman on the bill to advise her about everything from laundry problems to stage door Johnnies. On most bills there were family acts and the mother and eldest daughter had warm, understanding hearts and were eager to help the talented beginner in any way they could. The newcomers also quickly learned how to handle hecklers, amorous local managers, and other pests.

The singing women came in all shapes and sizes. Quite a few of them were tiny: Anna Held, Mae West, Nan Halperin, Fritzi Scheff, Irene Bordoni, Yvette Rugel, Frances White.

But most of these gifted girls, like the old-time opera singers, were of average height or more, ran to flesh, big bosoms, broad hips, powerful shoulders, and sizable bottoms. Since that was the fashion—not to say the ideal—it made it easier for their women admirers, usually well-stacked maids and matrons themselves, to identify with them. For the men these glorious singers combined the appeal of dear old

Mom, usually a busty lady herself, with the allure of that sexy young thing next door who had matured early.

In big-time vaudeville the women in less important acts also were paid more than men. Ed Albee once told reporters that "a minor two-girl dancing act is paid half again as much as a similar two-man act. This holds true, even when the men are better."

Women headliners were paid from $750 to $1500 a week, and played about forty weeks a year. The so-called Big Four —Eva Tanguay, Elsie Janis, Irene Franklin, and Nora Bayes —earned twice as much. This for going on twice a day for about twenty minutes, though they did have to pay all of their own expenses. But there was extra money from phonograph records. Song publishers paid them handsomely for singing new numbers; songwriters sometimes were so eager for one of them to sing a new tune that she'd be bribed with a slice of his royalties and also would share his byline credit.

And the big time's great woman singing stars were earning this kind of money in pre-World War I days when the average workingman's wage was $2 for a ten-hour day. There were few big-money women stars on the legitimate stage then—not many women operatic and concert stars earned that kind of money. The woman headliners were paid like queens and sometimes conducted themselves as arrogantly. Quite a number of them, however, shared one very rare human trait: the ability to laugh at one's self, on stage and sometimes off.

Nora Bayes was always joking wryly about her ill-starred marriages, her Jewishness, her "six note" voice. Irene Franklin told everybody she had no voice at all and insisted that without her husband–accompanist, Burton Green, she never could have succeeded. Elsie Janis, at 42, made fun of her virginity with the epitaph: "Here lies Elsie Janis still sleeping alone."

Trixie Friganza, a rollicking butterball, told newspaper interviewers, "When I started in show business I was thin enough to be blown through a keyhole. Now I can't even get through the door."

Emma Carus, who was not good looking, often got a laugh by opening her act with "I'm not pretty but I'm good to my folks."

Most of the singers lived extravagantly, heaping money and gifts on friends. Almost all came from poor families and had to help relatives and in-laws, who were not always grateful.

Some were good businesswomen besides—May Irwin, Sophie Tucker, Trixie Friganza, Emma Carus, and Fanny Brice. Miss Irwin was said to have banked more than a million on the investments made for her by admiring New York bankers and Wall Street barons. She was also the comedienne whom President Woodrow Wilson said he'd like to appoint Secretary of Laughter.

These colorful, exciting women were far ahead of their time in their attitude toward sex. Often they took their men where they found them and dropped them without a thought or qualm when bored, or attracted by a new admirer.

But there were other reasons their marriages seldom lasted. Because to reach and remain a headline attraction on the big time required (in addition to a monstrous ego) putting work before everything else. Few self-respecting men could take it. Those willing to accept the role of hand-

holder, emotional sponge, errand-boy, and sympathetic lis-
tener were quickly reduced to the status of despised lackeys.
Fed up with marriage, more than one of these electrically
charged women eventually solved her sex hunger by taking
home a husky stagehand for the night. However, Sophie
Tucker complained that the husbands and lovers in her life
had cost her over a million dollars, adding, "And I haven't
one damn thing to show for it!" Nora Bayes told reporters
that she had lovers between marriages, but didn't believe
in carrying on more than one affair at a time.

Unbelievable though it may seem, Eva Tanguay, the
greatest box-office attraction vaudeville ever developed, had
less talent than any of the other singing ladies. Her singing
and dancing were amateurish but prudish America should
have learned from Eva's success that sex conquers all, or
almost all.

For Tanguay was pure sex bomb, effervescent, vital, exploding with life. Unlike the public, newspaper critics from
coast to coast denounced her vulgarity and lack of talent.
One who did understand Tanguay's hypnotic effect on audiences was Ada Patterson, one of Randolph Hearst's crack
women reporters, who wrote:

> Everyone is filled with a breathless intensity . . . sitting
> up, straight and eager. The orchestra is playing with new
> vim. The instruments seem sharper and louder. The very
> lights seem to burn brighter, so tense is the atmosphere.
> . . . What is that noise that breaks upon our ears? A loud
> chattering voice, high-pitched, strident, voluble. Look! Here
> she comes with quick fluttering steps and restless, out-
> stretched hands, a dynamic personality all nerves and ex-
> citement . . . a trim, alert figure, held so tense and straight

that energy exudes from it . . . a wild mop of stiff, tousled blond hair which seems charged with electric vigor . . . saucy, broad, good-humored face . . . large, smiling mouth and pertly turned-up nose . . . her small, impudent eyes. Every inch of her is alive, nervous, vital . . .

Edward Bernays, inventor of the now prevalent blight called public relations, first saw Tanguay when he was a New York high school boy and, as an old man, remembered her. In his memoirs Bernays described Eva as "wild, bold, hectic, strutting up and down the stage . . . jolting us all . . . she was our first symbol of emergence from the Victorian Age."

The critics were indifferent—or at least pretended to be —to Tanguay's sex dynamics; they kept harping on her lack of ability. The choleric Percy Hammond of the Chicago *Tribune* wrote that he could think of no entertainer who entertained him less. Hammond compared Eva's singing to "the wail of the prehistoric diplodocus" and called her dancing "the very doggerel of motion." Another reviewer declared that her stage costumes ranged from the weird to the grotesque. Eva retorted that she paid more for her gowns than any other actress. Perhaps to convince the scoffer, she sang a number the next season in a dress made of one, five, ten, and fifty dollar bills that she had had sewn together.

Tanguay wore stage costumes that shimmered, gleamed, sparkled, and were befurred and befeathered. They covered her from shoulders to hips. Her "fuzzy-wuzzy" hair usually had a few ornaments and her gorgeous legs were sheathed in expensive sheer silk stockings.

During World War I she appeared wrapped in French flags to sing the "Marseillaise." In the New York *Tribune,*

Heywood Broun stormed, "There should be some moral force, or physical, if need be, to keep her away from the 'Marseillaise.' She should not be allowed to sing it even on her knees . . . it is monstrous that the great hymn of human liberty should be shrilled as a climax to a vulgar act by a bouncing singer in a grotesque costume begirt with little flags. I think she is the parsnip of performers."

Miss Tanguay responded with a full page ad in *Variety* of rhymed jingles depicting herself as the pitiful victim of venomous male jealousy and hate. She might have scored if she'd contended that Heywood should be the last person on earth to criticize anyone's wardrobe. Though a great journalist, Broun was a sartorial slob whose appearance had been compared to that of an unmade bed, or a tent that had folded.

But nothing the critics wrote diminished Eva Tanguay's popularity. It thrilled audiences to see her come racing out of the wings, screaming her theme song "I Don't Care!" whose chorus went:

> *I don't care! I don't care!*
> *What they may think of me.*
> *I'm happy-go-lucky*
> *Men say that I'm plucky,*
> *So jolly and carefree.*
> *I don't care, I don't care*
> *If I do get the mean and stony stare:*
> *If I'm never successful,*
> *I won't be distressful*
> *'Cause I don't care.*

While singing this, Tanguay ran wildly across the stage and seemed to carom from one corner of the set to another, wriggling her hips, waggling her breasts, kicking her legs wildly, and shaking that thing. Often she appeared to be having an orgasm.

Eva sang sexy songs over the objections of vaudeville tycoons and other prissy characters; their titles told all: "It's Been Done Before But Never the Way I Do It," "Go As Far As You Like," and "That's Why They Call Me Tabasco."

Along with squandering a fortune on her wardrobe, Eva spent more than any other big-time star on advertising and personal publicity. She often employed four press agents at the same time. One of their tasks was coining one-line descriptions of her for billboards and full-page ads in the theatrical newspapers. Among the results were:

The Girl Who Made Vaudeville Famous

Cyclonic Eva Tanguay

The Actress Loved More by More American Women
than any Other Actress

The Electrifying Hoyden

Mother Eve's Merriest Daughter

The Genius of Mirth and Song

Our Own Eva, America's Idol

The Girl the Whole World Loves

Vaudeville's Greatest Drawing Card

The Evangelist of Joy

Eva Tanguay was born in 1878 in the Canadian wilderness. Her mother was French-Canadian; her father, Dr. Gustave Tanguay, was a Paris physician who had heard the call of the wild. Eva was so tiny when born that her father put her in a small box and shoved it under the stove to save her from dying of the cold. Within a few weeks she grew to normal size. When Eva was seven, the family moved to Holyoke, Massachusetts, where Dr. Tanguay died soon afterwards.

During the next year Eva, her younger sister, and mother almost starved to death. They were saved by Francesca Redding, part owner of a touring troupe, who saw golden-haired Eva on the street. She told Mrs. Tanguay that she'd like to take the child into her company and could pay $8 a week. Most of this was sent home. In the next few years, Eva played all of the standard child roles with the company, from Little Lord Fauntleroy to the starveling in "The Face on the Barroom Floor."

During her teen years Eva worked with an acrobatic turn and as a chorus girl. The muscles she developed while accompanying the acrobats enabled her to become one of the most feared backstage scrappers in all show business.

Her first battle was with another chorus girl named Tessie Moody in "Hoo-Doo!," a musical with a Hawaiian setting. In one scene the girls slithered across the stage in grass skirts and gossamer blouses, danced briefly, then exited. One evening Eva dropped behind the others and did an unscheduled dance, wobbling, shimmying, and doing the bumps.

It brought down the house and also inspired some snappy criticism from Tessie. Without warning, Eva grabbed her by the throat and started to choke her. Tessie's tongue was hanging out and her face was turning blue by the time stagehands dragged Eva away. In retelling the story, Eva always boasted, "And Tessie was out for three hours!"

In her next show, "My Lady" starring Eddie Foy, Eva was given a number to sing all by herself. For this she stepped out of the chorus and walked to the footlights, with the other girls lined up behind her, listening. In the middle of Eva's song one of them—Jessie Jordan—threw a bun at a college boy suitor who was sitting in the front row. Laughter exploded and it grew louder when Jessie's admirer threw the bun back at her.

Eva finished her song, stepped back into line, and they all danced off. The moment they were out of the audience's sight, Eva leaped on Jessie and whacked her head against the backstage brick wall. Again stagehands had to stop the assault. This got Eva front page publicity because it happened on Broadway on Hammerstein's Paradise Garden Roof whose manager, Willie Hammerstein was a genius at getting newspaper space for his attractions.

"After that," Eva would reminisce, "the papers were full of me. My part was rewritten, my salary went up, and the place was jammed every night. Everyone said 'Don't go near Eva. She's crazy!' Ever since then the stagehands, the leader of the orchestra, and other people have been afraid of me."

It might be well to explain here why the tantrums of an obscure chorus girl should have attracted so much attention. Those were frivolous times and newspapers had lots of empty columns to fill, with their readers quite credulous about what went on in show business.

The manufacturing of myths about stage people is almost as old as show business itself. Florenz Ziegfeld, Jr., had made his wife Anna Held, the French singer, famous all over the United States with a single yarn: that she kept her schoolgirl complexion by bathing each day in a tub full of cow's milk. That encouraged press agents to prevaricate as never before.

The most popular phony press story for a few years was

the one about the star robbed of her jewels. After a while the editors began to refuse to print such hoaxes. But some publicity man got Olga Petrova's picture printed by a smart switch. Olga, a dramatic star who was touring in vaudeville, announced that she was suing a bird act. Petrova charged that the act's star parrot had gotten into her dressing room while she was on stage and swallowed one of her diamond earrings. Other odd attention-getters followed. Nora Bayes was reported to be oiling her vocal chords by sucking slowly on three lollipops every working day. And Madame Nazimova, the great Russian tragedienne, confided to interviewing journalists that she played tiddlywinks by the hour in her dressing room.

Occasionally the fake publicity backfired. Appearing at the Palace, Fanny Brice paid a publicity man $1000 to get her name in the papers. He sent out a story that Fanny, in spite of being Jewish, intended to work on Yom Kippur, the most important Hebrew Holy Day.

Fanny was not shown the story in advance. But it should not have caused any stir since for years Jewish vaudeville artists had worked on all religious holidays, just as Catholic and Protestant performers did on Christmas and Easter Sunday. And so did everybody in the legitimate theatre.

But protests against Brice erupted in the Orthodox Jewish community and there were threats to boycott the Palace while she was there. Fanny was forced to apologize for a statement she had never made.

Several hard-to-believe stories were published about Eva Tanguay while she was a featured player in "The Chaperones." One had her throwing a small comedian named Ed Redway at Walter Jones, the leading man. Another told of her discovering and capturing a Peeping Tom who was getting an eyeful of her roommate, Trixie Friganza, taking a bath.

But the most unbelievable story printed about Eva while she was in that same show may well have been true. This told of a dotty old multimillionaire, one of the Havemeyer sugar kings, who became infatuated with Eva after seeing her in the show. From that night on he traveled with the show, buying a front row orchestra seat for every performance. He was in heaven as he watched plump little Eva perform, took her out to dinner, and bought her furs and jewels. When she suggested that he take the whole company to lobster and champagne suppers he was enchanted. Eva even talked him into buying furs and jewels for her roommate Trixie.

Senile, cackling Mr. Havemeyer was a press agent's dream come true. He was delighted to give out long interviews to local newspapers. He said he thought of Eva as his adorable adopted daughter and explained to reporters that he was alone in the world, too old to undertake trips abroad, and did not like to play cards. All he enjoyed was seeing his friend Eva in "The Chaperones." He asked of her and the rest of the troupe only one thing: that they call him "Nunkey."

All through her career Eva continued to get more publicity than anyone else in vaudeville. Some of it was based on fact. Much of it was the sort of press notices other headliners on the two-a-day would have tried to suppress; they would never have boasted that stagehands and other coworkers were afraid of them.

One stagehand in a Midwest theatre had the temerity to

ask Eva what she would do if a masher flirted with her. "Watch!" she said. Picking him up, she threw him against the wall and knocked him unconscious. In Louisville, Kentucky, she pushed another stagehand downstairs. He was injured so severely that he had to be taken to the hospital. A court fined Eva $50. The stagehand brought a civil suit for damages that she settled for $1000. She liked to carry thousand dollar bills around with her and in this case she just peeled one off her roll and handed it to the stagehand.

Each of her violent acts got her more publicity. Eva's rages were genuine enough, but the fact that the unladylike brawls were publicized must have encouraged her.

In Evansville, Indiana, she slept through a matinee. When the house manager fined her $100 she pulled out a dagger and ripped the theatre's house curtain to shreds. In Sharon, Pennsylvania, Eva wanted the manager to replace the small mirror in her dressing room with a larger one. When he refused she complained to the audience. They proved unsympathetic and Eva committed the unforgivable professional sin: she quarreled with her audience, calling them "a lot of small town saps."

In her case it did not prove unforgivable at all. More and more people who'd read about her antics went to watch her act, hoping to see her explode. If there was anything vaudeville audiences loved it was being in on something that was not on the program. Vaudeville performers had always taken advantage of this and they'd have a stooge in the audience to heckle them or a kid with a golden voice in the gallery to get up and sing.

All of her life Eva was addicted to writing doggerel. She

also liked to talk doggerel. When anyone asked her how she became famous, she would say,

> When I put on tights
> My name went up in lights!

Some fans believed she didn't even wear tights for the performance that made her a big-money star. She was making $500 a week in vaudeville when she got the idea of presenting a sensational version of the Dance of the Seven Veils.

The dance had been a high point of the Richard Strauss opera *Salome* when it was first presented in Dresden in 1906. The New York Metropolitan Company put it on for a single performance. Then J. Pierpont Morgan (the elder), W. K. Vanderbilt, and August Belmont demanded that it be stopped. They found "revolting" and "disgusting" the Dance of the Seven Veils in which Salome fondles the severed head of John the Baptist whom she had ordered decapitated because he spurned her advances.

That of course made the dance, in which one after another of the veils is discarded, the rage of the decade. Maud Allan did it in a London music hall. Another first-rate dancer, Gertrude Hoffman, had a recordbreaking run doing it at Hammerstein's Victoria on Broadway, and then toured the country with it. Soon the dance was being performed in honkytonks and musical comedies. Comics did burlesques of it. Even Julian Eltinge, the country's favorite female impersonator, put it into his act. Martin Beck banned the dance on the stage of his theatres.

Reformers everywhere were outraged. Ohio, West Virginia, Pennsylvania, Kentucky, and many cities barred it. All this was like honey drawing flies to the box office. Nothing can help shows more than angry bluenoses.

But nobody's Salome dance enraged them as much as Tanguay's. When Eva first mentioned to C. F. Zittel, her press agent, that she was thinking of doing a sensational version of Salome in her act, he told her she was mad. He said, "You can't sing and you can't dance. If you go through with this I'm leaving town." He predicted she'd be hooted off the stage. She often took Zittel's advice, but he couldn't talk her out of this idea. Eva did the number wearing only the veils and a little jewelry. The night she first did the dance her sister, who was in the audience, fainted. She was convinced Eva would be arrested for indecent exposure.

"I was no classical dancer," Eva said years after her triumph, "so I mixed in some Highland Fling and Sailor's Hornpipe and everything else I knew. And I sang as I danced and dropped one veil after another.

"I also did something else that no one else had thought of. Instead of dancing around holding the papier mâche head I hired a Negro boy with big eyes. I sat him on the side of the stage, all covered up. As I began to dance, I uncovered his head which, to the audience, appeared to be resting on a silver tray. As I moved about the stage his huge eyes also moved, following me.

"The audience was electrified. But when the Mayor of New York heard about the dance, he sent word to me to put some clothes on or he'd close the show."

Before Eva had time to react to that, Florenz Ziegfeld sent for her. One of the star acts in his 1909 Follies, the singing team of Jack Norworth and Nora Bayes, had just walked out. Eva had been getting $500 a week. Because of the sensation she'd made as Salome, she was able to demand and get from Ziegfeld $1200 plus top billing in the lobby, on billboards, and in the newspaper ads. And five years later, helped by constant publicity, Eva was getting $3000 a week.

Throughout the rest of her career, Eva remained both a top money-earner and a newsworthy personality.

During an engagement in Chicago a man charged in a local court with making a 15-year-old girl pregnant was given the choice of marrying her or going to jail. "I can't marry her, Your Honor," he told the judge, "I've been married for ten years to Eva Tanguay." On hearing this Eva rushed to the court and convinced the judge that she didn't even know the upstart.

This may have inspired Eva to announce engagements to men without even bothering to tell them about it beforehand. She did this to Eddie Darling, a lifelong bachelor who was then Ed Albee's secretary, and at the moment in London signing up acts. He told British reporters it was all news to him. After a balloon trip over St. Louis with Tony von Phul, a well-known aeronaut, she told reporters that when they were five thousand feet in the air, von Phul had proposed to her and, swept away by the romance of it all, she had accepted. Von Phul said her announcement was as big a surprise to him as it must be to them, the gentlemen of the press.

At a time when sexual indiscretion could ruin the career of most other women stars, scandal only increased Eva's popularity. She was traveling on a train through the Middle West with one John Leech when they got into a slugging match with a conductor about an open window. Leech was accused of pulling a gun. But before he could fire it, he was jumped by other trainmen and disarmed. He and Eva were arrested and put off at Des Moines, the next stop. Taken to court, Miss Tanguay told the judge that Mr. Leech was her husband. His Honor told Eva that for years he had been an admirer of her art, and released them both. Leech disappeared at once.

Eva was involved in several other scandals. On one occasion she was caught in a hotel suite in bed with her press agent, C. F. Zittel, by his wife and private detectives. Another time, the New York police broke up a fistfight she was having with Roscoe Ails, a comedian whom she was living with in a New York apartment. Eva was losing that scrap when the boys arrived.

Later, Miss Tanguay, a Christian Scientist, announced her intention of becoming an evangelist. She said, "I'll use whatever I have to save people. If I'm a Cyclonic Comedienne, I'll be an Evangelistic Typhoon." But Eva remained in vaudeville until the two-a-day fell apart. Many of her full-page ads in *Variety* carried such messages as "God Is My Peace—Naught Can Disturb!"

So far as we know, she married only twice. Her first husband was Johnny Ford, comedian and extraordinary eccentric dancer, whom she wed in 1914. Thirteen years later she married Alan Parado, a musician in her act. Neither marriage lasted very long. One of her reasons for divorcing Parado, she said, who was much younger than she, was her discovery that his real name was Chandos Kaszkewacz which was "a real disappointment to me."

To the end she battled management, walking out of shows whenever she pleased, and boasted in one of her jingles,

I've been wired and tired and hired and fired
I've jawed with Frohman and Ziegfeld and Fields . . .

Toward the end of her career Eva announced that she was writing *A Hundred Loves* which she described as a "semi-autobiographical novel." It had long been rumored that she had black lovers.

"They also say I have illegitimate babies," Eva complained to one reporter, "and I don't even drink or smoke."

Elsie Janis was all talent. A slim, frail, ladylike creature, she was also Eva's direct opposite in personality and character. Throughout her long career, Elsie, a mouse, was utterly dominated by her mother, Elizabeth Cockerill Bierbower. The Cockerills were a distinguished Ohio family that had produced Colonel Joseph A. Cockerill, a Civil War hero, and his son John, a fighting St. Louis *Post-Dispatch* editor, who shot to death a political enemy who came to his office to settle the quarrel.

Liz, as Elsie's mother liked to be called, had inherited their battling spirit, and made war on everyone who got in the way of her gifted child's career. She was the epitome of the stage mother except that she was not as greedy as most. Elsie had been a highly paid child wonder but Liz had never permitted her to be overworked. All of the contracts she signed for Elsie stipulated that the fragile girl was to have two weeks of rest following every four weeks of performances.

When Elsie was a grownup star her mother continued to rule her life as she had when she was a tot. Liz nursed Elsie when she was ill, supervised her meals, woke her up in the morning, dictated her schedule, coached her, chose her wardrobe and material, told her when to go to bed. She even went along on Elsie's dates. Not so surprisingly, Liz managed to discourage all her charming daughter's suitors, including sons of this country's and England's most patrician families.

Elsie was over forty when Liz died. It had never occurred to her to rebel. But then she wrote, seemingly in wonder, "I was a strange little puppet. She pulled the strings. She turned me off and on at will, like a music box." But Elsie also added, "She gave up her whole life for me. Her only thought was furthering my career."

As a school girl in Columbus, Ohio, Liz had always been the life of the party. Everybody who heard her entertaining at church socials and picnics urged her to go on the professional stage.

"I was always the leader in everything as a girl," Mrs. Bierbower often told Elsie. Liz organized the church picnics. At sixteen, she got a job at a millinery shop and became "head trimmer" in no time.

At a bobsled party Liz insisted on steering, ran the sled into a tree, and went to the hospital with a broken leg. In her weakened condition she made what she always considered the worst error of her life. When Johnny Bierbower, a railroad brakeman, asked her to marry him she accepted.

Elsie was born on March 16, 1889, in Columbus, Ohio. Even before that, as a child wife and mother, Mrs. Bierbower had been very restless. In those days when women's place was supposed to be in the home Liz had established her own profitable real estate business. She would buy a house, move in with her husband, have the house painted and renovated, sell it at a profit, and move out. In their first year of marriage the Bierbowers, because of her transactions, lived in seven different homes. Liz in addition gave elocution lessons and served as a board member of the House of Fallen Women in Columbus. She also took advantage of the free passes on all lines then given to railway men and their families to visit relatives in all parts of the Midwest.

Young Mrs. Bierbower—in those days called Jennie—abandoned all of these interests after Elsie was born in 1889. She concentrated her torrential energy on preparing her child for the stage stardom she was convinced she herself had missed by being such a fool as to marry Johnny Bierbower.

From the time she could walk, Elsie proved superb material. A pretty child, she was pert, wistful, quick to follow instructions, and surprisingly inventive. As a five-year-old making her debut in a local church entertainment she stole the show. After doing her songs and dances, Elsie astonished even her mother by mimicking perfectly the speech the pompous Sunday School superintendent had made just an hour before. Thereafter "Little Elsie" appeared in one-tot entertainments at churches and schools in Columbus and many nearby towns.

Her mother had been a friend of President William McKinley and his wife since the years when he was Governor of Ohio. After they invited Liz to bring her *wunderkind* to the White House to perform, Little Elsie overnight became the country's most publicized child star. She'd performed in the White House and every newspaper in the United States described her impersonations of the President and Mrs. McKinley and how afterwards the President had taken the child on his lap, kissed her, and told her "You'll be a star some day!"

Liz, who later on again preferred to be called Jennie, capitalized on the McKinley blessing and prophecy by getting a tryout for her six-year-old at Mike Shea's theatre in Buffalo. When Little Elsie stopped the show, Liz demanded $125 a week for her, and got it over Shea's howled protests. She also insisted that her child be given the spotlight. Shea, a tough manager, pointed out that the spotlight was used only for headliners. Liz shrugged and started collecting the sheet music she'd distributed to the orchestra for use while Elsie was on. Again Shea gave in. Little Elsie started the week in the Number Two slot and ended it in the next to closing position usually reserved for the headliner.

Shea became so delighted with the little girl's work that he wrote to other vaudeville managers he knew recommending they hire her.

During the next few years, however, Liz had Elsie play in stock companies most of the time. They proved to be the best theatrical training schools. Besides playing child's parts in all of the standard plays, Little Elsie did her specialties between the acts, becoming the best-loved child performer in the country. Elsie was fifteen when she became the toast of New York after doing her "impressions" of stage stars of the day at the New York Theatre's roof garden. The following year she became the youngest star on Broadway in *The Vanderbilt Cup*. In those days musical shows were just vaudeville with a silly, meaningless plot running through. For ten years Elsie was one of the greatest names in both mediums and a beloved star in London.

As a mimic she had only one equal: Cissy Loftus, the

British charmer. Both had that remarkable ability of simply becoming for the moment George M. Cohan talking and singing out of the corner of his mouth; Eddie Foy strutting and doing his old Irish clog-dance; the majestic Ethel Barrymore; Nazimova with her huge tragic eyes and tormented mouth; Harry Lauder singing "You Take the High Road."

And somehow Janis, like Loftus, convinced audiences that they were not only hearing a song or speech, but getting insight into the real character of the celebrity. Both were not merely mimics but also singers, dancers, and actresses right out of the top drawer. Elsie wrote her own material and often made helpful suggestions when a show was struggling with a scene that just didn't play. Everybody who worked with Elsie found her sweet and sympathetic. While year after year, as she passed through her twenties and early thirties, they all waited for her to rebel.

It never happened.

Liz continued to be all over the place, fighting for Elsie's rights to this and that, insisting that Elsie get top billing, the big numbers in every show, the star's dressing room. And when Elsie was on, Mrs. Bierbower was back there in the wings, singing, dancing, saying Elsie's lines, rooting, and praying for her.

Charles Dillingham was a manager beloved by artists, but once Liz almost prevented a show of his from opening on Broadway because her Elsie had been promised sole star billing and would have to share it with veteran star Joseph Cawthorn. Cawthorn had been hired late in rehearsals as a replacement. Forgetting his commitment to Miss Janis, Dillingham also promised Cawthorn star billing. Until a few hours before curtain time, Cawthorn and Liz (on behalf of her daughter) were both refusing to go on. Dillingham foxed them at the last minute by having the electrician disconnect the lights on the marquee signboard. So the name of neither was up in lights. The stars both went on, the show was a hit. After reading the notices, Liz and Joe Cawthorn agreed to equal billing.

A letter Mrs. Bierbower wrote one New Year's Eve and left on Elsie's pillow just before the star became old enough to sign her own contracts illustrates how frightened Liz was of Elsie becoming independent of her. It read, in part,

> . . . As you grow older you will find much that does not please you. When such times come, when you think you know more than I do, you just say to yourself "Well, if I do know more, after all, it was mother who did most to help me." . . . I'm so anxious, worried, nervous, and not always reasonable, but I love you! . . . Mother

Irene Castle thought that Elsie's life contained more tragedy than anyone else she knew. Irene grants Ma Janis, as everyone on the big time called her, credit for guiding Elsie to the top. "She had a marvelous combination of business ability and unadulterated nerve and the producers were terrified of her." But she claims that Elsie was a normal, healthy girl and that caused the conflict. "If her mother ever thought for one minute that she was falling in love with a man," wrote Mrs. Castle in her memoirs, "she'd begin to stamp on his face and drive him away with sticks and stones. She managed to drive away everybody.

"I think Elsie had quite a crush on Maurice Chevalier at one time . . . but Chevalier ended up just a good and loyal friend."

Another time Elsie fell in love with her first cousin but her mother talked her out of it, calling it unnatural and monstrous and warned Elsie against "fouling the nest."

Mrs. Castle listened to Ma Janis until she could stand no more, then asked, "How dare you be mad at her after the way she's loved you all these years?"

"Ma Janis never felt the same way about me after that," Irene said.

Mrs. Bierbower got another shock when Elsie was in her late twenties. In London the star fell in love with Basil Hallam, an English actor. The newspapers there said they were engaged. But the war had started by then and Hallam enlisted in the Royal Flying Corps. Shortly afterwards he was killed in a parachute jump.

"Mother was my greatest comfort. She's never left my side," Miss Janis told friends after she recovered from her grief.

Elsie was starring in a London revue when the United States joined the Allies. She quit the show and left for France, intent on entertaining our troops at the front, with mother going along as always. It was some time before the doughboys arrived and Elsie wangled permission from the French and English commanders to visit the battlefields. She had a difficult time persuading the French that it was all-important for her mother to accompany her.

Elsie Janis was there with Ma to greet the American troops when they arrived. She sang to the boys behind the lines, in hospitals, and at the front. She became the best-known, best-loved actress, and the first great star to risk her life, day after day, singing often within the sound of shellfire.

War correspondent Alexander Woollcott wrote in the

New York *Times*, "When the history of this great expedition comes to be written, there should be a chapter devoted to the playgirl of the Western front, the star of the A.E.F., the forerunner of those players who are now being booked in the greatest circuit of them all, the Y.M.C.A. huts of France."

Ward Morehouse, later a star on the New York *Sun*, described how "Elsie Janis, the official sweetheart of the A.E.F. . . . sang, talked and did handsprings as she toured the Western front, her black tam pushed back on her tossing hair."

The greatest triumph of Elsie's career came the night General John J. (Blackjack) Pershing, the Allied Commander in France, told her, "Elsie, when first you came to France someone said you were more valuable than an entire regiment, then someone raised it to a division, but I want to tell you that if you can give our men this sort of happiness, you are worth a whole Army Corps."

After the Armistice Elsie produced, directed, wrote, and starred in a musical show she called "Elsie Janis and Her Gang," with an all-soldier supporting cast. The troupe—all amateurs—was trained by Elsie to sing, dance, and act like old pros. It toured successfully across the country and played more than 800 performances. Then Elsie returned to vaudeville and the Broadway musical theatre. But some of the pep and sizzle and joy seemed to have gone out of her work. And years later, as a mature woman, she wrote,

> There is no doubt that with the end of the war came the death of something inside of me. Pride? Perhaps, for I have never really felt proud of myself since. I've been pleased with work that I've done and grateful for the success that I've had in several different lines, but the war was

my high spot and I think there is only one peak in each life.

Her career was not as successful as before, it was true. Yet her mother was still with her morning, noon, and night. And it was not until after Mrs. Bierbower died that Elsie, at 42, became a bride. Her husband was Gilbert Wilson, 26, an actor who hadn't enjoyed much success. Elsie said she wanted him to manage her financial affairs. She announced her retirement from the stage, and set about to write books, magazine pieces, movies.

There was plenty else Mr. Wilson had to manage. Elsie, the resourceful enchantress on the stage, was as helpless as an infant in the house. She had never learned to shop for groceries, sew on a button, or cook an egg.

"Mother always did everything for me," she kept repeating. "Liz sacrificed her whole life for me."

Irene Franklin, the redhead and the only one of the Big Four to make a happy, lasting marriage, was a busty woman with a genius for portraying both resentful little girls and an assortment of amusing women characters: an old farm woman, a flirtatious school teacher, a Childs Restaurant waitress, a hotel maid who'd been wronged and abandoned by a handsome traveling salesman. Often when she sang, with her husband Burton Green at the piano, she used her flaming waist-length red hair to thrill audiences. Instead of leaving the stage for a costume change, she'd do all sorts of tricks with her hair, working with the skill and speed of a professional hairdresser. She'd put it up into one type of knot to portray the old farmwife, another to satirize a saucy school teacher. Irene in an instant could roll it into a bun, make spit curls or bangs, braid it, or let it fall full length. She also wrote all of her own material except for the music which Burt supplied.

A wit with a gay, glad heart, Irene combined talent with true humility. She often said, "I sing badly, have only two notes. If I had seven and sang well, I'd probably be studying for opera and starving to death."

She never failed to credit her husband for guiding her to stardom, never lost her wonder at his gift for accompanying her like a mindreader nor missed an opportunity to tell friends that Burt was capable of composing for concert artists and orchestras and was wasting his time setting her lyrics to music.

And Burton Green was a remarkable man. He had started in life as an iron-moulder and was a self-taught musician. He scoffed at his wife's idea that he was responsible for her success, saying, "I'm just part of the scenery of Irene Franklin's act."

Irene's parents were stock company performers. She was born on June 12, 1876, and six months later was carried on the boards in the hearty old melodrama, *Hearts of Oak*. When she was twelve years old Irene, with her mother and her younger sister, went to visit her mother's family in Australia. Her father remained here and Irene never saw him again for he died while they were still away. She lost her mother soon afterwards.

Irene was a teenager when she and her sister returned to the United States. She had a difficult time making a living, couldn't find enough work and never was able to earn more than $25 a week.

Whenever Tony Pastor needed a substitute act for a night in his New York theatre, he'd give Irene a chance to go on. But something was lacking and she knew it. During one of her nights at Pastor's she met Burton Green. He had formerly been the pit pianist there but that evening had come just to see the show. Tony Pastor introduced them and Green told Irene what was wrong with her act. He said he liked her work but she was not getting over as she should because the house piano player was playing her numbers exactly the way he played for everybody else. "You're special," he told Irene, "and the songs you sing should have special arrangements."

At the next show that evening he took the place of the pit pianist—it was before the day when single singers carried their own accompanists with them—and played her numbers as he thought they should be played. Irene relaxed and the applause that greeted her was encouragingly enthusiastic.

He watched her work at other theatres and finally told her, "What you must have, Irene, is an accompanist with intuition. You never sing the same song the same way twice in a row. You'll never get anywhere until you find a piano player who can sense your mood each night, and be able to anticipate your approach at that show."

"I've found the man," she told him. "It's you."

Irene always believed that her meeting with Burt Green was the miracle that changed her life, and remained grateful to him for the rest of her days. Burt was a good-looking, mature man and, at 20, Irene was bewitching, witty, gay, a redhead as feminine as silk stockings.

"It would be wonderful working together," he said. "But

it's impossible." He explained that he was married to Helen van Campen, a columnist on the New York *Morning Telegraph*. He had given up his job at Pastor's to become an advertising salesman for the *Telegraph*, which at the time devoted most of its attention to Broadway.

But he kept working with Irene in his spare time and wrote orchestral arrangements for her. His wife was just as enthusiastic about the girl's future as he was. She urged Green to get a temporary leave of absence from the *Telegraph* so he could help Irene break in a new act.

Early in their partnership they started writing songs together. Irene told Burt that when she was a little girl she had heard her father play some musical phrases on the piano. After he died she wrote words to the melody as she remembered it. Whenever she met a songwriter, she had tried to get him to write down the music to the tune she hummed. She hummed the music to Green and he set down the notes. Together they wrote the song "Redhead," in which a little girl tells of the woes and aggravations of being called redhead, firehead, bricktop, and other names by little boys, and it was Irene Franklin's identification song for the rest of her life.

They broke in their act in Ashland, Pennsylvania, and played in other small towns until they were ready for a tryout at a big-time theatre in New York. They were always big-timers after that, and among the best paid.

But before they got into the real money they decided they wanted to marry. Green liked and respected his wife and they had a child. Fortunately for them, Helen van Campen Green had ideas about marriage that were a half-century ahead of her time. She had gone with men on hunting, fishing, and mining adventures around the world, and believed that husbands and wives should live in separate apartments if they wished, meet only by appointment, and need not ask or answer questions of their mates.

Nevertheless, Green, who knew about the inexplicable whims of women from working with actresses, was not at all sure how advanced her ideas of marriage would remain when it came to divorce. But when he asked the all-important question, she said, "Is Irene Franklin the new love?"

He nodded.

"Then I'll give you a divorce. If it was anyone else but that angel, I'd just hold on to you until you tired of her and came back." She left for Reno almost immediately. While waiting for her decree she wrote a short story based on the triangle.

Besides "Redhead," Irene and her husband wrote other kid songs like "I Don't Care What Happens to Me" and "Somebody Ought to Put the Old Man Wise" which she sang dressed as a little girl in short dress or rompers.

During the more than twenty years that the Greens were the country's most admired man-and-wife team, they got several complaints that puzzled them. One was from a hotel chain asking them to drop their song about the chambermaid who bemoaned the loss of her traveling salesman admirer. The letter said it was bad for the hotel business. While Childs Restaurants objected to one of their waitresses being portrayed as supercilious, saying "they're not all like that."

Suffragettes and other early women's rights advocates disapproved of something Irene had said in an interview. Asked "Is woman's hardest job getting a man?" Irene replied, "No, holding him!" The ladies seemed to think that men were conceited enough without this flattery.

The Greens retained the songs and Irene continued saying what she pleased. After Green died, Irene came back to vaudeville with a new pianist. She tried several including Jerry Jarnigan who turned out to be a fair substitute for Burt. She became Mrs. Jarnigan but that marriage ended in the never explained suicide of Jarnigan, who was much younger than she. In 1929 Irene made her final appearance on Broadway in the hit musical, *Sweet Adeline,* in which she triumphed.

Nora Bayes was the big time's singer–actress supreme. No one was in Nora's class when it came to dramatizing a popular song. Though she had a gift for self-depreciation, Nora billed herself "Empress of Vaudeville." She was madly extravagant, adored children, and was gracious and kind to young performers who worked with or for her. The first four of her five husbands found her impossible to cope with. Her neurotic behavior distressed even calm managers. Though she always needed money, she once quit a thirty-week tour at $1500 a week when refused an extra $75 which she demanded after signing the contract.

Nora was born Nora Goldberg in 1880 at Joliet, Illinois. Her parents were devout Orthodox Jews who regarded the theatre as a house of evil. But they permitted Nora to take singing lessons after she convinced them she wished to sing only at religious ceremonies.

Her first singing teachers encouraged her to study for the opera. But apparently Nora, even as a teenager, knew her own limitations. Whenever it was Amateur Night at the local vaudeville house, Nora would sneak out of her home and go on. She never forgot the sign put out on the stage just before the amateur part of the show started. It read: "Don't Throw Anything!"

Nora ran off to Chicago at 18, met and married Otto Gressing, an undertaker. Her first professional engagement was at the Chicago Opera House which played melodrama. Vaudeville turns were put on between the acts.

Jay Rial, the manager, refused to give her a chance. But Nora told him, "I'll work for nothing if I'm not better than anyone else in your show." She got the job. Rial, who paid her $25 a week, told her she'd need a fancier dress for the evening performance. Nora ran home, decided that the fanciest dress she had was her wedding dress. She wore that. Her first big hit "Down Where the Wurzburger Flows," was a drinking song and she had no trouble after that getting work. It was no accident that Nora became the two-a-day's greatest singer–actress. Early in her career she had gone out to San Francisco and played for months in a stock company. Also for the first and last time she saved her money so she could go to Paris to study singing.

Nora had a natural elegance, along with her talent. But it was the season in stock and the singing lessons in Paris that taught her to dramatize her songs so effectively and use her fine contralto voice so magnificently. Yet she waited several years before invading New York, the capital of the kingdom of vaudeville.

Critics raved about her voice control, diction, and enunciation. Her personality charmed. One woman critic wrote of Nora, "Is there such a thing as languid glamor? If so, she has it. She appears a little wistful as though she'd hate to think you might not like her . . .

"Nora sings a song so simply and naturally it is hard to catch the artifice of it—her roguish smile, a certain delicacy that makes you want to meet her half-way. She needs no bursts of energy, doesn't have to work too hard. She can emphasize a point with a slight glance. . . . There is something of a quality of sadness, even in the merriest of her moments . . ."

Her marriage to undertaker Gressing went on the rocks after nine years. Nora afterwards said that her husband was a very merry mortician indeed who spent almost no time at all at home with her—but it was Gressing who brought the divorce action. Suspicious that she was not all that a wife should be he hired private detectives to follow her. They got the evidence he needed: proof that she had spent one night at least sleeping on an excursion steamer with Frank McKelvey, described in the court papers as the "scion of a Pittsburgh cement tycoon."

Nora met Jack Norworth, who became her second husband, while she was headlining the bill at Proctor's Fifth Avenue Theatre in New York. She had triumphed in the first two editions of the Ziegfeld Follies by then, raising her Follies salary from $75 to $450 a week.

While passing Norworth's dressing room she heard him humming a tune. She stopped at his doorway to ask him what it was. When he told her it was a song he was writing, she offered to work on it with him. The song was "Shine On, Harvest Moon," and when it was published the credits read "Words and Music by Nora Bayes and Jack Norworth."

Nora, incidentally, loved to have her name as a writer on

songs she hadn't written. In 1919 Ring Lardner, the famous short story writer and humorist, sent her his "Prohibition Blues" suggesting she might want to sing it in her show *Ladies First*. When Nora got it published the credits read "by Nora Bayes and Ring Lardner." Lardner, a glum man whose real ambition was to write songs, was very bitter. "She'd changed two words in the lyrics," he said.

Norworth and Bayes married in 1908 and appeared as a team in the 1908 Follies. They were the hit of the show. When they sang "Shine On, Harvest Moon," they seemed a young couple completely in love. Sometimes the curtain would go up after their act and reveal the pair embracing. And to them it was the love of their lives—for a time.

One trouble was that Bayes was a bigger name than Norworth. When they became partners, Nora earned $450 a week, almost twice what Jack was paid. She ordered him around almost as though he were a servant. And she was insanely jealous of Jack who loved and was loved by ladies of all types. Catching him kissing another girl backstage—this was in 1909, the year after their marriage—Nora humiliated him by insisting on billing the team:

NORA BAYES
ASSISTED AND ADMIRED BY JACK NORWORTH

She made him walk her pet dog. He was not allowed to smoke in the house. Norworth also had contracted the habit of chewing tobacco in the Navy which, she said, she found more horrifying than leprosy. She bossed him around so much that one Broadway wag, seeing them rolling by in their limousine, said that Jack must be winning the fight "because

Nora was letting him sit in the rear seat with her, instead of up front with the chauffeur."

During the 1909 Follies, Norworth walked out in a huff. Soon afterwards Nora also left the show. Ziegfeld got an injunction barring them from appearing in the United States. They went to England where they scored a walloping success.

The Ziegfeld suit dragged on for a long time. Nora claimed at the trial that she had quit after Ziegfeld insisted that she wear tights and ride an elephant, both of which she contended were beneath her dignity. Broadway said that she had driven Jack out of the show with her abuse for being too attentive to a madcap star named Lillian Lorraine. The lawsuit was different from the usual theatrical set-tos which simply result in the lawyers on both sides getting richer. In this case, as a result of the publicity, the salary of the team Norworth and Bayes more than doubled, going from about $1000 to $2500.

The roof fell in on Nora in 1913, a year before the Great War started. The team broke up and the marriage of the "happiest couple in show business" ended in divorce. Jack Norworth then went to England where he scored a tremendous success in vaudeville as a single. Nora followed him there and begged for a reconciliation. Jack rejected the idea. He was so angry that he never again sang "Shine On, Harvest Moon." But he wrote other hit songs including "Honey Boy," "Take Me Out to the Ball Game," and "Come Along, My Mandy!"

In England, after the war started, Jack wrote a tongue-twister called "Sister Susie's Sewing Shirts for Soldiers." The British loved this as well as a second that Norworth sang: "Which Switch is the Switch, Miss, for Ipswich." He stayed in wartime London until 1916 when he got tired of German bombs drowning out his applause.

Meanwhile Nora's act had flopped in London. And in the summer of 1914 her doctors told her she couldn't last for six months unless she stopped her stage work at once and took a complete rest. She told reporters that she was suffering from anemia and complete exhaustion.

After being divorced by Norworth, Nora married on the rebound a minor actor named Harry Clarke, who said he was a nephew of Edwin Booth. How deeply hurt she had been by Norworth's loss may be judged by a statement she made for publication:

"Marriage is the only state to be in. I believe a woman should have as many love affairs as she likes, but only one at a time. Also I am sure that a woman may be in love many times, but I cannot understand how she can be on with the new before she is off with the old.

"A man or woman can go directly from one love affair to another and be quite happy. People always have said that it was impossible for a married couple on the stage to be happy. Once I proved the fallacy of this for five years, and now I am proving it again. Happiness is right up to the individual every time."

Her London doctors may or may not have told Nora that she had a malignant cancer but she certainly learned the truth in the sanitarium in Kissingen, Germany, to which they sent her for six weeks of radium treatments. She hurriedly left there on August 4, 1914, the day after the Kaiser's troops invaded Belgium. Her new husband was in Paris and she was unable to reach him. One day her death was announced by a wire service, and the false story was published all over the world. Flowers and messages of condolence flooded the Kissingen sanitarium as Nora fled Germany in a car. She was arrested at the border. Asked her name by the German soldiers on the frontier she wrote "the immortal Nora Bayes of America." She was released, and with her husband sailed home on the *S.S. Rotterdam.*

The worldwide publicity about her "death" and subsequent "escape" from Germany made Nora a national heroine. She opened at the Palace in a wildly acclaimed act with three men supporting her. Hardly anyone noticed that Harry was missing. She and Clarke were divorced on April 12, 1915.

By that time Nora had either introduced or helped make popular a long string of song hits. The first had been "Down Where the Wurzburger Flows," a turn-of-the-century drinking song which she sang in Chicago. Audiences at the Follies had gone wild when she put over "Has Anybody Here Seen Kelly?" They sang the next line "Kelly with the green necktie" with her. In 1917 when George Cohan wrote his wartime song "Over There," he asked Nora to introduce it. The patriotic song—a natural—became America's number one hit. She also made a best seller out of Irving Berlin's "Tell Me, Pretty Gipsy."

During the next few years her salary soared—to $1750 a week, to $2250 and $2500. In 1928 the MGM presentation house, the Capitol, in New York paid her $5000 a week. A Broadway theatre was re-named "Nora Bayes." Nora produced shows there and later took them on tour. Sunday nights she put on one-woman shows in which she sang over two hundred songs. She went back to London and at first flopped there. Nora shrewdly figured out that it was because she'd been presented as a famous headliner. Patrons didn't like a foreigner pushed on them as a star. Nora offered to tour the provinces for only $300 a week. London then "discovered" her and after that she could do no wrong in their music halls.

All through her years of fame Nora's quips were published in newspapers. When she was interviewed by Oscar Hammerstein about an engagement in his vaudeville house his office was being painted. She was horrified because as they talked he'd stop smoking his cigar to spit on the walls.

"I see," said Nora, "that you do your own decorating, Mr. Hammerstein."

She walked into the Broadway restaurant Shanley's one day in a dress so décolleté that her women friends there gasped.

"I understand your astonishment," Nora told them. "When my modiste first tried it on me I asked her if she was dressing me for an opera or an operation."

The failures of her marriages worried her. Yet once boarding a ship for home she smiled because the vessel's orchestra was playing "Lohengrin's Wedding March" in honor of a young couple just married who had walked up the gangplank. "That's my theme song they're playing," whispered Nora to a traveling companion, "my national anthem."

During her middle age the flood of undignified Nora Bayes publicity increased, if anything. There were many stories about her romances, backstage tantrums, and broken contracts. She was single for five years after the Clarke divorce. Then she married another actor, Arthur Gordon, who was playing a small part in her 1920 show, *Ladies First*. They separated after a short while.

Much was published about Nora's extravagances. She adopted three children and took them with her wherever she traveled, along with a half-dozen or more friends. She rented a private railroad car, sometimes a whole train, when she toured. She took half a floor in deluxe hotels.

More should have been published about Miss Bayes' generosity. After the Actors' Fund was established, she pledged her earnings at private entertainments to the Fund. And no star was ever kinder to young performers. In their memoirs both Fred Allen and Harry Richman, whom she hired for her shows, tell of her courtesy, consideration, and encouragement. Richman's story is extraordinary. She had come to his Long Island estate and was watching him play in a baseball game with other young actors. During the game Richman slammed out a foul that struck Nora in the face. Appalled, he ran up and, not knowing how else to comfort her, he started singing to her. Nora, seeing how anguished he was, said, "Would you like to appear in the new show I'm putting on?" Richman accepted with delight.

Helen Clement, a teen-age vaudevillian, was on a bill on which Nora was the headliner. Miss Clement, later Mrs. Russ Brown, was trying to make up and making a mess of it when Nora passed by and saw her. Walking in, she picked up a towel and wiped off the makeup.

"Dear child," she said, "you don't need makeup. You are so young. Your skin is beautiful as it is. Later on, when you're as old as I, you'll need it. You'll be glad of makeup then." Patting the youngster on the shoulder, she left quietly.

In 1925, when Nora was 45, she was proposed to under the most romantic circumstances imaginable. She was sailing for England and among those who came to see her off was Ben Friedland, a banker. As he bid her goodbye he asked her to marry him. Nora accepted. Friedland immediately booked passage for himself so they could be married on board ship.

New York's governor Alfred E. Smith and Mrs. Smith were among the witnesses.

Though happy with Friedland, her fights with her vaudeville bosses became even more tumultuous. Finally, Ed Albee notified all of his bookers that she was never to be allowed to appear in a big-time theatre again.

One day in March, 1928, Nora invited Eddie Darling, the Palace booker, to her home. (He'd forgiven her by now for announcing their engagement without consulting him.) She sang several songs for him and asked him to put a billboard in the Palace lobby, announcing that she would appear there the following week. Darling said, "Mr. Albee would fire me." She said she'd work for no salary. He promised to arrange it.

The next day, Nora sang for the derelicts in Tom Noonan's Bowery Mission, something she had often done. On the way home she stopped off in front of the Palace and walked into the lobby. The billboard was there and she smiled as she studied it. Then she walked to her car and told her chauffeur to drive her home.

A few days later Nora died after an abdominal operation in a Brooklyn hospital. The cancer that had been rotting her insides for so many years had finally killed her.

The only service was private and conducted by a Christian Science practitioner. She was insolvent at her death. In her will was a clause stipulating that she not be buried until her husband died, when they would be buried together. Nora's remains were kept in a vault at Woodlawn Cemetery, New York, until Friedland died, eleven years later. By then he had re-married, but his widow insisted that Nora Bayes' last wish be fulfilled.

CHAPTER THREE

Legends

Perhaps it was really the "Big Five," for Sophie Tucker, massive and homely, had the biggest, brassiest voice of all. The beat in her voice made your heart pound with it, and in syncopated time. With the same gusto she sang everything from the sentimental ballad "Mammy's Little Coal Black Rose" to her cathouse special, "There's Company in the Parlor, Girls, Come On Down."

Soph was one singing single who lived up to her billing, "Last of the Red Hot Mammas." She was still in demand at top money for years after all of the other big-time singing singles were either dead or retired. When old Soph died in 1966 at 82 she was booked ahead for months in night clubs from Miami to Las Vegas.

Young or old, Soph was always hot stuff. A vulgar, loud-spoken woman, she was interested in everybody and everything, loved to play poker and swap dirty stories and hot track tips.

But in her early days, the critics were not friendly to Sophie

at all. In their attempts to describe her tones they would em-
ploy such phrases as "The voice with a stucco finish," "a
booming buckshot voice," and "Tucker's voice combines the
diction of a burlesque theatre's candy seller with the roar of a
steam boiler, hynotic rhythm, and a combination of large and
small bells."

For years reviewers kept attacking Tucker's work. But she
outlasted them. And their successors gradually came to accept
Soph for what she was, a force of nature.

Chicago's savage Percy Hammond described her as "a squat
and sophisticated Maypole" who sang "her lavendar anthology
of night songs, voicing the desires of the ardent female for her
mate. Miss Tucker's repertory comes, in a way, under the
classification of chamber music since its contents are intimate
almost to the point of privacy." But he added ruefully that
"her other hearers were enraptured."

His colleague Ashton Stevens opened his review, "And
speaking of elephants" and then went on to compare Sophie
to vaudeville's most popular female impersonator, saying,
"She has a voice—well, if Julian Eltinge's was as virile as Miss
Tucker's, he would be executing a long over-due male impersonation . . . but she is my headliner . . . some of her songs are
red, white and blue." He cited one number which "becomes
a syncopated hari-kiri before Miss Tucker has finished with it.
Miss Tucker can move an audience or a piano with equal
address . . ."

Chicago, a great show town in those days, was jumping with
Soph's admirers. If they read such criticisms, they probably
were mystified. They turned out in mobs every time Tucker
came around.

Her voice was also baffling to science. A throat specialist, while treating Eddie Cantor for laryngitis, said he'd examined Sophie's throat just two weeks before and predicted, "If she doesn't cut down on her work schedule and take breathing lessons, she'll have no vocal chords at all in five years."

A short time later Cantor asked Sophie how her vocal chords were doing. She gave him one of her big booming laughs, and said, "These aren't vocal chords, Eddie. They are bands of steel!" And they never did wear out.

Soph, who weighed 192 in her prime, sang one song, "Nobody Loves a Fat Girl but How a Fat Girl Can Love!" to prove she didn't care. She did care, of course, but lived with it, being a girl of bouncing spirits and grateful heart. She'd come most of the way on her own and thanked God for giving her the strength and vitality to take it on the chin and keep going.

Sophie was born Sophie Kalish in 1884 while her mother was on the way to America from Southern Russia to join Soph's father who had fled to escape the Czar's military service. She was eight when her family moved to Hartford and started a Jewish restaurant there. It served full course dinners for twenty-five cents. All through grammar school and high school Sophie was the restaurant's girl of all work.

Her one relief came from singing. In the summer she'd stand in the restaurant doorway singing, "Just Break the News to Mother," or the rollicking "Hello, My Baby." Whenever passersby stopped to listen, Sophie would urge them to come in, saying: "Do you know any other restaurant in Hartford where you can get a full course dinner for twenty-five cents, with grand entertainment thrown in free?"

There were tips for Sophie which she was allowed to keep.

But she spent seven days a week, from morning to night except when at school, washing dishes, scrubbing floors, waiting on tables.

Soph was still in high school when she started dating Louis Tuck, a good-looking truckdriver. He proposed to her the night she graduated. She became Mrs. Tuck a few days later and moved into a little home of their own. Within a year, Sophie had a son whom she named Burt. Her husband only made $15 a week and, unable to live on that—Louis was a fancy dresser who liked to go out dancing—they moved in with her mother. There was a quarrel and her husband left, moving to New Haven.

Instead of following him, Sophie and her baby remained and she resumed the old girl-of-all-work routine in the restaurant, and sang whenever she had a spare few minutes. It was near the railway station and more and more vaudeville and burlesque performers while playing Hartford were discovering the place. Willie and Eugene Howard, among others, kept telling her that she ought to try her luck in New York.

Sophie thought it over for quite a while. She was devoted to her baby and her family, and she was not yet twenty. For a young woman brought up in the orthodox Jewish faith to leave her baby and run off to Broadway was something her family and everyone she knew would condemn. They might never forgive her.

But with a hundred dollars in tips that she'd saved, Sophie one night took the train to New York. In a letter she wrote to her mother on the train, Sophie tried to explain her reasons and promised to send money every week for her child's care.

Sophie's first New York singing job was as a coonshouter in the German Village, a huge beer hall in the Tenderloin. It was a place where streetwalkers, closely watched by their pimps, met customers. Sophie was paid $15 a week, plus tips which averaged $85. She sang about a hundred songs a night, everything from heartbreaking ballads about home and mother to the bawdiest numbers she could find, plus songs the customers requested. Every week she sent home what she could for Burt's care.

One hundred dollars a week was a great deal of money for any young woman to be making then. But Sophie saw that she could sing in a beer hall for the rest of her life without getting a chance on the stage, or becoming known anywhere else.

She decided to try small-time vaudeville. That would mean giving up $100 a week for $15 or $20, and a big $25 on the road. But even to get that kind of money, one had to audition at an Amateur Night. Sophie was preparing to go on for her tryout when she heard the booking agent tell his assistant, "This one is so big and ugly the crowd up front will razz her. Better get some cork and black her up. She'll kill 'em."

And Sophie, in blackface, did.

Her agent kept her in blackface for years. He also changed her name to Tucker and billed her as "The World-Renowned Coonshouter," then as "Sophie Tucker, the Ginger Girl, Refined Coon Singer" and in New York as "Sophie Tucker, Manipulator of Coon Melodies."

Sophie quickly caught on to the fact that vaudeville audiences enjoy something new. As she finished each date, she'd ask the manager to book her again, and promised, "I'll sing different songs next time. Maybe some that your customers never heard before."

In *Some of These Days*, the autobiography Soph wrote with Dorothy Giles, she describes how tough she found working the small time, particularly on the road. Out of her twenty-five a week, she sent home five dollars. There was also the five percent, $1.25, her agent got. She could afford only to buy lisle stockings—three pairs for a dollar. Each night she washed the pair she'd worn that day together with her other laundry.

And she was lonely. There were few other women singles playing the small time then. The men on the bill never asked her out. Soph thought later that she may have intimidated them because she never asked for advice, took care of her own luggage, bought her own railway tickets, and found a boarding house for herself in each town. There were the usual small town sports hanging around the theatres but they seemed the same kind she had avoided at the German Village.

After a year of tough trouping, Soph moved up to $40 a week in burlesque. Shortly afterwards, she got the big break she'd been waiting for—a job in the new Ziegfeld Follies in which Nora Bayes and Jack Norworth were to be featured. Tucker was given four songs to sing.

At the opening in Atlantic City, she stopped the show with a wild, bombastic number called, "It's Moving Day Way Down in Jungle Town."

Miss Bayes, as the star, resented Sophie's applause and got Ziegfeld to give three of the four songs to her. When Bayes and Norworth walked out, Soph expected to get back the songs. But Eva Tanguay who replaced the team liked them all and insisted on keeping them. That left the newcomer with nothing to do and she was let out.

Later Sophie said that this crushing disappointment taught her the most valuable lesson of her life: the theatre might seem glamorous but it was first of all a business. And she ran her career with that in mind from then on.

Following the Follies debacle, she returned to vaudeville at $40 a week and soon was raised to $75. Wherever she played, she tipped the head stagehand and orchestra leader a couple of bucks each, increasing the tips as her salary grew.

She also started building her own following. Whenever she met people in her travels she'd ask for their names and addresses. Then when she was to play that city again, she'd write them postcards announcing "Sophie Tucker, the greatest vaudeville act in the world, is returning to the Orpheum in two weeks. Be sure to come to see me and drop back afterwards to my dressing room to say hello."

Tucker kept that up through the rest of her career. Eventually she was writing 7000 postcards a year to her friends out front, along with birthday and Christmas presents to those who had become pals. Ultimately she had to get a secretary.

Sophie spent a fortune each year on new gowns, jewels, exclusive songs and material, and considered it an investment. She believed audiences wanted to see her do something new in something new every time they saw her. "Every time I step on a stage there's fifty thousand dollars riding on me—twenty-five thousand in clothes, twenty-five thousand in new songs and material."

But her taste in clothes did not improve as her star rose. One uncharitable soul observed, "When she was young, Soph dressed and looked like a hooker. After she became a headliner, she dressed and looked like the madame." Her idea of elegance was almost on a level with Tanguay's.

The songs specially written for her were often first rate. As Sophie got older, she would interrupt her great singing to philosophize like Pearl Bailey. Her favorite homily came in a song about "life's highway." She'd pause in the music to say that there was "always a turning" on that road—sooner or later philanderers and crooks got it in the neck. Even then, as a truth, it seemed dubious but the remarks were applauded by audiences everywhere.

Soph always liked to reward her admirers with a naughty song or two, but the big time frowned on this. When the manager of the Keith theatre in Atlantic City insisted she eliminate "Who Paid the Rent for Mrs. Rip Van Winkle while Rip Van Winkle Was Away?" Soph walked out. John Royal from Cleveland sent a report on March 31, 1917, to the New York office saying he had cut that same song from Miss Tucker's routine, adding: "This woman must be watched carefully. It is unfortuate that a woman of her talents must stoop to such a low type of song. . . . She goes very big, however."

This was the kind of censorship that caused vaudevillians to refer to the Keith chain as "the Sunday School circuit." Sophie always believed it was this prissiness that kept her out of the Palace after it opened. Consequently she was first booked there only because they needed a last-minute replacement for Ruth Roye, who'd suddenly been taken ill. Soph almost caused a riot. *Variety* reported: "She just walked out and owned the place."

Years later Sophie was on stage at the Palace singing when fire broke out backstage. She calmly told the audience to leave quietly and the newspapers devoted much space to the efficiency with which the house staff got the crowd out safely and extinguished the blaze. But there were other headlines too: "RED HOT MAMA BURNS UP PALACE THEATRE" and "SOPHIE'S SONGS SO HOT, THEATRE BURNS UNDER THEM!"

As a big-timer, Sophie also found a great many friends

among her fellow artists. She loaned money to those down on their luck, played benefits whenever asked, and gave advice when she thought it was needed. One benefit that she organized herself netted $12,000.

But when it came to her work, Soph was both martinet and perfectionist and she behaved like a queen with those she employed in her act. Her piano player Ted Shapiro never dared call her anything but "Miss Tucker" during the 42 years he worked with her. She was also tough with the five musicians in the band added to her act after she became a headliner. Their billing read: "Sophie Tucker, the Queen of Jazz and Her Five Kings of Syncopation." The week before the act was to play the all-important New York Palace date, the five bandsmen presented her with an ultimatum for more pay. Sophie felt they had come to think themselves more important to the act than she and told them, "Okay, boys! The act closes on Sunday night. No more Sophie Tucker and her Five Kings of Syncopation." She went on at the Palace alone.

Sophie Tucker always believed she began cabaret in this country when she was booked into Reisenweber's restaurant on New York's Columbus Circle as mistress of ceremonies and chief entertainer. Though she spent most of her long career in vaudeville, she admitted that she preferred night club work. She loved taming down that most difficult of all audiences and her language could be rough as a sailor's with them if necessary.

Harry Richman learned that the hard way. Sophie had praised and encouraged him when Harry was a child pianist in Cincinnati. After being discharged from the World War I navy, Harry went to see her at Reisenweber's. But during Sophie's act he got into a panic—he was afraid he couldn't pay the bill, got up from his table, and walked out. Sophie saw him leave and refused to speak to him for years. When she did, she told him: "Listen to me, kid, and never forget what I'm telling you. Not even Jesus Christ Himself walks out on Tucker."

Sophie got Joe Frisco and other vaudevillians their first New York break at Reisenweber's. But she was much prouder of her matchmaking. She introduced Gil Boag, a fast buck promoter, to Gilda Gray, the shimmy queen. Boag married Gilda and then managed her career very successfully.

Soph got even more satisfaction pairing Belle Baker and Maurice Abrams. Belle had seen Abrams and told Sophie she was eager to meet him. Shortly afterwards, Abrams brought Tucker "Yiddisha Mama," a song he wanted her to introduce. Though she liked the number, Soph suggested that Belle was the singer who could really put it over. Their marriage was happy and lasted. And later Tucker often used the song herself.

Sophie lamented her own love life, though readily admitted: "If you've got a man you can take whatever life deals you. There isn't a woman in the world who doesn't feel like that—no matter what she tells her hairdresser."

For some time she believed that Frank Westphal would turn out to be that man. Frank was tall, handsome, and much younger than Soph and they met shortly before Louis Tuck, her first husband, died. Westphal was a low pressure comedian who also sang and played the piano in his act. He was amusing and so was his casual way of coming on stage. Dressed for the street and also wearing rubbers, he pushed his piano on stage himself. He took off his hat and raincoat, hung them up, then took the bench off the piano and sat on it to take off his rubbers. While doing this, he chatted with the audience as though he were in their parlor. Then he'd play, sing, and tell a few jokes.

When Westphal finished, he'd put on his rubbers, hat, and raincoat, return the bench back to the piano, bid his audience goodbye, and leave, pushing the piano offstage.

One week when they were both on the bill he made a second appearance while Sophie—the headliner—was on without warning her about it. He told her gravely: "Excuse me, Miss Tucker. I forgot to play one of my numbers while I was on. I know you won't mind if I do it now." Sophie was surprised but she knew how enchanted audiences were to see something unexpected happen. So Westphal played a song and she joined him in singing it. The stunt got a big hand and Sophie kept it in her act.

After they were married Westphal became less amusing, both on stage and off. She was still the headliner, with Westphal just another act on the program. He became restive. Once an auto racer, he still loved to tinker with cars and told Sophie he wanted to get into the car business. Sophie bought him a garage out on Long Island. But when she took him to see it, he shuddered on seeing in big lights the sign: SOPHIE TUCKER'S GARAGE. That ended the marriage. Sophie blamed herself, saying she'd thought only of what wonderful publicity that sign would be.

Her third husband was Al Lackey, a man about town who became her manager. Soph divorced him in 1934, after four years of marriage. Al walked into the Lambs Club one day and told the assembled thespians: "Well, I'll say this for Old Soph. None of the checks she gave me ever bounced."

Sophie answered the ungrateful Lackey in a song that went,

"There is not going to be any fourth Mr. Ex. I'm darned if I'll pay any more alimony checks. I'm living alone and I like it."

Sophie never tried to appear more refined off stage than on. She remained raucous, loud-mouthed, and would do such things as shouting in a restaurant to friends at other tables. After her son Burt grew up, he worked as a salesman in I. Miller's New York shoe store. Then Sophie's shouting across the restaurant became a sales pitch for him: "Know you need shoes, Helen. Why not go over to I. Miller's and ask for my son, Burt? He told me they just put in a new line of beautiful shoes."

Sophie did act unlike herself one week while playing the Palace. She had just come back from a triumphant tour of English music halls, where she saw acts she admired billed "Madame." So Soph had herself billed at the Palace, "Madame Sophie Tucker"—but only for a couple of days. A friend, seeing the billing, yelled to her on Broadway, "Hey, Sophie, what kind of business did you do at your cathouse last Saturday?" Sophie had the "Madame" removed at once.

Even as a beginner, Mae West apparently knew that it was sex rather than her performing gifts that would make her rich and famous. When she was sixteen, Attorney Jim Timoney, her first important lover, brought her to his friend Ned Brown, sports editor of the New York *World*. Timoney, a Brooklyn lawyer and politician, asked Brown, "Can you get this little girl's picture in your Sunday theatrical section?" Ned, a Broadway rounder, said he thought so and suggested she wear a bathing suit for the camera study. "No," said Mae, "I want to wear this." She took her coat off. The dress she wanted to be pictured in had a round piece cut out of the upper section, exposing her entire left breast. Mr. Brown recalled later, "It was the only time in my life I ever regretted working for a family newspaper."

Mae was born in Brooklyn in 1893. Her father was Battling Jack West, who came of Irish-English stock. The battler was so pugnacious that when he couldn't get paying engagements, he fought all comers for kicks as a bouncer in Coney Island dives and on the street. Mae's mother, Matilda Doelger West, was a blonde beauty of German descent. Mae, like Eva Tanguay, was pretty much of a loner after she made her reputation, but adored her mother and loved her sister and brother. As a child she got her first stage training in amateur night contests and with a Brooklyn stock company, playing in everything from low comedy to low melodrama. Later, again like Tanguay, she worked in an acrobatic act. Then followed a song-and-dance act with Frank Wallace, a song-and-dance man. At seventeen she was briefly married to him. After they broke up their act, Mae simply forgot him, not bothering to divorce him. He popped up again in the thirties, only after she was established as Hollywood's sexiest actress and box office queen.

In vaudeville, Mae developed her trick of singing suggestive songs two ways: with the leer of a hopeful woman rapist, or (when a cop or one of Mr. Albee's spies was in the house) as an innocent child who did not really know what the naughty lyrics meant.

The manager of one New York Keith theatre made such a critical report to Ed Albee, the big time's czar, that he sent for Mae and had her do her whole act for him and his secretary, with her accompanist Harry Richman at the piano in the otherwise empty Palace. The song, "If You Don't Like My Peaches Why Do You Shake My Tree?" was the number that had most upset the manager. In his theatre, Mae had sung it using all of her vocal and physical equipment to appeal to her male listeners' baser instincts. But before the head of the Keith Circuit, she sang it in her childlike voice, clasping her hands to one cheek and casting her eyes upward like an innocent little girl.

Instead of cancelling the act, Albee told the manager he had a dirty mind. Booked into another theatre, Richman recalled, Mae delivered the lines with the most suggestive movements he ever saw on a stage.

Unlike the giddy Tanguay, Mae always knew what she was doing—and why. She boasts in her autobiography of her dozens of lovers. At one point, she explains that strong and important citizens were attracted to her because they were aware that, "I was not like the other women they knew. They soon discovered I would not conform to the old fashioned limits they had set on a woman's freedom of action . . . but none of them left me: my problem was how to get rid of them." Like Miss Tanguay, Mae neither drank nor smoked. She says that though she did not invent sex she "rediscovered it."

Not long after the episode with the *World*'s Mr. Brown, her appearance in a Philadelphia theatre was advertised: "She does a muscle dance in a sitting position. It is all in the way she does it, and her way is all her own." Sime Silverman, editor of *Variety*, thought she could get by on talent alone. Reviewing her act at Hammerstein's, he wrote: "She's one of the many freak persons on the vaudeville stage where freakishness often carries more weight than talent, but Miss West

should be coached to deliver the full value of her personality."
At another Broadway vaudeville house, Mae had a shoulder
strap that broke at almost every performance. Later she did an
act with her sister whose finale had her come out in a male
dress suit, fully testing her control of her many muscular
protuberances.

She scored a hit at the Palace in 1922 with Harry Richman
still at the piano. But Mae never played as much vaudeville
as she could have. Richman says it was not her sexy gestures
and wigglings that lost her dates, but rather money. Mae insisted on getting $750 a week and Keith would pay no more
than $500. She held out while bills for both of them piled up.
Richman's pleas that he was hungry and about to be kicked
out of his hotel failed to move her.

"Let 'em pay me what I'm worth," said Mae, and that was
that.

In 1918, Mae had made a hit in Ed Wynn's musical show
"Sometime" in which she did the shimmy, along with her
other specialties. Her role as Mayme Dean, a wisecracker, was
tailor-made.

Mae has always claimed she introduced the shimmy to
Broadway. She first saw the dance—then called the "Shimmy-
shawobble"—in Chicago's Negro dives. There the patrons, "to
the music of 'Can House Blues' " says Mae, "stood in one spot
with scarcely any movement of their feet, and just shook their
shoulders, torsos, breasts and pelvises. We thought it was
funny, and were terribly amused by it. But there was a naked,
sensual agony about it, too."

Gilda Gray, who specialized in this non-dancing art form,
insisted she'd done it first on the big white street at Reisen-

weber's Cabaret. Gilda became famous with her shimmy. So did another beautiful blonde, Bee Palmer.

Mae West wrote and acted in shimmying sex plays in the mid-twenties which made her more famous and better paid than both of them. She then crowned her career by becoming the star of very funny movies which are still being shown in art theatres and on TV. Her double entendres made hits all over the world and in her scenes with Cary Grant and other masculine idols Mae never made a secret of what part of their anatomy interested her most.

Few vaudeville fans thought of Emma Carus as a sexpot. She had long blonde hair that she coiled in braids on top of her head, blue eyes, and too much chin—she was built like the powerful German servant girl she once had been.

Emma could belt out songs in five dialects—Scotch, Dutch, Irish, Negro, and British—and for a time billed herself, "The Human Dialect Cocktail." Her best trick was switching without warning from her contralto to a deep baritone. Because she usually did this during her Scotch number while dressed in bonny kilts she was called, "The Kilted Baritone."

Amy Leslie, then the Midwest's seeress on the drama, acclaimed her: "Emma Carus is about the only one of the big-time singers who has a cultivated and genuine voice. It is a sweet contralto voice with excellent mezzo register and she uses it well."

Not everyone agreed, of course. In fact, the noise Miss Carus projected when making her voice switch caused the Kansas City *Post* critic to warn her in his review: "When singing, remember you are in an enclosed building and not trying to be heard throughout the whole city, including the stockyards."

Emma was born in Berlin in 1879 and brought here as a baby by impoverished parents. Her mother died when she was four and a few years later her father became an invalid whom she supported for the rest of his life. An attempt had been made to present her on the stage as a child singer but it failed.

When Emma was eleven she was working as a slavey in a boarding house in New York for her meals, a bed, and $1 a week. Her duties included taking care of two little children. She kept them quiet while doing the dishes by singing German lullabies. One day Morris Rosenthal, a music publisher, heard her as he was passing the house. He went in, found her in the kitchen, and told her she had a "valuable timbre" in her voice and said he might be able to get her a job as a singer.

The job involved singing two songs at the eighteen shows a day put on by a New York museum; her pay was $2 a day. These museums had sprung up all over the country following Barnum's success. Besides the shows at the five-and-ten cent theatre, there were exhibits of freaks, fossils, curios, and wild animals.

Nine years later Emma, at twenty, was making $100 a week on the big time. She knew she was no beauty and could hardly believe it when Sture Mattson, a Yale graduate who was heir to a fortune and member of an illustrious family, fell in love with her and asked her to marry him. There was irony in what followed.

Other thrifty vaudevillians existed, but Emma was just about the most frugal of them all. Fellow artists claimed she made her own clothes even after she was earning $750 a week. Some of her competitors declared that only Sandow, the world's strongest man, could have squeezed a loose quarter out of her.

To her Sture represented everything she wanted in a husband. But the marriage didn't last long for a curious reason:
he loved her too much. Every night, after a few drinks at a
saloon, young Mattson would start boasting about his talented bride. Insisting that they all see and hear her for themselves, he would invite everybody in the saloon to the theatre
as his guests.

Though Emma loved adulation this was too much. She
urged Sture to get a job but he said he was too busy building
up her following. "He had $800 a month income," she later
told reporters, "but he was spending more on tickets than I
earned. No one was ever more devoted to a woman but his
love for me never drove him to work."

She had little luck in subsequent marriages, even though
she usually went to the trouble of establishing businesses for
her men. These included a talent agency and a company to produce plays and operate theatres. None of these earned much
money but one of the clients she discovered was Carl Randall,
a sensational young English dancer. She put Randall in her
act and though Emma weighed 197 pounds she told friends
she intended to dance with him. In eighteen months, by
heroic slimming, she got down to 127 pounds and amazed her
fans by shaking a wicked shimmy on stage and dancing like a
mad young thing with her phenomenal hoofer. Emma died in
1927, leaving more than $200,000 in real estate, household
goods, and cash.

Like Emma, Ruth Roye—one of the big time's best loved
singing ladies—spent almost nothing on wardrobe, written
material, exclusive songs, a special drop, or an accompanist.
Ruth was a cute little girl with a turned up nose, but she was

not really pretty. Anyone seeing her walk on for the first time might easily have thought she'd somehow wandered on stage by mistake. But the moment Ruth started her first number, she tore the house apart. There was a beat to her singing that made your own heartbeat increase. She created excitement with everything she sang. She delivered ballads well but her explosive handling of such comic numbers as "Mooching Along," and "He's a Devil in His Own Home Town," were what made her a sensation. In 1915 Ruth started singing "Waiting for the Robert E. Lee!" This popular number had been published three years before and was sung everywhere by big-timers and many lesser shouters. But Ruth Roye's delivery, which consisted of sounding and puffing like a tiny, turbulent steamboat and shuffling her feet in time, was so explosive that it became her song. And Ruthie never went on after that without the audience screaming: "Waiting for the Robert E. Lee!"

Miss Roye gave few interviews. In one she explained, "I didn't go on the stage. I was pushed on by my family. When I was a very young girl my brother opened a nickelodeon in Brooklyn. Business was so bad that to cut expenses they fired a singer who was getting $20 a week, and the ticket-taker who was getting $15. I had a strong contralto voice and they paid me five dollars a week for doing both jobs. I had such a good time singing and I enjoyed it so much that my brother said I shouldn't be paid anything. Like a boob, I agreed with him!"

Ruth, billed under her real name, Ruth Becker, next worked in small-time vaudeville for a year at $35 a week. It was there, she said, that she learned how to use her voice properly in putting over a song. A smart agent got her up to $500 a week on the big time, but in the summer of 1913 he accepted $400 a week for her at the New York Palace which, unlike most theatres, stayed open in the hot weather. The Palace, which had just opened, already had become the best showcase in America for theatrical talent. Many acts took reduced salaries for the chance to work there. Ruth Roye killed them at the Palace, just as she'd done everywhere else. That first week was additionally impressive because she'd come on booked into the Number Two spot (second on the bill) when the patrons—they drifted in late at the Palace—were still arriving. Her reception was so uproarious that she played there for several successive weeks and remained a beloved act everywhere until she retired.

More than one of the singing singles enjoyed her first real success when she sang what became her identification number. A young rosy-cheeked, blonde farm girl named Louise Kerlin was all but starving the day she walked into the Chicago office of a song publishing house to request professional copies of its new numbers. A tall, corpulent, middle-aged man heard Louise give her name to the receptionist, and asked, "Are you any relation to Billy Kerlin who years ago was an engineer on the Terre Haute and Evansville Railroad?"

"I am his daughter, but he's dead," she said, bursting into tears. "He was killed in a train wreck."

The man seemed shocked. He told Louise that he was Paul Dresser. She was awed. Dresser, whose real name was Dreiser, was then the country's most successful song writer and publisher. He'd made—and squandered—the half-million dollars he'd earned on his own hits, including "On the Banks of the Wabash Far Away" and "Just Tell Them That You Saw Me."

Dresser explained that when he was a boy he had sold magazines and candy on her father's train. The rest of the crew was forever taunting him because he was fat and one day her father walked into the crew car and caught them teasing him so much that he was crying. Kerlin told them to quit bothering the youngster. And if they didn't, he said, he'd fight them all one at a time. Paul had no trouble after that. But Dresser had never thanked Billy Kerlin.

On questioning Louise, he got her to admit that she'd been having a hard time getting even church jobs. She'd gone hungry more than once since coming to Chicago. After asking her to sing for him, Dresser told her, "As I said, I never got the chance to thank your father. But I think I can do something for his daughter." He loaned her some money to tide her over. When they next met, Dresser suggested that she might have better luck if he introduced her as his kid sister. He would also write a song for her debut.

The song was "My Gal Sal," which turned out to be one of Paul Dresser's biggest hits, and launched her—as Louise Dresser—on a long career, first as a singer, then as a dramatic actress.

Everybody on Broadway believed Louise was his sister. That caused her some embarrassment a year or two later when Dresser died, and the obituaries listed her among his surviving relatives. Paul's brother Theodore Dreiser, the novelist, insisted that the papers publish a correction.

It hurt her feelings, but not her career. She was well-established on her own by then and out of gratitude to Paul Dresser, she kept the name he'd given her. She later married Jack Norworth but that lasted only until she discovered that he had become infatuated with Trixie Friganza. Later still, she appeared in vaudeville sketches with her second husband, Jack Gardner, and ended her career as one of Hollywood's favorite character actresses.

Trixie didn't keep Norworth's affections for very long. Nora Bayes quickly got him. Not that Trixie seemed to mind. She was always too interested in having a good time to worry about losing a man. But to have taken away the flibbertigibbet Romeo even briefly from Louise Dresser was quite a triumph. At the time of their amorous caper, Trixie weighed 190 pounds and was a dozen years older than Louise.

Trixie was a rollicking butterball who sang and danced with skill and zest. She delighted audiences with her comments about her size: "When I started in show business I was so thin that you could blow me through a keyhole. Now you have to take down the whole door to get me through. Being fat may be a tragedy to the society dame, but not for me. By putting on one-third more weight I doubled my salary. And look at how many other hefty women are vaudeville headliners: Marie Dressler, Stella Mayhew, Emma Carus, Sophie Tucker, and May Irwin."

Trixie was born in 1870 in Ireland. Her real name was Brigid O'Callaghan, her father Irish, her mother Spanish. She borrowed her mother's name for stage purposes. Trix grew up in Cincinnati. At 15, she was a $3-a-week salesgirl when she ran away with *Pearl of Pekin*, a touring musical. Her mother went to the Cincinnati police to help her get her under-age daughter to return. After talking to the runaway, the police chief convinced her mother that Trixie's morals would be no more endangered as an $18-a-week chorus girl than they would be as an underpaid salesgirl.

By the turn of the century Trixie was being acclaimed "Broadway's Favorite Champagne Girl." Nobody had any idea that she had once been married. That only came out when Trix, at forty, decided to marry Charles Goettler, the company manager of a musical show she was touring in which that week was appearing in Cincinnati. Trixie, a good Catholic, insisted on having a church ceremony. She readily admitted to the priest she talked to that she had been secretly married once before in a civil ceremony but refused to tell him the man's name. That angered the priest and he refused to marry her and Goettler.

The couple then spent frustrating hours going from parish house to parish house with the same result. Finally, while telling their story to a Jesuit, it occurred to Trixie to mention that her husband had died. In that case, the cleric decreed, she did not have to reveal her dead spouse's name and he married them.

Trixie, like Emma Carus, tried to establish a business for her bridegroom. A travel agency, it failed to make money and apparently the marriage also failed. As far as we know, Trixie Friganza never re-married.

Miss Friganza was herself a good businesswoman and among her properties at one time was a plantation in South Carolina. She always planned to retire while still on top, which she did in 1927. Trixie moved to Hollywood to be close to her many friends in show business and lived happily there until she died at the ripe old age of 85.

*   *   *

Opera singers were among the classiest headliners on the big time. But Fritzi Scheff, a one-time member of the New York Metropolitan Opera Company, was about the only one who made the two-a-day the chief source of her income throughout the rest of her career. The adorable little Fritzi was born in Vienna on August 30, 1879. Her mother was the opera singer Anna Yeager and her father, Dr. Gottfried Scheff, physician at the Emperor's court. Fritzi made her debut at eighteen when she sang the title role in *Martha* at the Nuremberg Opera House. Three years later she made her first appearance here at New York's Metropolitan Opera. In the three years she remained under contract to the Met, Mlle. Scheff sang in more than thirty operas with Caruso, Melba, Calve, and the other great stars of that Golden Era. By offering her a better salary, Charles Dillingham got her to star in his operetta *Babette*. It was two years later, in 1905, in *Mlle. Modiste,* another Victor Herbert operetta, that Broadway took her to its heart. The first nighters went wild when she sang "Kiss Me Again."

Fritzi, who had auburn hair, a doll-like figure, and the *hauteur* of a great opera star, had not wanted to sing the song that was identified with her until the end of her career. While in vaudeville, she spent money wildly in the tradition of giddy opera larks. Buster Keaton lived through Hollywood's gold bathtub and custom-made yacht era without being unduly impressed. But he never forgot how amazed he had been by Mlle. Scheff's life style when the family act "The Three Keatons" played on a bill with her at the Grand Theatre, Pittsburgh, while Fritzi was the headliner.

"This little lady," recalled Buster more than forty years later, "carried 36 pieces of luggage with her and an entourage consisting of her pianist, a chauffeur, a footman and two French maids. One maid served her at the theatre, the other at her hotel suite. A week before Fritzi arrived in each city on her route an interior decorator redecorated and refurnished the suite and her dressing room. The decor of the dressing room featured magnificent mirrors with gold frames and drapes suitable to one of the fabulous boudoirs at Versailles.

"Fritzi traveled in a private car. Attached to this was a flat car carrying her Pierce-Arrow. She used the Pierce-Arrow only to travel between her hotel and the theatre, or when there was only a short jump to the next city on her tour. Carrying the car on the flat car on long jumps made sense, if the rest of her grandeur didn't. In those days the roads were too rough for long trips."

Fritzi Scheff was married and divorced three times, which seems to be about par for singing ladies. Her husbands were Baron Friedrich von Bardeleben, John Fox, Jr., and George Anderson, actor. Fox was an author. His most famous work *The Trail of the Lonesome Pine* was a long-time best seller dedicated to Fritzi; it offered the most heartwarming view ever taken of Appalachia.

When Fritzi went broke it was with a bang, naturally. She was playing in Cincinnati in 1914 in a show called *Pretty Miss Smith* when her gowns were claimed by Henri Bendel, Inc., who said Fritzi's unpaid bill was $700. Other creditors were swarming all over the theatre. *Variety* commented that the show (which closed immediately) had more attachments against it than any in theatrical history.

CHAPTER FOUR

Bring on the Clowns

Over the years the big time marshaled and presented thousands of clowns and comedians. They came in all shapes, sizes, and guises and some of the funniest were women. Fannie Brice, Marie Dressler, Gracie Allen, Ray Dooley, Patsy Kelly—all made audiences laugh with joy.

They worked in every way imaginable, in black face or white face, in street clothes or costume, as a single act, girl and boy team, two man or two girl act, in trios, quartets, family acts. Some standard acts—like Victor Moore and Emma Littlefield and Imhof, Conn and Corinne—never changed their routine, coming back year after year with the same gags and still getting howls.

Others were forever switching their partners and costumes. Men just introduced by their agents went out as brother acts, girls as sister acts. Many came to the big time from minstrel shows, the circus, burlesque, the sports world or legitimate theatre.

Usually the comic had a straight man as a foil. He'd repeat the comic's questions to heighten interest or challenge him with taunts. Certain fine comedians could never learn to work effectively with another straight man after their first one died, retired, or quit the team. Others continued as stars without their original partners: Bobby Clark without Paul McCullough, Fred Stone without Dave Montgomery, Willie Howard without his brother Eugene.

The history of the Broadway musical theatre is studded with the names of vaudeville comic teams whose shows ran for years and coined money: Weber and Fields and Montgomery and Stone down to Olsen and Johnson. All but one of the brilliant funny people in the Ziegfeld Follies had learned or sharpened their art in vaudeville: W. C. Fields, Will Rogers, Ray Dooley, Ed Wynn, Eddie Cantor, Leon Errol, and Bert Williams. The exception was Fannie Brice who came to Zieggy's attention while in burlesque.

Every day for the fifty years that the big time was the biggest business in show business, its army of laugh-makers brought forth smiles, chuckles, and belly-laughs all over the country. And vaudeville's best-loved graduates continued doing it in the fifty years that have followed—in radio, movies, night clubs, and on television. For a whole century, through wars and all other sorts of hell, they have blessed us with a Golden Era of Laughter.

These mountebanks, clowns, and satirists romped, climbed walls, mugged, and made gags about almost everything on earth, including floods, earthquakes, hanging judges, and death itself. They imitated each other and did priceless takeoffs on the latest Broadway plays. Nothing human escaped their jesters' eyes. Among favorite targets were generals, admirals, congressmen, trolley-car conductors, bricklayers,

firemen, hotelkeepers, truckdrivers, thieving tradesmen, sales-
men, spendthrifts, old maids, schoolma'rms, hillbilly grand-
mas who drank, misers, gamblers, conmen, waiters, braggarts,
punch-drunk fighters, mothers-in-law, wives, husbands, maids-
of-all-work, janitors, clergymen, tax-collectors, city slickers,
country jakes, indignant citizens, ballet dancers, bumbling
magicians, Negroes, haughty Englishmen, French Casanovas,
shrewd Jewish peddlers, German street musicians, Irish blar-
ney slingers.

Their great accomplishment was enabling millions of men,
women, and children not only to forget their troubles for
a few hours, but to laugh at them.

Being uneducated street kids, many of vaudeville's satirists didn't even know what the word satirist meant. Charlie
Chaplin, who did know, thought of himself purely as a clown
until intellectuals convinced him that he was a social critic.
It turned his head, made him self-conscious, and certainly
did his subsequent films no good. Buster Keaton, who also
knew, once read a piece in an art magazine that bewildered
him. "Why," he asked a friend, "do they call me a creative
artist? I'm only a comedian, an expert at throwing custard
pies and taking pratt falls."

"It's because you *are* a creative artist. In your work you
have made an original and authentic comment on society."

Buster gave a skeptical look, and walked away.

The most famous family act was "Eddie Foy and His Seven
Little Foys" which Pop Foy kept on the big time for more
than ten years. In 1913, when he first offered it, Eddie was
57. He had been a great star in musical extravaganzas and
other singing shows for thirty years as well as a producer.

But he'd retired some years before with his wife and seven kids to a farm in the New York suburb of New Rochelle.

Foy had wanted to name his first son Eddie Jr.—if the child looked like him. But when the boy was born Foy found no resemblance and had him christened Lincoln Bryan Fitzgerald Foy. He explained that Lincoln was for the infant's birthplace, Lincoln, Nebraska, Bryan for that state's leading citizen, and Fitzgerald because that was Eddie's real name. The second son didn't look like him either and, at his Italian wife's request, he was given the name of Giovanni Vittorio Emmanuel Fitzgerald Foy, in honor of the King of Italy. Eddie's eldest, however, always used the one name, Bryan, and the second asked that he be called Charlie. It was not until his fourth son was born that Papa Foy, after pronouncing him "the dead spitting image of me," acclaimed him Eddie Foy, Jr.

The Foy kids—five boys and two girls—were famous long before they stepped on a stage. Their father took them on tour with him when possible and wherever they went newspapers ran feature stories about them as the largest and most uninhibited family in vaudeville. After they moved to the farm they continued to be good copy. To visitors Eddie seemed like one of the kids, playing ball, flying kites, and shooting marbles with them. He bought all kinds of animals for the children to study and play with: a cow, horse, chickens, ducks, rabbits, and, of course, many cats and dogs. Eddie was often interviewed about his theories on child-rearing.

One afternoon a neighbor and friend of Foy's, arrived to find Bryan hammering nails into the front door with a croquet mallet. Young Eddie was pulling stuffing out of a davenport in the living room. Charlie was happily making wigs

TONY PASTOR'S THEATRE IN TAMMANY HALL

Jimmy Savo

Both photos by UPI

Mae West, circa 1919

Culver

FRITZI SCHEFF

PAUL MCCULLOUGH AND BOBBY CLARK

AL JOLSON
Culver

LOUISE DRESSER
UPI

BERT WILLIAMS

FRANK FAY

THE DOLLY SISTERS

IRENE FRANKLIN AT
THE PALACE

Both photos by Culver

A. ROBINS

ADELAIDE AND HUGHES AT THE WINTER GARDEN

NORA BAYES

Both photos by Culver

JACK BENNY, AGE 15

Culver

ABOVE: ELSIE JANIS

ELSIE JANIS AND HER MOTHER
SAIL FOR EUROPE

Culver

EDWARD ALBEE

OSCAR HAMMERSTEIN

UPI

SOPHIE TUCKER

WILL ROGERS

Culver

Culver

HERB WILLIAMS

Culver

EDDIE FOY

and false beards out of the stuffing. Irving, the youngest son, was trying to saw the legs off a table.

The other children were making so much noise on their own that Foy and his visitor couldn't hear one another. But the comedian did not tell them to quiet down or to stop their assault on the furniture. He did ask Bryan not to drive the nails through to the door's other side where they might snag visitors' clothing. He also urged Eddie to pull out the divan's stuffing evenly so it wouldn't be lopsided. He had the same advice to Irving about cutting each table leg at the same height so the lamp wouldn't fall off.

When the friend was leaving, Eddie explained, "They're understudying the Katzenjammer Kids."

The kids got the surprise of their hellraising young lives when their father started rehearsing them for their debut. He turned from adoring father to complete martinet. "We learned everything we know about acting from him," said Eddie Jr. many years later, "but he could be a stern disciplinarian. And it's not easy to keep seven kids in line and attentive. If we did something wrong, he'd step down hard on our foot. It hurt. But he gave us good advice: 'If you can't dance good, dance fast.' After showing us a routine, he'd say, 'That's how I do it. But you do it your own way.' If one of us did something wrong, he'd warn, 'Watch that tonight!' Sometimes he'd tell us 'You don't need talent to get by in show business, you need courage.' If we were on a bill with a dancer with a new routine, he'd get him to show us the steps. He'd give the dancer a tie or something.

"Whenever he'd show signs of blowing up in a rage, one of us would run out, find a priest and bring him back in a hurry. We knew that the old man, being a devout Catholic, would restrain himself with a priest there."

From the beginning Eddie paid the kids salaries of $75 a week each with no restrictions on how they spent it. Mrs. Foy was kept busy making certain that the endless small and large articles they bought were not left behind in hotel rooms or on trains. Their purchases included musical instruments, giant dolls, mechanical toys, bearskins, and live pets. The pets, of course, were the most difficult of all to keep track of.

Eddie took no chances when he first showed the act—"Fun in the Foy Family"—to the public. He chose a benefit in the New Rochelle theatre, knowing the place would be packed with friendly neighbors and their kids. And he hired Billy Jerome, a big time expert, to write his material. The kids went on first. While waiting in the wings to join them, Eddie decided he didn't like his opening line. To Jerome, who was at his side, Eddie implored: "Give me another opening line." Jerome whispered, "Try 'If I moved to Bayside it would be a city!' " Eddie strutted out, and the line brought a roar. They used it everywhere they played with Flatbush substituted when they played Brooklyn, Englewood when they played Chicago, and other small local communities near other cities. Later he found a second good opening line. Looking at his kids, Eddie would step to the footlights and confide to the audience: "It sure took me a long time to put *this* act together!" In the first years of the act, Eddie also counted the kids and would discover Irving, his youngest, was missing. He'd ask the others, "Where's Irving?" One of them would run off and return lugging a suitcase. On opening it up, Irving would step out and blow kisses to the audience. The applause that scene brought caused Irving to go into an exultant dance until Eddie stopped him and angrily reproached him for trying to steal the show.

Critics rejoiced. "One big scream from the start to the finish, an irresistible stage frolic that the audience is loath to have finish," was a typical review.

Yes, everybody loved the act except, of course, the Gerry Society.

Eddie ran into trouble after the act's very first big-time showing at Brighton Beach, a New York seaside resort. The Gerry Society, which tried to stop children from working on the stage, got an injunction to prevent the little Foys from being cruelly exploited. This puzzled and angered Eddie, who had known terrible poverty in his childhood and also knew that youngsters were still being worked ten to twelve hours a day for starvation pay in factories and on farms all over the country. But the Gerry Society was interested only in the children of the stage.

Foy was able to cope with the misguided do-gooders. It helped that for years he had been the drinking companion, wherever he went, of local judges and politicians. He also was able to prove that his kids were over-protected, if anything. His wife and her sister saw that they ate properly. A governess with credentials as a high school teacher gave them daily lessons. To make sure that they got to bed early he insisted their act, though a headliner, go on third at evening performances. Finally, Eddie argued that all seven intended to continue acting when they grew up. So this was a valuable part of their education.

In dozens of cities Eddie Foy was dragged into court but

invariably the case was dismissed by judges who either knew him personally or had seen and enjoyed the family act.

But in Louisville, Kentucky, after being arrested three times, Foy cancelled the engagement and took his group out of the state. And it was quite a group. In addition to the family, Eddie had his own orchestra leader, a teacher, and two stagehands traveling with his act. The Foys' departure inspired indignant editorials by the distinguished Henry Watterson of the Louisville *Courier-Journal*. These continued until the State Legislature amended the child labor law. The governor sent Eddie the pen with which he'd signed the legislation permitting children to work on the stages of Old Kentucky. Naturally this all made great publicity for the act.

The kids loved their father who in turn was a loving father most of the time. But besides having a bad temper he could be the worst ham in show business. When he got into a dispute with the management over billing or anything else, he would start packing and order his valet to "take my trunk out to the alley" which meant the express company could be called to take it away, leaving the theatre without a headliner. Almost always Eddie got what he wanted. On one occasion he refused to share top billing with the distinguished dramatic star, Tyrone Power. "There is nothing personal in this," he told reporters, "it's purely a matter of business and I'm withdrawing from the bill." Eddie and the seven little Foys appeared at Hammerstein's big time New York showcase in its last days. To make sure nothing would go wrong with the music accompaniment, Eddie talked his friend Victor Herbert into leading the pit orchestra the day the act made its debut. But when the beloved operetta composer received a standing ovation, Foy complained to Willie Hammerstein that Herbert had put his whole turn in the shade. It was also at Hammerstein's that Pop Foy did something that bewildered his kids.

Diamond Jim Brady was in the front row one night. While the Foys were taking their bow, he tossed a little chamois bag up on the stage. It contained seven diamonds, one for each child. But their old man had a jeweler set them in a ring for himself. It was the sort of thing children remember all their lives.

Eddie Foy was what his own Irish call "a darlin' man." No one was ever more admired by young performers. They would cluster in groups in the wings to watch him at every performance and Eddie invariably was kind to them, advised them, told them how to improve their acts.

And it wouldn't have been strange if elfish little Eddie had turned out to be a cold, glum, bitter man off-stage. He had survived as crushing a childhood as one could imagine. He had also participated in many violent and colorful events in American history, and had made friends—and in one case an enemy—of some pretty salty characters.

Eddie was born Edward Fitzgerald in New York's Greenwich Village on March 9, 1856. His father, a tailor, was wounded in the head during the Civil War, went insane as a result, and died in an asylum. Eddie, his two sisters, and their mother never saw him after he was taken away. Little Eddie also witnessed the street fighting during the New York Draft Riots and the corpse of a lynched Negro whom a hate-maddened mob had left hanging from the corner lamppost near his home.

The Fitzgerald family had a harrowing time trying to survive during the war and in the years that followed. Eddie's mother worked as a washerwoman, a nurse, anything she could find. His sisters ran errands, did nursing and sewing. Eddie shined shoes and sold newspapers. He had plenty of competition. At the time there were ten thousand abandoned boys wandering the streets of New York, all trying to make their living as shoeshine boys and newsboys. They stole, begged, fought each other, slept at night in alleys, doorways, or in the back of any wagon parked for the night on a street or in a stable. A number even died of exposure and hunger. Eddie became a street entertainer after watching vagabonds do their turn, then pass a hat around the crowd. He began to sing, dance, and do cartwheels and collected a few coppers a day to add to what he made shining shoes and peddling papers.

After a while a 30-year-old fiddler named Huggins became his partner. Together, they entertained all over town, passing a hat on streets, in backyards, and saloons. Sometimes they'd take the three-cent ferry across the Hudson to Hoboken, Weehawken, and Jersey City to do their stuff there. They drew far bigger crowds together than Eddie had attracted alone. But somehow Eddie never seemed to get any more money. Years later it dawned on him that this was because it was Huggins who always passed the hat.

The Fitzgeralds moved to Chicago when Eddie was eight. His mother's brother had sent them train tickets and written that they could do better there. In Chicago the widow Fitzgerald was hired to be nurse-companion to Mary Todd Lincoln, the martyred President's widow, who was living in Springfield. The girls stayed with relatives and Eddie went to the Chicago Newsboys Lodging House. But Mrs. Lincoln proved so difficult that their mother soon came back. It is a measure of her desperation that she returned to Mrs. Lincoln in Springfield six different times and each time came back to Chicago because the former First Lady was simply impossible.

Meanwhile Eddie had run into so much competition as an entertainer that he returned to shining shoes and selling newspapers full time. At night, at the Newsboys Lodging House, he was a great hit with his fellow urchins, particularly when he turned his coat inside out for heightened comic effect and it was there that he learned to be a great mugger. Eddie seldom had a spare dime to buy a gallery seat at a show. But he hung around the stage door just to catch a glimpse of what was going on, and to see the artists come and go.

The next event of national importance to touch Eddie's life was the Great Chicago Fire of 1871. Eddie was separated from his family for three days. When he reappeared, his mother told them that Jim Fisk, the Robber Baron "who loved the poor," had offered free passage back to New York for ex-New Yorkers made homeless by the fire, on the Erie Railway of which he was part-owner. The forlorn little family went back only to find work there more difficult to come by than ever.

Finally, Mrs. Fitzgerald went to Jim Fisk's office and begged him for tickets back to Chicago. He told her to return for them next day.

The next day, January 6, 1872, Fisk was shot to death by Edward Stokes, a business associate and rival for the love of Fisk's mistress, the actress Josie Mansfield. But he had signed the passes a few hours before he was killed.

As a teenager in Chicago, young Eddie hooked up with another hopeful, Jack Finnegan. Since there was great prejudice against the Irish in those days the boys decided they might get more work if the act was called Edwards and Foy. They played beer halls, honkytonks, wine rooms, and rode the freights to Milwaukee and worked there whenever they thought they might be wearing out their welcome in the Windy City joints. They would move on to another town at the slightest tip that a few days' work might be had in the new place. When thrown off a train for lack of fare the young troupers would walk the rest of the way, though their promised pay for a one-night stand might be only two or three dollars.

In Chicago they finally got a whole week's engagement at the Cosmopolitan Beer Hall only to be hissed off the stage on their opening performance. Foy's partner, attempting a somersault, had fallen on his face.

Foy had other partners and wilder times the next few years. Once a fifty-cent job as a super in Edwin Booth's Shakespearean company kept him from starving. Then he was with a wagon show whose owner clipped the customers at crooked gambling games. Eddie's pay was often weeks in arrears and in Galena, Illinois, the manager ran off with the box-receipts.

One of the swindler's shortchange workers then organized another show. In this Eddie, his partner, and a sad-faced old fiddler furnished the entertainment with their new boss as interlocutor. Their exhibition, which played single night stands, was billed "A Grand Minstrel Show and Dance." Their pay was in arrears again when the aged horse that pulled the equipment wagon dropped dead. When the head man suggested that Eddie steal a farmer's horse for him, young Foy and his partner headed for home. They walked most of the way. Foy was then 21.

His mother did not greet him as a prodigal son when he at last arrived broke, hungry, and dirty. It appeared that Mrs. Fitzgerald had been patient with him until then because she had hoped he would turn into a great Shakespearean star like Edwin Booth. In Mrs. Fitzgerald's opinion, her son's tumbling, clowning, joke-making, and burlesques of popular songs was nonsensical foolishness, just his way of getting out of working. Every time she washed his dirty tights and hung them on the line to dry, she felt ashamed, was sure her neighbors were ridiculing and pitying her for having a bummy of a son. But that fall Eddie's luck changed. He teamed up with Jim Thompson, a tenor with an ingratiating personality who turned out to be a true-blue pal.

After engagements in Chicago and Kansas City, they arrived in Dodge City, Kansas, "the wickedest little city in America," where he and Thompson were to get $20 a week for appearances at Ben Springer's place, a combined dance-hall, saloon, and gambling casino. Springer and everyone else in town sober enough to walk was at the station to greet the boys whom Springer advertised as "a star attraction direct from Chicago." Each carried only a pair of dancing shoes and no other stage clothes though their routines included sketches in blackface, acrobatics, and songs old and new.

In the crowd that acclaimed them at the station were Bat Masterson, Luke Short, Doc Holliday and Wyatt Earp, who are all now enshrined as folk-heroes of the Old West. On opening night Foy, who was a pretty cocky young actor, made a few slighting remarks about cowpokes. The boys in the front room and those in the back too were not amused. In addition they did not care for the young fellow's flashy clothes and the waggling walk that later became his trademark.

At an ungodly morning hour Eddie was dragged from bed and trussed up like an ornery steer by the whooping cowboys. They threw him over a horse and took him under a big tree from which a noose was hanging. "Eddie Foy, Esquire, have you anything to say before we string you up?"

"Yes," said Foy, "but I'd rather say it while I'm standing at the Long Branch bar."

The "lynchers," who had merely intended to shake the cockiness out of Foy, admired him for his courage and quick wit. Not that this stopped them later from throwing him into the water trough in the fancy new togs he'd just bought. But soon he became one of them after taking all their roughhousing in stride.

One night while he was sleeping someone took two shots at him that narrowly missed hitting him. Foy was always convinced that the would-be assassin was another actor, Charles Chapin, who became infamous years later as the madly sadistic editor of the New York *Evening World,* and ended up a lifer in Sing Sing for killing his wife.

Everybody else in the so-called "Bibulous Babylon of the Frontier" was a wholehearted Foy fan. Though Eddie and his partner kept playing engagements in other Western frontier towns, they always came back to Dodge City for triumphal return appearances.

Once Foy saw both Dodge City sheriff Bat Masterson and Doc Holliday drop their poker hands and hit the floor when two drunken Texans started shooting up the place. After which the two celebrated gunfighters got up and chased the cowboys out of the saloon and into the hills. However, in this real life thriller, the bad guys got away. When Eddie went backstage, he found three bullet holes in the new $11 suit he had just bought. One hole was still burning around the edges.

On another wild day Sheriff Masterson deputized Eddie into a posse to round up some drunken Indians. Foy was relieved when the posse rode up to find the Indians now sober and willing to go to jail quietly. In Leadville the boys got plenty of throw money and met "Silver Dollar" Tabor whom the local papers called the town's "ten-millionaire." In Canon City the saloonkeeper didn't pay them so the team stole a barrel of his whiskey and sold it for enough to cover their pay which was now $25 a week.

In many lawless towns the actors had to go back to their rooming house each night, protected by armed guards. While appearing at Birdcage Varieties in Tombstone, Arizona, Eddie saw an insolent faro player shot by a killer who picked up the dead body, hurled it out into the street, then calmly returned to the game. In Denver, Foy watched a race riot in which 200 Chinese were beaten, hounded, and had their pigtails tied together. That week the team was playing at the Palace, a concert hall with fifty-two gambling games, located over a feed-store.

Eddie got married during this tumultuous tour. His bride was Rose Howland of the Howland Sisters, who were traveling through the rootin', tootin' Old West with their mother as chaperone. A short while later his partner married actress Millie Thompson and the two couples traveled in a foursome, playing in gold camps, copper towns, and ending their tour in a San Francisco stock company. Like many other stars, Eddie always said that whatever he knew about acting he learned by playing stock.

They resumed touring with a company playing "Muldoon's Picnic," which ended disastrously when the lead burro died and the company couldn't scrape up enough money to buy another.

After playing an engagement in Philadelphia with the famous Carncross Minstrels, the team of Foy and Thompson broke up. Thompson wanted to go back to the Coast. Eddie thought he'd find better opportunities in the East. They'd been together for six exciting years. The men cried and hugged each other as they said goodbye.

Not long afterward, Eddie's wife died in childbirth.

Losing Rose seemed the end of the world to the little clown with the curled-up mouth. All he could think of was how beautiful she was and how sweet. Eddie couldn't forget the night he'd come home and told Rose he'd lost his week's pay, playing faro. Money badly needed for rent and food.

"It's all right, darling," Rose had said, kissing him. "We'll make some more money. But don't do it again!"

For a whole year after her death, he did little work. His heart was no longer in it. At one point, to avoid starving, he took a job in a dime museum where he had to do ten shows a day.

Foy's tragedy was repeated a few years later when he married Lola Sefton, also an actress. She, too, died in childbirth. But by that time, Foy had become successful and could divert himself by working hard. His break had come in New York while he was appearing in *Jack in the Box*. He had taken $20 a week with a promise of $40 if he made good. But on opening night, he was scarcely noticed by the reviewers. One even called him Mr. Fry.

Eddie was doing a dozen bits in this show, including a burlesque of an Italian ballerina. On impulse one night and without consulting the management, Eddie walked out dressed up like the great English Shakespearean star, Henry Irving in *Hamlet*. Irving was scoring a brilliant success in New York that season and Foy's burlesque stopped the show.

When he came off, the manager of *Jack in the Box* followed him to his dressing room and offered him $75 a week. "Please stay with our show," he pleaded. "Tomorrow everyone in town will be trying to sign you up."

Foy promised and even went on the road with the show when it left New York. The star of the troupe, Carrie Swain, did flip-flops which were advertised, "Can a woman turn a somersault and remain a lady?" The tour ended in San Francisco where Eddie completed his stage training working several months with stock companies.

By the nineties, Eddie was a leading star in extravaganzas. These were musical shows based on such stories as Sinbad, The Silver Slipper, Bluebeard, Ali Baba and the Forty Thieves. One reviewer's description tells why Eddie was perfect in these entertainments: "A thin, elfish fellow with blue eyes and light brown hair, usually covered by a wig, he has a wide comic mouth made up to look wider, a hoarse, hissing voice and his pantomimic clowning and eccentric dancing is done with a great deal of grace."

Another compared his work to that of a well-mannered child: "If he exaggerates any personal trait it is that air of wide-eyed and wondering innocence that sits so well upon him, suggesting a Rip Van Winkle wandering on Broadway." His salary, of course, kept rising, $75 a week to $150, $250, $350, and it continued to increase.

Eddie always reveled in doing the unexpected on stage. Among his greatest assets were the grace and expressiveness with which he used his hands. He managed to play farce so casually that audiences often forgot he was acting. He was mild and unobtrusive, the opposite of those artists who come on like whirlwinds.

In 1896 Foy married again, this time with happier results. His bride was Madeline Morando, a young Italian ballet dancer who bore him eleven children. Seven of them became the Seven Little Foys. The other four died in childhood.

In 1903, Foy became the hero of the most disastrous fire in theatrical history. Eddie had opened his latest extravaganza, *Mr. Bluebeard,* at the Iroquois Theatre in Chicago. This was the city's new architectural showcase, supposedly fireproof, a plush marble palace with a ceiling sixty feet high. Its dressing rooms and backstage space were as large as those in opera houses.

With Foy as the drawing card, the show, ideal for children, sold out for the Wednesday matinee of Christmas week far in advance. When the curtain went up that afternoon the theatre's 1600 seats were filled, and there were several hundred standees. Eddie was unable to get a seat at the last moment for his eldest child, Bryan, who was then six. He put the boy on a stool in the wings and told him to stay there. Foy was putting on a grotesque costume for the second act—wig with a pigtail, smock, and oversize shoes

—when he heard an unusual noise outside. He ran out of his dressing room, found Bryan, and also discovered two stage-hands trying to put out a fire in the flimsy scenery back-stage. One had a fire extinguisher, the other only a stick.

Disturbing noises were coming through the curtain from the lighted stage. He entrusted Bryan to a stagehand, telling him to take the boy outside and to stay with him there.

Then Eddie stepped on stage where sixteen chorus people were bravely trying to sing "In the Pale Moonlight." The orchestra had stopped playing. Foy told the chorus people to leave, slowly and quietly, then whispered to the orchestra leader: "Play something, for God's sake, anything, but *play!*"

Out front the audience was streaming toward the doors. Eddie attempted to distract them by clowning for a moment. Then he called: "Go quietly! Please! Everything will be all right if you remain calm!" And he ordered the asbestos curtain brought down so they couldn't see how the back-stage fire was growing.

The audience applauded him as they started out. And there would have been no panic if the stagehands had been able to bring down the asbestos curtain. But twelve feet from the floor it stopped. It had somehow got entangled with a heavy electric light reflector. The blazing scenery crashed to the stage and flamed over the pit. That started the panic. In the rush bodies started piling up before the closed exit doors, little ones mostly, the bodies of children. The cruelest part of this holocaust was that though 588 persons were killed because of panic, there was small damage to the thea-tre itself. Only one person backstage died, an aerialist who had been waiting high in the wings to do her act.

During the next ten years, Foy had a string of successes

in such Broadway hit musicals as *Piff! Paff! Pouf!*, *The Earl and the Girl*, *The Orchid*, and *Mr. Hamlet of Broadway*. For years Foy had one publicity trick that he used again and again. This was an announcement that he would play *Hamlet*. Eddie would then deny the story, reaping more news space.

He always recalled those turn-of-the-century days as the happiest of his professional life. It was the custom in those years to keep a musical show on Broadway only a short time before sending it out on tour. Because that's where the big money was then—in the towns, not in New York. They opened there mainly so they could advertise on tour "Direct from Broadway, Original Cast!"

Foy, in his later years, was fond of pointing out that the troupers then felt much closer to their audiences, particularly in the smaller communities. Crowds welcomed them at the station and went there again to see them off. Well-wishers greeted them on the street and in the hotel lobby.

Yet one could not imagine anyone happier than old Pop Foy seemed when he had all his kids in the act. In 1917, shortly after the United States entered World War I, the Seven Little Foys became six. The boys in that year's act wore sailors' uniforms for one number and at a performance in Indianapolis, a real sailor in the audience yelled at Bryan, still in his teens, "Why don't you join the Navy instead of prancing around up there in that kid sailor suit!"

Bryan interrupted the number and walked off stage. He went straight to the nearest recruiting office and enlisted.

The following year Mrs. Foy died. She had never danced professionally after her marriage, but in at least one of the family acts, "The Old Woman Who Lived in a Shoe," she came out and sat on a chair at one side of the stage sewing, while her husband and children made jokes, danced the tango, mimicked Pop, and sang the current hits. Bryan never rejoined the act. In 1922, he wrote "Mr. Gallagher, Mr. Shean" which made the team of Ed Gallagher and Al Shean the rage of Broadway, but sold it to them for fifty dollars. Their names, not his, were credited with both words and music.

On January 10, 1923, while their act was headlining at Keith's Alhambra Theatre in New York, Eddie Foy, then 64, took a fourth wife. She was Marie Combs, a striking young brunette from Sedalia, Missouri, who said she was part Cherokee. None of Foy's children attended the ceremony. When interviewed in his dressing room that evening, Eddie said, "I see my children growing up and away from me. I don't intend to be left alone in my old age. I love children and I'm going to raise another family. I want a home with little ones in it."

His seven children never commented on the May and December marriage. But soon afterwards they quit working with their father. Madeline married and the five remaining little Foys tried an act of their own which didn't last long.

Soon Eddie announced that he was retiring once more, and with his wife he lived for a while in a New York apartment before moving to Westchester County. But like most old actors, he came out of retirement at the drop of a decent offer to make a few movies that weren't so successful and appeared briefly in the play, *That Casey Girl*.

Then the miracle happened. Eddie, whom Broadway had written off as an old has-been, suddenly popped up in *The Fallen Star*, a one-act by Tom Barry that was tailor-made for the sexagenarian elf. In it, Foy played a stage doorman whose name had once been in lights but now is forgotten. The old timer gives advice to a boy-and-girl dance team and when they leave, he falls asleep and dreams of the past. He acts it all out: the days when, after the show each night, he went to Rector's, Shanley's, and Considine's old Metropole and met all the wonderful people of the turn of the century New York—Lillian Russell, Diamond Jim Brady, young Georgie Cohan, Al Smith, the East Side politician with such great things ahead of him, writer Irvin S. Cobb. An instant hit, the act was booked for a year.

In August, Eddie played the New York Palace. Though his autobiography, which appeared that year, stated he was born on March 9, 1856, the Palace's press agents said it had happened in August so they could announce his 71st birthday would be celebrated on their stage. Tom Heath, of McIntyre and Heath, the great blackface team, who were also on the bill revealed he also would celebrate his 74th birthday and the fifty-fourth anniversary of the team's partnership. The Palace brought in all of the old timers they could round up to participate in the celebration, making it old home week for everybody.

Shortly afterwards, Eddie began to suffer angina pectoris attacks. Yet he resumed working after each attack. He died in Kansas City on February 16, 1928, while headlining a bill at the Orpheum Theatre. The children, five of whom were doing their act in Wisconsin, joined the funeral cortege at Chicago. They, along with Bryan and Madeline became reconciled with their stepmother as the train proceeded to New York.

Of the seven little Foys, only Eddie, Jr., remained an actor.

Charlie, a compulsive gambler, ran a night club near Holly-wood before marrying a wealthy woman. Eddie says, "You might call him a retired night club owner." Bryan became a successful film producer at Warner Brothers.

Other acts featuring kids were great favorites on the big time. George M. Cohan was the star of The Four Cohans when he was in his early teens. And almost as soon as Buster Keaton learned to walk his father featured him in the family act.

In 1913 *Variety* counted sixty-two school acts playing big-time vaudeville. School acts cost very little to put on since the props consist of school desks and seats, a blackboard, and teacher's desk. There were gifted boys and girls everywhere whose mothers let them work for little in order to get them started.

The routine of these school acts seldom varied. If they began with the teacher calling the roll, one boy would answer, "Absent. I couldn't come to school today." When the teacher left the room for a moment, the kids started fighting, chasing each other around the room, jigged, did flip-flops and wrote sassy things on the blackboard. Some-times the gifted ones had a chance to do a number or two. Then when the teacher returned she (or he) found the pu-pils studying hard. Lessons began with questions and an-swers:

"What is an island?"

"An island is a wart on the ocean."

"Give me a sentence with the word delight in it."

"The vind blew in the vindow and blew de light out."

The best-loved kid acts were put on by Gus Edwards, starting in 1905 and continuing into the thirties when vaudeville was dying. Gus was a lantern-jawed, long-faced man who came to New York from Germany, where he was born in 1879, as a boy of thirteen. For a while he worked as a tobacco stripper and went to night school. But his true love was show business and, like other vaudevillians, he started singing on ferryboats and in saloons, at club parties or from a balcony seat during acts. His first real stage appearance came as one of the four youngsters in "Newsboy Quartette."

Gus started writing songs by accident. He had a job singing between the acts as colored stills illustrating each number were flashed on a white sheet. Ex-World Heavyweight Champion John L. Sullivan, a mighty drinker, was headliner on the bill. One night Sullivan stumbled into Edwards's dressing room and sat on the chair where Gus had put his stills, shattering them. Doubting that the audience would care for his singing old songs without the stills to distract them, Gus thereupon composed a brand new number "I Wants My Black Baby Back." It scored a success and soon the bill's star, May Irwin, and others were making it popular. Among later Gus Edwards song hits are a few still being sung today "School Days," "By the Light of the Silvery Moon," "In My Merry Oldsmobile," "Sunbonnet Sue," as well as "Good-by, Little Girl, Good-by" of World War I days.

Successful though these songs were, the real genius of genial Gus Edwards lay in his gift for discovering dozens of talented kids. He pulled Lila Lee off the street when she was eight years old, and as "Cuddles" she remained the star of his act for eight years, playing opposite Little Georgie Price. When Price grew up, he quit show business to become a Wall Street stock broker. But he was an exception. Among the Gus Edwards troupers who became name players were Eleanor Powell and Mae Murray, dancers who became Broadway and Hollywood stars; Sally Rand, the Duncan Sisters, Hildegarde, Groucho Marx, Bert Wheeler, Eddie Cantor, Jack Pearl, Helen Menken, Gregory Kelly, Georgie Jessel. Phil Silvers was a boy soprano with one of Gus Edwards' acts but when his voice changed at ten he had to quit.

Edwards and his wife Lillian had no children of their own. Gus was like a Dutch uncle to the boys and his wife mothered the girls, saw that they ate nourishing meals, comforted them when they were discouraged or homesick, made certain that they were getting their sleep, and encouraged the youngsters to save most of the decent salaries her husband paid them. Both had their hands full coping with Georgie Jessel, who had already started chasing girls, as well as with the street fighting of Bert Wheeler and the hell-raising of several other little rascals.

Eddie Cantor joined the group in 1912. He had already worked two years with an act called Bedini and Arthur; and though he was a hit, he was getting only $35 a week. A friend urged Cantor to ask Edwards for fifty a week expecting he might get forty. But when he did so, Gus told Cantor that he admired him greatly, adding, "I wouldn't think of paying you less than $75 a week as a starting salary."

"Kid Kabaret" was the Edwards act that year. Cantor recalled, "It was not only first-class vaudeville, but the best and only acting school of its kind, where poor boys and girls could learn the art of entertainment in all its forms and get paid for learning. Gus Edwards has done more for the youth of the stage than any other man I know. He not only schooled a large number of our present-day stars, but composed songs that suited the needs of the youngsters."

There were sometimes as many as fifteen youngsters for Mrs. Edwards to mother. Cantor himself took over the rearing and civilizing of his roommate and best friend, Georgie Jessel, initiating him "into the mysteries of bathing." "I also taught him to save money but he spent it between lessons," Cantor quipped. Eddie, who did save his, died a millionaire, while Jessel, his protégé, both a spendthrift and one of the softest touches in show business, dissipated for decades the huge sums he made.

Another Gus Edwards protégé was Walter Winchell, who later became the country's most widely read newspaper columnist. His daily gossip hurt hundreds of persons in and out of show business. When one old timer was reminded of this, he said, "Well that—hurting people—was one thing Winchell never learned from Gus Edwards."

Of course, not all of the kid act producers were as kind as Mr. and Mrs. Gus Edwards. In fact a lot of youngsters had stage mothers working them like horses. Yet very few of vaudeville's tough, smart kids became human wrecks as so many of Hollywood's child stars did.

In the first place, vaudeville was not nearly so hard. The child performer was on twice a day for fifteen or twenty minutes at most, leaving him plenty of time to himself. And then when he went on stage, he was on his own.

In pictures the tot had to be awakened at a very early hour, dressed in the dark, rushed to the studio to be made up, costumed, rehearsed endlessly, and sent to the studio school between takes. The Hollywood child grew up in an adult's hurry-up, no-play world.

The large sums the Hollywood child made were, except in a few cases, squandered by his greedy parents. The vaudeville child was usually part of the family team and as soon as he was old enough to know what money was he got his fair share. Most of it remained in the family pot for emergencies which helped strengthen the bonds.

There must have been jealousy in some family acts when one member rose to stardom. But few knew of it. Marilyn Miller, a great Ziegfeld star who had started in a family act, The Five Columbians, certainly retained her family's love. While Sidney Chaplin, a gifted actor, quit his career to manage Charlie's affairs.

Buster Keaton, Chaplin's closest rival in silent film comedies, kept supporting his family through good times and bad until the end of his life. Buster recalled with pleasure how Joe, his convivial father, would meet and drink with old vaudeville pals at every town on the big-time route. "In each town we played, there would be long nightly sessions of drinking beer, eating free lunch, and swapping hilarious reminiscences." The act was one of the roughest in vaudeville. Once, while playing Pittsburgh, Joe tried to punish Buster, then seventeen, for smoking at a matinee performance, and the battle was so furious that it required the services of two doctors and two masseurs to get father and son back in shape to go on that evening.

Buster only threatened to break up the act when his father started drinking whiskey instead of beer. This threw his timing off. "In an act like ours," wrote Buster, "precise timing was all important. Being a half-second off in throwing a punch or ducking a kick meant broken bones sooner or later."

When Pop Keaton paid no attention to Buster's threats,

Buster tried roughing him up on the stage, punishing him a little. After talking to his mother, Buster quit and went to New York. There he was immediately signed for the Shubert *Passing Show* at $250 a week in New York, $300 on the road.

Before Buster could get to a rehearsal, however, he met Fatty Arbuckle, who hired Buster to make movies with him. And that's how vaudeville lost one of its funniest men to Hollywood.

Harpo Marx once told a story that illustrated how rugged life could be playing the small time with his brothers in Good Old Dixie.

"All of us used to dream of eggs," said Harpo, "and discuss tenderly the vegetable soup our mother used to cook for us. Gastronomically speaking, we had to live in the past during our non-triumphal tour below the Mason-Dixon line. We were hungry from Atlanta to the sea, famished all the way from Tennessee to Texas.

"We Marxes were treated, to tell the truth, like direct descendants of General Sherman until we reached Biloxi, Mississippi, which was then a whistle stop.

"In Biloxi, our luck seemed to change. At ten cents a head admission, the little tumbledown theatre there was jammed to the doors. And unlike theatre owners in other towns, the Biloxi Belasco manager didn't claim, when it came time to pay us off, that 'all those people out front tonight were mah relatives and I had to let them in free.'

"He was so overjoyed with our performance that he invited us to play there again the following night. He even commented favorably on a song that Groucho sang. It was called, 'I Love My Wife, but Oh You Kid!' At the finish Groucho would get a laugh by pointing as he sang the word 'kid' at the lady piano player in the pit. She was usually middle-aged and shaped like a wrestler.

"In high spirits we went to our boarding-house. Five minutes later a tornado started blowing in from the Gulf of Mexico. It didn't come in empty-handed. It carried mosquitoes the size of teddy-bears into our room. At the foot of each bed was a pail of oxalic acid. This was supposed to keep the ants from getting under the covers with the guests. But the big wind blew the ants right past the oxalic acid and all over us. The next afternoon the natives told us we were lucky. The big wind was dying down. It had only lasted 18 hours.

"That evening, Groucho was sitting on the porch alone when a cowboy on horseback, with a six-shooter on his hip, came riding up.

" 'Tell me, pardner,' he says to Groucho. 'I seen you in the show last night. Which one of you gentlemen sang that song, 'I Love My Wife, but Oh You Kid!'?

"Groucho, thinking he was about to be taken out to dinner, grinned happily. 'Why, I sang that song, pardner. I'm glad you liked it.'

"The cowboy drew his revolver, 'I didn't say nothin' about likin' it, pardner! I jus' come to warn you not to insult my little sweetheart again tonight. If you do, I'll shoot you down, sir, like the rattlesnake you are!'

" 'How could I insult your sweetheart, when I haven't met her?' asked Groucho, getting ready to run. 'Sure you insulted her,' insisted the cowboy. 'You pointed at her when you sang 'Oh, You Kid!' Down here in Texas it's an insult to point at a lady. Don't do that again, or I'll have to shoot you down like a dog. Remember what I say, pardner.' 'I'll remember sure nuff,' said the scared Groucho. That night he sang his song with his hands tied behind his back. He wanted to make sure he didn't point at the cowboy's girl at the piano."

Harpo sighed, "That was our introduction to old-fashioned Southern chivalry. We were happy to leave Biloxi by train. But ten miles out of town, at four in the morning, our train broke down. The conductor said he was going home as it would be a few days before the train could be repaired.

"At six in the moning, we got hungry. My brothers and I got out of the upper berth we were sharing—yes, three of us were in the upper berth—and walked for miles until we came to a farmhouse.

"We knocked at the door and asked for food. You never saw such graciousness. The farmer invited us in, sent his wife into the kitchen to cook ham and eggs, coffee and those wonderful southern biscuits. After their sixteen year old daughter served us—and we ate four portions of ham and eggs each, dozens of biscuits and drank quarts of coffee—the farmer had the girl wave a big palm fan over us to keep us cool.

"We offered to pay for the food. The farmer was insulted. We were trying to figure out some way of repaying him and his wife for their kindness. We thought of doing a show for them but our efforts in the south had been so badly received, except in Biloxi, that we weren't sure they'd consider the show a favor.

"While thinking, Groucho pulled out his pipe, stuffed it with tobacco and lighted it. The farmer got red with rage. He ran into the kitchen and reappeared with a shotgun. Pointing it at Groucho, he said,

"I'm gonna shoot you, sir!"

"What for?" asked Groucho.

"What for?" the farmer exploded. "How can you ask that? You've *smoked* in front of my daughter! Don't you know a girl's reputation is ruined in these parts if it gets known that she let a stranger *smoke* in her presence?"

"I grabbed the gun and held it up so he couldn't shoot

Groucho," Harpo concluded. "At least, until Groucho could explain that we came from up north where chivalry wasn't so highly developed.

"Up north!" cried the farmer in a fresh rage. He said a lot more but we didn't hear him. We were running too fast down the road towards the train. We haven't been south since, except with armed guards dressed as Confederate soldiers."

One never heard of disputes or jealousy breaking up a real sister act. But sometimes they split up when one or both got married. The Courtney Sisters, Fay and Florence, separated temporarily when Florence, a beautiful girl, married George Jessel the first time. But they came together again after the divorce and did not split apart when Florence became Mrs. Jessel for the second time which also ended in divorce. Gracie Allen was on the Three Allen Sisters before she married and became the partner of George Burns. However, the Duncan Sisters who started as a singing team but developed into headliners as comics stayed glued.

Lillian and Ann Roth, as kids, had a sister act. Ann later became a much-sought-after Broadway dress designer. Lillian married a New York judge, became an alcoholic, and later made a fortune out of her drinking experiences by writing about them in *I'll Cry Tomorrow*, which became a best-seller. Hannah Williams was one of the cute Williams Sisters before she married Roger Wolfe Kahn, orchestra leader and son of financier Otto H. Kahn, and later Jack Dempsey.

The Dolly Sisters were the most beautiful identical twins ever. Born in Hungary on October 25, 1892, they grew up on New York's Lower East Side. Both were small, dark women with almond-shaped eyes who were charming dancers and dressed like queens. As teenagers they achieved headline status in vaudeville and became Ziegfeld Follies stars. Their lovely figures and oriental looks enchanted Broadway and its wealthiest profligates paid tribute to their beauty with furs and jewels. Diamond Jim Brady sent them a Rolls Royce tied up in satin ribbons. One Dolly sister seemed a marvel, two strained credibility.

Early in their careers Jennie (Yansci) and Rosie (Rozicka) married songwriters they'd grown up with. Harry Fox, Jennie's first husband, worked with her in vaudeville for a while. Rosie's husband, Jean Schwartz, wrote songs for her dancing act with Martin Brown. But the marriages were brief and the girls were soon re-united on the big time.

In the early twenties the Dollys went abroad, conquering audiences first in London, then Paris. There they acquired as admirers the Prince of Wales and, reportedly, the kings of Portugal and Spain, Lord Beaverbrook, the English newspaper tycoon, and Sir Thomas Lipton, the tea baron and jolly international yachtsman. The girls lived like royal personages at their chateau at Fontainbleu, and entertained there the crème de la crème of international society. Eventually they both married American millionaires.

The Dolly Sisters were supposed to have broken the bank at Monte Carlo—again and again. Each time, the report won headlines around the world. The strangest thing about these glamorous twins was that being pampered and adored never caused them to lose their sense of humor.

In 1924, along with Al Jolson, Ed Wynn, and other Broadway stars, they were invited to have breakfast at the White House with President Calvin Coolidge. The party came down from New York by train and a line of Cadillacs waited at the

Washington Railroad Station to whisk them off. Edward Bernays was in charge of the party but at the last minute he couldn't find the sisters.

He did discover them after a time in the station lunch room, having breakfast. "Girls!" exclaimed Bernays, "do you realize you are keeping the President of the United States waiting?"

"Let him wait. What is he, anyway? Only a Vermont farmer," Jennie replied. And they kept on eating.

CHAPTER FIVE

"The Asylum Had
to Keep Him"

WILL ROGERS made his first public speech on a vaudeville stage. His admirers saw him as a wise man of the vanishing frontier, plain-looking, clean-living, decent in every way, smart as a man could be, a fellow who always talked sense while making them laugh. And it was all true. Rogers was a rare fellow indeed. He could see through the pretences and pomposities of others, expose them with a winning grin, and love them just the same.

In 1905 Will Rogers, then 26, was stranded in New York and going broke. His spectacular riding and rope-throwing tricks had just made him the sensation of Zach Miller's Wild West Show at Madison Square Garden. But Will was intent on getting into vaudeville which promised steadier work and better pay. On the two-a-day he hoped to save enough money to marry his sweetheart back in Oklahoma.

148

All of the vaudeville managers and agents Will begged for a chance told him that audiences in big cities were not interested in watching fancy riding and trick roping stunts. Finally, though, to get rid of Rogers, the house manager of B. F. Keith's Union Square Theatre on East Fourteenth Street, agreed to let Will do his stuff at one supper show. That was the performance at such three-a-day houses between the matinee and the evening show. All artists hated to play the supper show especially one in such a tough neighborhood since the theatre usually was half-empty and most of the customers seemed to come there to sleep, read newspapers, and sometimes eat sandwiches they'd brought with them.

Jean Brown, the comedienne, never forgot one supper show she played at the Union Square. During her act she was interrupted at regular intervals by a loud *clunk, clunk*. Ushers who rushed to investigate found a man in a back orchestra row eating oysters. On opening and eating each one he dropped the shell into a tin-pail he'd brought with him. The ushers who escorted him and his pail to the street were loudly jeered by the rest of the audience.

Before this most difficult audience Rogers was a hit. They sent him off to wild applause. He stayed the week and was then booked into Hammerstein's where everybody in show business had a chance to see him. While there Will decided to show the crowd a much more difficult stunt—lassoing horse and rider with two separate ropes, both thrown at the same time. Until that night he had never uttered a word to an audience anywhere. But he wished to give himself an out, in case he missed.

Walking to the footlights, Will gestured to the house orchestra leader to stop the music, and announced in his thick

Oklahoma drawl, "I want to call your sho nuff attention to this little stunt I am going to pull on you next. I am going to throw out two of these ropes, catching the horse with one and the rider with the other. I don't have any idea that I'll get it, but here goes."

The audience, amused, roared. Will was hurt, thinking they were laughing at him. But when he did the trick successfully he was wildly applauded. On going off he told a stranger standing in the wings, "Those folks out front laughed at me, thought I was a damn fool, I guess, for opening my big mouth."

"You got a big laugh, son, didn't you?" the stranger replied. "You are new to vaudeville but you'll soon learn that every laugh you get is like money in the bank. You get every laugh you can any way you can."

Will kept the speech in his act but for a long time he couldn't believe the audience was laughing with him, not at him. For one thing, he'd been talking exactly like that to other cowboys all of his life without drawing a smile. But gradually he added lines to his act and did less and less roping. The jokes went over so well that after a while Rogers gained confidence enough to send home his rider and horse.

But he didn't change his mannerisms—moving his chewing gum from one side of his mouth to the other, taking off his big cowboy hat to scratch his head, fiddling with his rope as he talked. For a long time he went on in his cowboy outfit. When a new line fell a little flat Will would throw out the rope. He seemed able to make it come alive with a flip of his wrist and it made the audience forget the last line. Will's manner was so casual that it seemed unrehearsed. But he spent hours every day studying the newspapers. Nothing, he knew, went over better than a joke about something familiar. His whole personality warmed the audience the moment he shambled on. But he liked to come up with something new at every performance. His one stock line, "All I know is what I read in the newspapers," was almost true and fitted the audience's impression of him.

His most famous lines are quoted often. They include: "Everybody is ignorant, only on different subjects . . . Everything is funny as long as it is happening to someone else . . . The good old horse-and-buggy days: then you lived until you died, and not only until you were run over . . . Spinning a rope's a lot of fun—providing your neck's not in it . . . A comedian can only last until he takes himself serious or the audience takes him serious."

Will once explained his method:

"I start in on a subject and if it's no good, then I have to switch quick. Lots of times when I come off I have an entirely different act. Sometimes an audience is not so good and then you see the old rope commence to do something. It gets their mind. Then I reach back into my back pocket and dig up a fine gag." He thought one of the reasons for his success was that he did a very short act "never more than ten minutes, sometimes only six."

Audiences loved it when he confided, "I've been getting away with this junk so long that I thought that you would get wise to me sooner or later, so I went and dug up a little new stuff with which to bunk you for a few more years."

Will Rogers was born on his father's ranch in what was then Indian territory and is now Oklahoma. The date was November 4, 1879. He was part Cherokee and proud of it. Will told many an audience, "My folks didn't come over here on the Mayflower. They met the boat when it arrived. They should have sent it back."

Will became a crack roper as a boy. After a short spell at Kemper Military School in Missouri, he worked as a cowboy in Texas. Will had wanderlust and his exceptional talent for plain and fancy roping took him around the world, though often on short pay and occasionally with none at all. He joined Zack Miller's Wild West Show in Australia as a rough rider and lariat artist. It was Colonel Zach's show that brought him to Madison Square Garden.

Rogers spent nine years in vaudeville before becoming a star of the Ziegfeld Follies. When he left Ziegfeld it was to go into the movies. He also became a syndicated newspaper columnist. His column, which soon surfaced all over the English-speaking world, achieved the unique distinction of appearing daily on the front page of The New York *Times*. But he was never as funny either in print or in Hollywood as he was in person. His warm, friendly personality and perfect timing added much to his effectiveness.

During the national political conventions Rogers was invariably a wildly applauded speaker. No one before or since has been so successful in making fun of stuffed shirts, fakers, and liars in Congress and the White House. He even had the politicians, saintly and otherwise, laughing at themselves with such lines as: "Congressional investigations are for the benefit of the photographers . . . I don't make jokes, I just watch the government and report the facts . . . No party is as bad as its leaders . . . The United States never lost a war or won a conference . . . The Income Tax has made more liars out of the American people than gold has . . . What the country needs is dirtier finger-nails and cleaner minds."

Many other great comics that the big time developed entered vaudeville as "dumb acts." Fred Allen, the intellectual, started out as a juggler but proved so inept he changed to self-deprecation and gags in self-defense. He even billed himself as "the world's worst juggler."

One of his tricks was juggling three cigar boxes. Whenever he dropped one he'd tell the audience, "It's your own fault that you didn't see this stunt succeed. If you'd come last night you would have seen me do it right. Yes indeed, that's the night I made it."

Allen also got a big laugh with a sign that was lowered on the stage just before he came on. It read:

MR. ALLEN IS QUITE DEAF

IF YOU CARE TO LAUGH AND APPLAUD

PLEASE DO SO LOUDLY

After a joke or sight gag he would step to the footlights, hand cupped to his ear, and listen to the applause which always came.

The incomparable W. C. Fields also started in vaudeville as a juggler and was so fantastically nimble-fingered that his billing, "World's Greatest Juggler" went unchallenged. He performed in a tramp outfit while gradually working in sapient comments and starred in the Follies before going to Hollywood and becoming a legend.

Most dumb acts that became comedians, however, were by accident. Jimmy Savo is the perfect example.

One afternoon in a small Indiana mining town there was sub-zero weather and the theatre was unheated. The hands of the miniature strong man and juggler became so stiff from the cold that he kept dropping the cannonballs he was trying to keep in the air.

"Get him a clothes-basket," yelled a miner in the crowd. A sadistic stagehand found one backstage and kicked it out to the appalled Savo. The audience roared. Jimmy smiled his

sad, wistful smile but on an impulse used the basket to catch
the cannonballs his hands couldn't control—and went off to
applause. He kept the clothes-basket in the act and little by
little worked up a comedy act as a substitute for his juggling
tricks.

Savo was so short that on stage he looked like a man standing in a hole. He increased the effect by wearing a coat and
baggy pants far too large for him, a derby that threatened to
fall down over his face, plus an oversized umbrella. With his
huge black eyes he expressed the bewilderment of a tiny man
in a world that had never given him a fair shake. But he also
looked valiant and impish, a child-sized chap who while taking it never stopped hoping his fortunes would change for
the better.

Jimmy Savo sang songs like "That Old Black Magic" in a
way no one else could. As a pantomimist he was at his best
singing "River, Stay Away From My Door" and the comic
ballad "One Meatball."

In the first, he mimed the tiny human confronted by overwhelming disaster, a surging flood. He did much with his eyes
that reflected, in turn, surprise, indignation, panic, and finally
the determination to survive. You saw him trying to fan back
the swollen river with his derby, then leaning over fastidi-
ously to repel the thundering water by cupping drops of it in
his hand and flinging them back. He's upset by the water
lapping at his shoes. He jumps on a chair, rolls up his pants
and does his feeble best to fight the flood, flipping it back with
one hand.

In singing in his small, sweet voice, "We Don't Serve Bread
With One Meatball," he was the same little fellow, half dead

from hunger, valiantly approaching the counter of a cheap restaurant. He looks in his pocket, finds only a single nickel. When he is served one meatball there is no bread and, the picture of disappointment, he pleads for a slice but is told:

> *In a voice that rang out through the hall,*
> *'We don't serve bread with one meatball.'*

Savo was one of the five children of a poor Italian cobbler. The seven Savos—children and parents—all slept in one room in a shanty store-front on a rural Bronx road. Papa Savo had his workbench in a corner of their other room.

Savo always remembered that their poverty once saved their lives. A typhoid epidemic swept the neighborhood one year when Jimmy was quite young. Only the Savos, the poorest family, survived without losing at least one youngster. The health authorities solved the mystery after they traced the typhoid to a cow on a nearby farm. The Savo children had not been stricken because their father couldn't afford to pay the four cents a quart then charged for fresh milk. Instead, he had given his children watered condensed milk which was cheaper.

Poverty, Savo said, was also the reason that he became a "miniature strong man" and juggler. Being undernourished, he was always the smallest boy in his class whom the bigger kids pushed around, and to defend himself, Jimmy spent hours every day in the gymnasium.

He started juggling because his father never had enough cash or credit to keep extra pieces of leather or a pair of rubber heels on hand in his shanty shop. Jimmy was sent racing each time a customer came in for a repair job to a cobbler's shop twelve blocks away for the needed material. Mr. Savo paid for it after the customer paid him. Bored on the way back, Jimmy juggled the heels all the way home, becoming quite adept at it.

When he was thirteen, Jimmy entered an Amateur Night contest as a "miniature strong man" and won first prize. A booker saw him and booked him into a string of New England vaudeville houses. That gave him his start. If there was any snobbery in vaudeville it was toward the dumb acts, a category that included acrobats and others who spoke not a word on stage. The rise to stardom of such former dumb acts as Savo, Bill Fields, Will Rogers, and others should have ended that. But it never did. They continued to be classified as dumb acts right along with Fink's Mules and Powers' Elephants.

Starting with his years as a kid street entertainer Eddie Cantor's ambition was to become a comedian. One of Eddie's most amusing tricks, however—running up and down and all over the stage as he sang a number—originated because he was afraid. In the Gus Edwards act he sang Irving Berlin's "Ragtime Violin." But when they were to open at the Jefferson Theatre on East Fourteenth street, near the Union Square, Cantor tried to beg off. "I'm afraid to sing here," he told Gus. "There are always a lot of goons out front. If they don't like you, they throw rotten apples and bananas, even watermelons."

"But Eddie," Gus told him, "if you run up and down as you sing, they'll never be able to hit you!" Cantor tried it. He proved a sensation and stopped the show. The tough audience went wild, applauded and stamped. That is the way the roughnecks were—they loved you or they wanted to kill you.

And that night little Eddie Cantor found the perfect way to

deliver his songs. His tiny body would throb with rhythm when he stopped near the wings to finish a number.

Cantor, a bundle of controlled dynamite, occasionally got swept away. One night at the New York Hippodrome, Cantor spotted Sir Thomas Lipton sitting in a box. Cantor got so excited that he ran off the stage, out the stage door, down the alley to the street, in the front door, down the side aisle, and got into the box where he kissed Sir Thomas on the top of his bald head.

Reproached later for his bad taste, Eddie said, "I really couldn't help it. I thought of his racing yacht and said, 'Here is the guy who *really* owns all the tea in China and can bet it —I had to kiss his bald spot.' "

Bad taste or not, the audience loved it. So did Sir Thomas.

Jack Benny, of course, started in vaudeville as a serious musician. He and his piano partner played the big time, and even made the Palace with their highbrow offering. But their reception at that Taj Mahal of the two-a-day was so cool that Benny did not think he'd ever see it again. Yet the moment he started talking he found that audiences everywhere loved him. And why not? Jack, from his beginning days as a comedian, was all class, urbanity personified, and had an irresistible amiability.

Long after he knew that his engaging personality and his conversation were what the folks out front wanted, he kept coming out with his violin even though at many performances he didn't play it. Now, having made millions with his amusing act, Jack still wishes he had kept on studying for the concert stage. When he practices, which is every day, his wife

Mary Livingstone insists that he take his Stradivarius out to a motel so she can't hear him.

Our own favorite among the musician-comics was Herb Williams. He and his wife Hilda Woolfus also started in vaudeville offering the better (and less popular) sort of music. Herb was a pianist, Hilda a singer. Like all such acts, they did not attempt anything esoteric or too complicated.

The couple worked for years preparing for their debut. They took lessons from the best voice and piano teachers they could find in their native Philadelphia. For a long time, Williams supported himself as a bank teller but quit that to become the pit pianist in a Gus Sun theatre in Ohio. On the Gus Sun time, the pianist was the whole house orchestra and the butt of the comic acts' jokes. Whenever he got the chance, Herb told audiences he was really a three-piece orchestra— "Williams, Piano and Stool." In the music he played before and after the show, Herb interpolated comic trills, original cadenzas, and plaintive passages.

Williams tried to get friendly with the small-time artists who played the Sun time, but was rebuffed. They considered pit pianists their professional inferiors.

When he told them, "I'll have my own act some day, you'll see!" They simply laughed.

It is curious that Williams wasn't a comedian from the start. Even his real name—Herbert Schussler Billerbeck—was worth a laugh. As a school kid, he'd invented trick devices to make his friends laugh at Hallowe'en parties, picnics, and Sunday school entertainments. And he was plenty mischievous as well.

He had additional natural equipment for a comic—he was near-sighted, bald, and clumsy. Herb wore pince-nez spectacles, badly fitted clothes, and yellow button shoes. Hilda was a blonde and had a pretty face, but she was skinny as a broomstick and just as flat-chested.

At their vaudeville debut, both were gripped by stage fright and stumbled all over each other as well as the piano stool. Herb kept knocking the music off the piano. Their ill-fitting clothes and terror had the audience laughing from start to finish. They were so well received, for the wrong reason, that they got bookings for three months.

Stage managers kept telling Williams what a howl his act was. In the end, he accepted the idea that he and Hilda should *try* to be funny. And he began working on original comic devices.

Almost from the day that Williams and Woolfus got on i ıe big time, they were show-stoppers. Their act wasn't always the same but this is how we remember it.

Herb comes out first in a wrinkled evening suit, baggy at the knees, and a funny hat—a large, blinking, bumbling man, with his yellow button shoes on the wrong feet. On entering, he shouts "Spot l-l-light!" accompanied by a lordly gesture. Immediately the stage is plunged into darkness.

Confused, Williams goes off and returns a moment later holding a lighted candlestick above his head and yells again "Spot l-l-l-i-i-ight!" But it remains so dark that he stumbles against the upright piano. When the footlights come on again, he bows ceremoniously and adjusts the piano stool which is too low. But it whirls on, rising until its seat is above the piano. Williams mounts it but no matter how he stretches, his fingers don't reach the keyboard. Dismounting, he tries to lower it. When it was at a height that suits him, he sat on the stool which immediately sinks so low that his fingers still can't touch the keyboard.

On finally adjusting it, he once again screams "Spot l-l-light!" The spot appears and wanders all over the stage. When it centers on his face, he begins to play only to interrupt himself. "That l-l-light is blinding my eyes!" he shrieks. Herb then sings in his squeaky voice, "Hark, Hark—" a takeoff on a popular opera singer. He puts his cupped hand to his ear so he won't miss the response he expects from one of his feathered admirers. He looks chagrined when this does not come.

While all this is going on, Hilda slips out and speaks to Herb who claims he cannot see her. It turns out the candle on the top of the piano is between them, hiding her. Hilda starts to sing a song and steps in front of him. He observes that her legs can be seen through a big round hole cut in the bottom part of her skirt. Herb, shocked, reaches down and pulls down a tiny green shade on which is printed "Censored!"

While playing a solo Herb notices that some of the keys seem to be stuck. Reaching into the piano, he pulls out a cat. On finishing, he is perspiring. This time he pulls a beer spigot out of the piano, draws a stein of beer, and drinks it.

The spotlight then shifts to a new leader in the pit who is red-wigged and its glare drives him crazy with ambition. He starts whirling his baton, bobbing his head, doing everything to steal attention away from the comedian at the piano. Appalled by his behavior, Herb grabs the baton and raps the leader over the head with it. But when the baton only bends, Williams hands it back, apologetically, whimpering to the audience in a heartbroken voice, "This is so embarrassing for me!"

Another delightfully inventive clown was A. Robins, a Viennese. Robins, carrying fiddle and bow, would walk on dressed in a Swiss Alpine outfit: green suit, coat with long tails, hat with feather, and red tie. As he started to play, he'd see a spot on his tie. When he tried to brush it off, the whole tie disappeared—it had been painted on his shirt. Next, the unbelievable happened. The violin Robins had been playing began to shrink. Though it got smaller and smaller until it almost vanished, its music continued.

Then Robins reached into his coattails and produced all sorts of other instruments—a cornet, trombone, bass violin, drums, everything but a piano—and played each in turn. He also pulled out a bouquet of flowers, a music stand, and a campstool. As he explained years later, the trick was one he had perfected himself. The instruments, stool, and stand had been collapsed to take up small space. As he pulled each from his coattails, he would touch a spring that released them. Meanwhile he hummed the music. "You might call me a ventriloquist of musical instruments," he observed. "I learned as a youngster of 14 how to imitate all these instruments I seem to play." The full set of props in his coattails weighed sixty pounds.

Several other of vaudeville's funniest, rowdiest acts were also built around musical instruments—pianists played standing on their heads, others played one tune with the right hand, another with the left. Violinsky, who was funnier offstage than on, played the piano and fiddle at the same time. Sitting at the piano, he'd play that with one hand and do his fingering of the violin with the other. The bow was strapped to Violinsky's right knee in such a way that it produced music from the strings whenever he moved his knee.

Solly Violinsky was the funniest man at the Friars Club, and he wrote a couple of song hits, including one with Billy Rose called "When Frances Dances With Me." But he could hardly get work in his later years and out of this starvation situation came one of his funniest lines: "I have laid off under every Administration since William Howard Taft."

The big time's monologists (today they are called standup comics) had to be the bravest vaudevillians. Try to imagine a kid coming out alone on a stage before a theatre full of people who had never heard of him before. No props, pretty girls, or sight gags. All he had to do was tell jokes and anecdotes that would bring waves of applause and laughter.

If he could dance and sing a little, it might help; in Milton Berle's case, it didn't. There may have been other child monologists more offensive offstage, but onstage Milton Berle (later, of course, one of the world's beloved comedians) was without competition as an insufferable child ham.

Milton's mother, Sandra, became known wherever her little horror played. From a lower box, she would laugh herself into hysterics every time Miltie went on. Since laughter's contagious, she soon had others chuckling as well.

The other acts hated Miltie. He stole everybody's gags. Nothing could stop him—threats of lawsuits, exposure in the theatrical press, ridicule, personal threats. Miltie and Sandra believed that any joke stolen by him became his property by right of genius.

The wonder of Milton Berle is that his mother's worship did not ruin him permanently. On the contrary, the fantastic success of his mature years, crowned in the dozen seasons he was "Mr. Television," turned him mellow; he became a star known for his loyal friendships with other stars and for the pains he took in helping talented young comedians just starting on the long way up. Not that Uncle Miltie has lost his self-esteem. A part of the fresh, cocky young Milton remains, but the kid who was once the most hated brat in vaudeville is now a loved and respected Elder Statesman in the rollicking country of professional comedy.

Miltie, of course, was not the first or the last of the big time's joke-stealers. Most beginners relied on the gags of former clowns and old joke books. But once they learned their trade they worked up original material for themselves or bought it from gag-men. We know of only one other old timer who made a career of swiping others' jokes.

This was Marshall Wilder, who got up to $600 a week in turn-of-the-century vaudeville, plus additional tidy sums for lectures and after-dinner speeches. If Wilder was never physically assaulted for his thefts it was probably because he was a dwarf. And he was cunning enough to credit the source with flattering remarks like "as my good friend, that prince of a fellow, Jim Thornton, was telling me the other day—" before repeating Jim's latest gag.

When he matured, Berle naturally became clever enough to work up material that was fresh or at least sounded new. But the impudent Mr. Wilder never bothered.

Julius Tannen was one of the best monologists. His own personality was so glum and discouraged that he needed a superior wit to please audiences. You could not imagine him getting away with what his rival baby-faced Frank Tinney did: whispering "backstage secrets" to the audience about the other acts, telling pointless jokes, asking the orchestra leader to help him out—with something or other always going amiss.

Like so many vaudevillians, Julius was orphaned in early boyhood. The New York Hebrew Orphan Asylum tried to bring him up but when he proved unmanageable, they decided that a home atmosphere would bring out his lovable side. Consequently, they paid a needy, respectable Jewish family to take him in. The family soon brought him back, saying they had tried everything they could think of but Julius appeared to have no lovable side. Several other poor families reported the same result. The Asylum had to keep him.

In his teens, Tannen had a series of poor-paying jobs, some around the theatre. At one time though he was a secretary to one of the Armour family of meat barons.

Julius quit the business world to become a vaudeville mimic and he was brilliant at it. Abel Green and Joe E. Laurie say he invented the much admired curtain speech attributed to George M. Cohan that all other mimics of Cohan used forever after. George was supposed to have said: "My mother thanks you! My father thanks you! My sister thanks you! And I thank you!"

Cohan, who detested almost all impressions of him, liked Tannen's speech so much he started using it himself.

Tannen was something new in monologists. He came on in an ordinary business suit and talked very quickly and spontaneously. At one performance a stagehand behind the curtain dropped something with a resounding bang. Tannen, pretending to suspect the stagehand was spying on his act, informed the audience, "Sneak thieves!" Once when heckled, he told his would-be tormentor, "Save your breath. You'll need it later to clean your glasses."

A great many veteran vaudevillians who didn't like slim, dour-faced Julius Tannen personally believed that he was the wittiest of all the monologists. If you said you thought Will Rogers or Walter Kelly (billed "The Virginia Judge") or James Morton or some other stand-up talker was funnier, they would reply, "They are humorists, Tannen is a wit." If you asked them what wit was, you'd be told, "Funny stuff with a bite to it that they might not like hearing but that makes them think." Among Tannen's best lines were:

I'm as welcome as a wet goat . . . Those paper cups give me a sensation of drinking out of a letter . . . Pardon me for being late. I squeezed out too much toothpaste and couldn't get it back . . . A lady has the right to be as homely as she pleases—but this one abuses the privilege . . .

One of Tannen's stories was about a young man whose girl's father told him, "Remember our lights are put out at ten-thirty." The youth replied, "You can expect me at eleven o'clock."

If that young man doesn't sound naughty now, he did sixty years ago when Julius told the joke. Tannen also had the gift of compressing into a few words an anecdote that could have been used as a plot for a short story—as in the following illustrations.

"A friend of mine had a fine looking blonde stenographer who did not meet the approval of his wife because of the girl's good looks. The wife got so jealous she told him to discharge the girl and that she would act as his secretary, thus saving the girl's salary. She showed him that over a period of time they could buy a home with what they saved.

"The man consented, the blonde left and the wife took

her place. Sure enough, things went better afterwards. Business picked up to such an extent that in time the husband saved up enough to buy a new house, and he did buy it—for the blonde."

One day, while selling World War I Liberty Bonds to a crowd, Tannen wasn't doing very well until a sailor in uniform bought one.

"Ladies and gentlemen," Tannen asked the crowd, "a highwayman says 'Your money or your life.' Shall we be worse than highwaymen, saying to this boy, 'Your money *and* your life?' "

Plenty of the fund-raisers at bond selling rallies afterwards used the same approach, planting a serviceman in the crowd to buy a bond as a come-on.

Tannen was rarely as successful outside New York as he was at the Palace and the city's other big-time houses. Once when he and another smart comic were doing badly in Kansas City, the other laugh-maker said in despair, "We might as well hire Madison Square Garden and fill it with our enemies and do our act there." Tannen replied, "When you had your enemies seated, where would I put mine?"

Another top-ranking monologist was James Thornton, the songwriter whose pranks and misadventures as a drinker "of everything that flows" got as much attention on Broadway as his act and his songs combined. Jim's appearance, like Tannen's, could have been described as sepulchral but that, and wearing pince-nez glasses, was all the two had in common. Jim would come out, dressed like a minister, look over the audience and say, "Well, I'm glad *you're* all sober."

It always got a laugh. Those out front who knew of Thornton's hard drinking especially roared.

Thornton could say anything on the stage and get away with it. He even got a laugh in that tough town, Steubenville, Ohio, when he called it "Stupidville."

After falling off the stage at Tony Pastor's, the drunken Jim told the audience it had watched history being made. "You have seen many an act open in the pit and finish on the stage. But I'm the only act that ever opened on the stage and finished in the pit."

During a quarrel with the manager of the vaudeville house in Bethlehem, Pennsylvania, Thornton threatened to walk off the bill. When told "You can't do *that!*" Jim shouted back, "Can't I? Jesus Christ walked out of Bethlehem, and so will I."

James Thornton's life could be used as a testimonial to the preservative quality of alcoholic beverages. Born in 1861 at Liverpool, he came to Boston with his parents as a small boy. He graduated from the Eliot Street School where he was a classmate of John F. Fitzgerald, "Honey Fitz," who became Mayor of Boston, father of Rose Fitzgerald Kennedy, and grandfather of her large and distinguished family.

At 20, Thornton was the night watchman of a Boston printing plant where his principal duty was to keep the fire going in the coal furnace. While shoveling coal one bitter night he got an idea for a song and wrote it on a piece of paper. Then, with the words on the paper and the music in his head, Jim stepped out in the street for a breath of air. Hearing musical sounds coming from Mother Crowley's "Free and Easy," a cellar drinking joint down the street, he went in and found Will Fox at the piano. Fox, who could write a tune to almost anything, looked at the paper, listened to Thornton humming the tune, and composed music to fit.

Mother Crowley then gave Jim permission to sing, and his song "Remember Poor Mother at Home," went well with the customers. On the spot, Thornton was given the job of singing waiter for $2.50 a week and tips. As soon as he (or any of his drinking companions) could afford it, he began to consume between three and four quarts of whiskey a day. As an old man of 79 he explained, "Not that I confined myself to whiskey. I drank all sorts and conditions of booze. In fact, you might say I drank anything that flowed. But I always kept up with my work and wrote my best songs when under the influence. But I say this was my failing and my strength. I made lots of money and drank it up. The truth is that even in this dry prohibition time, I do not want the wide-open saloon. I ask only that it be open wide enough to let me in."

Jim said that he loved life as a singing waiter in Mother Crowley's so much that he never even went back to the printing plant to get his pay. A couple of years later in New York he got a job as a singing waiter at the notorious Theodore Allen's Jardin de Mabille. This dive had a dance-hall in the basement and a concert hall upstairs. "There," says Herbert Asbury in *The Gangs of New York,* "dissolute women in gaudy tights danced and sang ribald songs."

Jim fell in love with petite sixteen-year-old Bonnie Cox of Brooklyn after seeing her in this wicked establishment Music publisher Edward Marx didn't think highly of Bon nie's voice but believed her to be "the only technically vir tuous woman employed in any East Side resort."

Thornton wrote many of his song hits in the eighties, when songs dedicated either to Mother or to moon-kissed romance were enormously popular. They included "My Sweetheart's the Man in the Moon" and "She May Have Seen Better Days." But some of his songs—"When You Were Sweet Sixteen" and "On the Benches in the Park"—were not published until the nineties. He sold all rights to many a song for $15, $25, and $50 each and these numbers made fortunes for those who bought them. It was not an uncommon practice in those days when the revenue from songs came from the sheet music sales.

After a vaudeville tour as the monologist partner of Charles Lawler (composer of "The Sidewalks of New York"), Jim returned to New York and Bonnie, who was appearing at Tony Pastor's Theatre on Fourteenth Street. Soon afterwards they were married. Jim loved Bonnie but not enough to stop drinking. She often collected his week's pay and invested it in jewelry for herself. Many show people put their savings in diamonds and little Mrs. Thornton soon developed a passion for adorning herself with sparkling baubles.

Jim came home more inebriated than usual the night he wrote his greatest hit. On seeing him, Bonnie burst into tears and sobbed, "Jimmie, don't you love me any more?"

"Bonnie," he told her, "I love you now just as I did when you were sweet sixteen."

Jim said he thought then, "What a swell title for a song." He explained, "Now I know as much about music as I do about hieroglyphics on a Babylonian spittoon. But I have a mental piano that works overtime. So right off I went to a park, sat on a bench, and the song came—words and music. The next day I went out to sell it to a music publisher.

I said, 'I'd like $15 as an advance on this song.' After listening to me sing it, the music publisher agreed." The contract was signed and Jim was given $15 for all rights to the number. The publisher made $200,000 from the song. Jim was not able to recover the rights to this number and other hits he sold for a little drinking money until he was an old man.

For years Jim and Bonnie were a standard act on the big time. And each week there was a good deal of maneuvering by both to collect their pay. Even when Bonnie did get it, there were always deductions for advances that Jim had drawn.

The most interesting stories about his drinking bouts date from the time he worked for the Hammersteins, and their efforts to keep him sober. These included putting him in a room at the Hotel Metropole between shows. The Considine Brothers, who owned and ran the Metropole, promised to instruct the staff not to give Jim any alcohol.

But Jim was a wily one. Several days later he phoned for a bellboy, and when he appeared, Jim opened the door a crack and said, "Some friends have just dropped in. I want drinks for them." He then called over his shoulder, "What do you want, Harry? A bourbon each for you and Jack and Bill? Tom Collins for you, Henry? Pete, scotch and soda for you and Al? What about you Sam? Straight rum? Hal the same?" Jim concluded, "And for me, son, I'll have a sarsaparilla—with plenty of ice."

When the drinks came, he was waiting behind the closed door. He tipped the boy, took the tray and began drinking the moment the youngster left. Of course there were no guests, and Jim was soon swacked to the eyeballs, having consumed everything but the sarsaparilla.

They locked him in the room after that. But one day Thornton talked the cleaning woman into buying him a pint. Another day he sent for a bellboy and slipped a bribe under the locked door. The boy brought him a pint but said he'd lose his job if he opened the door. Jim, according to legend, told the boy to get a straw. Then he had the boy hold up the bottle so he could sip it through the keyhole.

Many years later, after Bonnie died, Jim did a single act, coming on stage carrying a newspaper which he pretended had funny headlines that he read to the audience. One day while playing the Palace he forgot to bring in a newspaper and only remembered it when the call to go on came. Thornton rushed out of the stage door, found a paper in an ashcan on West 47th Street, and went on stage with it. There he was surprised to find he'd carted in a *Jewish Forward.*

Holding it up so the audience could see it, Jim said, "Didn't know I could read Yiddish, did you, folks?" And he pretended to do just that.

Jim stopped drinking when Prohibition became the law, probably because good liquor was hard to get at first. So his indignation was aroused one day when he was stopped by a drunken border guard on the way home from a Canadian engagement. In the Thornton car, the guard found only his stage equipment, an invitation to address a temperance society, a Gideon bible, and three receipts for alimony paid to his second wife. Jim, when cleared, told the guard in his most stentorian voice, "My dear man, kindly turn your face from the wind. The tonic you have been partaking of suggests a concoction of ether, chloride of lime, asafoetida and chloroform. As a detective, you're a perfect vacuum. You couldn't detect a herd of elephants swimming in a bucket of dishwater."

Joe Frisco, who stuttered, was the big time's fastest extemporaneous wit. The unlikely combination made some of Broadway's wisest wise guys suspect that he stuttered on purpose to add suspense to his punch lines.

They were wrong.

Joe stuttered naturally but, like so many other great two-a-day artists, he was able to convert a handicap into an asset. As a celebrity, his stutter became his trademark. He could devastate almost anyone with a stammered line. And Frisco was merciless.

In his early years, Joe had been a rail-riding bum and a street entertainer, hoofing for pennies in Chicago. He had the crude features of an alley character and all his life retained the smart bum's sharp eye and scorn for the pretentiousness and fakery of those who considered themselves his social superiors. Frisco could see right through them. Like George Bernard Shaw, our century's most brilliant gagman, Joe got his laughs by simply telling the truth as he saw it.

His impersonation at the Palace of the torch singer Helen Morgan, who drank too much and cried too much, was superb.

During the twenties, Joe spoofed Frank McGlynn, a veteran actor who had portrayed Abraham Lincoln for so long that he was beginning to think of himself as the martyred President reincarnated. When appearing on Broadway, Old

McGlynn took to walking about Times Square wearing Abe's beard, tall hat, and shawl and on seeing him, Frisco said, "That p-p-poor son of a g-g-gun won't be happy until someone s-s-shoots him."

During that time also vaudeville's young singing comics were all imitating Al Jolson in blackface. Frisco came upon a group of them—Eddie Cantor, Georgie Jessel, Lou Holtz, among others—talking in front of the Palace. Joe took off his hat, removed his cigar, and with a sweeping bow said, "Why, good afternoon, Mr. Al Jolson!"

Cantor, usually good-natured, didn't like that at all. He growled, "Why don't you try being funny on the stage, Joe, instead of out here on the street?" Cantor was referring to Frisco's refusal to work for less than $1500 a week, a policy that often resulted in long spells of unemployment.

At a benefit in which Enrico Caruso and Frisco were stars, Joe asked the world's greatest opera singer, "Don't use 'Dark Town Strutters Ball,' willya?" Caruso looked at him in bewilderment. Joe explained, "I'm using it for m-m-m-my finish."

We are indebted to Peter Lind Hayes, the radio comedian, for the story of Joe's early life and for preserving in print many of Joe's witticisms. Hayes considers Joe "the most literary illiterate" he ever met.

Joe Frisco claimed he was descended from the bewhiskered Franz Joseph, Emperor of the Austro-Hungarian Empire, which was put out of business in World War I. Joe told Hayes that he adopted his stage name in his hobo years, after seeing "Frisco" on the side of a freight car. His real name was Louis Joseph. In addition to the Austrian blue blood in his veins, he had ordinary red blood from Irish and Polish forebears. He quit school in Rock Island, Illinois, in the third grade. At fifteen, with a partner, he was bumming around the country eating doughnuts—when they could find work. His partner was named Andrew Coffee, which gave Frisco the idea of calling their team "Coffee and Doughnuts," but they had a hard time making enough to keep alive.

Joe's second partner was Loretta McDermott, a beautiful girl dancer, but with her too it was rugged going. Peter Lind Hayes' mother, Gracie Hayes, only a pretty young thing at the time, was working at Big Jim Colisimo's famous cafe in Chicago. When Big Jim was not around, Gracie and her roommate would sneak Frisco and Loretta in to do their act for throw money.

Gracie Hayes was a redhead with a red hot temper. After Frisco became a big Broadway star, she ran into him at parties and expected him to give her a big hello. But each time he gave her only a very small one. Finally, Gracie dragged him into another room and started reminding him of what she'd done for him when he was starving. For a moment, he didn't answer. Then he held his finger to his lips. "Q-q-quiet, girlie. I'll n-n-never give you away."

We don't know when Frisco started talking on the stage. But it was as a hoofer, introducing a wild, barbaric dance he called the Frisco shuffle, that he made it in New York.

Vernon Castle, then the country's number one ballroom dancer, saw Frisco doing this jungle-like number and told him, "Stay with that, kid. It's the coming thing."

Sophie Tucker introduced Frisco and Miss McDermott to New York, at Reisenweber's cabaret. They made an immediate hit and were booked over the Keith Circuit. He wore a derby and smoked a big cigar then, and these became his trademarks. With his crude features he always looked like a street tough who had come into money unexpectedly.

We first saw Frisco dance at a Keith theatre in Brooklyn. Besides the girl, he had an old bummy pal, Eddie Cox, as a singer in the act. Frisco's specialty was the wildest Apache-like dance we'd ever seen. Right in the middle, with the savage music pounding, he stopped at the front of the stage, got down on one knee, twirled his derby and then sent it rolling up the arm and down the other, while furiously puffing perfect smoke rings until he was ready to resume dancing.

Miss McDermott's big number was a shimmy and she also danced with Joe. Frisco never uttered a word.

It was his pal Eddie Cox, also sporting a derby, who swept off his hat to expose a head of hair parted zigzag and told the audience, "Where I come from the guys are so tough they comb their hair with broken bottles."

Frisco spent the last part of his life in Hollywood where he continued his pattern of living, refusing to work for less than the $1500 a week he'd set for himself. But he would do a stint in Gracie Hayes' Lodge for $20 a night or for his pal Charlie Foy, who briefly had a night club there.

All he seemed to want was a little betting money. The jokes he made about his insolvency, income tax troubles, overdue hotel bills, and track wagers were published frequently in the movie trade dailies. Some of them are classics: "Timing is everything. Look at Gary Cooper. He gets $10,000 a week for saying 'Y-y-y-yup!' and 'N-n-n-nope!'"

Think how much he could m-m-m-make if he could learn to say 'Lemme think it o-o-over.' "

Of a famous comedian he thought was a phony, Joe observed, "After they made him, they threw the shovel away."

"I go back four generations in horse-racing. That is, I'm losing now on horses whose great-grandfathers I lost on years ago."

When broke, Joe would borrow money from Bing Crosby. One day at the track Bing saw Frisco counting a big roll of bills which he'd just won on a long shot.

"How about paying me back some of that money?" Bing asked.

Frisco didn't even look up. He peeled off two ten-dollar bills and handed them over, saying, "Now w-w-what about a couple of choruses of 'Melancholy Baby?' "

Our own favorite Frisco joke concerns the day he saw a friend in the waiting room of the Los Angeles Income Tax office. The friend told Joe he had been called there to explain why he was behind in his payments.

"I'll f-f-f-fix it," Frisco assured him and went to the office of the bureau chief to tell him about his pal.

"Don't b-b-b-bother him, sir," pleaded Joe. The official was astounded. They'd been trying to wrestle Frisco out of his own overdue taxes for years. "What about his payments, Joe?"

"Just p-p-put them on my t-t-t-tab."

One of the most startling spectacles on Broadway throughout the twenties was Frank Fay, the big time's standup comedian supreme. No one in vaudeville achieved such complete rapport with audiences at the Palace, in night clubs, and at spots everywhere else that attracted the worldly-wise. The elegantly dressed Fay was the racketeers' *beau ideal* because of his many love affairs, barroom brawling, and wiseguy manner. He of course shared their uncritical esteem for his own personality and talent.

Fay was a handsome man with over-large County Kerry blue eyes, a long, aristocratic nose, ruddy complexion, and flaming red hair styled into perfectly formed waves. He had the forehead of an intellectual and his only imperfect featture was his slightly receding chin. Fay referred to himself variously as "The Great Faysie," "Broadway's Favorite Son," "The King," and "The Great One."

His fellow headliners had unrestrained admiration for his stage appearances but his egocentricity and the lordly airs he displayed at the Lambs Club and their other hangouts were considered ridiculous.

Fred Allen, who once worked for Fay in a show, wrote: "The last time I saw him, he was walking down lover's lane, holding hands with himself." Oscar Levant, also a fellow performer, remembered: "He suffered from total self-enthrallment." While another comedian could have been speaking for most vaudevillians when he said sadly, "I'd go half around the world to see Faysie perform but if I saw him lying dead drunk in the gutter, I wouldn't cross the street to pick him up."

The wise and witty publicist Dick Maney explained the ambivalence. "Though a megalomaniac with a genius for creating hostility, Fay was one of the most gifted performers ever to tread a variety stage. Suave and sardonic, with a superb sense of timing, Frank was an incomparable master of ceremonies."

Fay shared Mae West's gift for exaggerating his personal obsessions to the point of burlesque. Hers was sex, his was self-worship. His manner, like Mae's, carried the suggestion that his eminence was permanent—so secure that he could joke about it.

After he established himself as a Palace idol, Fay would saunter on in his flashy street clothes. He'd lean against the proscenium arch, take off his hat, loosen his tie, and do his stories and songs. Fay had been a fair hoofer before he dropped dancing.

Following a long period of unemployment, Fay told a Palace audience, "What Fred Astaire is to dancing, I am to leisure." It wasn't possible for Faysie to exaggerate his self-adoration, but he tried with, "Pour me a cup of coffee. I don't want to get sleepy while I'm boosting myself."

And when Fay went in for such jokes as, "I just made a date with a newspaperwoman. Yeah, she runs a newsstand on West 45th Street," the combination of self-deprecatory remarks with his hauteur made the gags sound better than they were.

He was greatest when working with stooges. On being insulted, he'd again poke fun at his own conceit. Occasionally he had Jane Brown, who was working in another act on the same bill, come in on his turn. Asked who she was, Jane—a dainty and pretty gal—would tell him,

"I'm the iceman."

"You look like a golddigger to me," Fay would reply.

"What's a golddigger?" Jane then asked.

"If you took fifty dollars out of my pocket you'd be a golddigger."

"I wouldn't be a golddigger, I'd be a magician." Then came Faysie's punch line.

"Take care, you are talking of the man I love."

Frank Fay's utterly relaxed manner was irresistible. His mimicry was also superb. With a drooped eyelid or a pursed mouth, he could make you see the person he was talking about—an uncle with a passion for string saving, another who was a paper bag putter-awayer—and have you enjoy their misadventures. One of his best vignettes concerned a prissy old maid who, with mounting delight, pushes her way through the crowd gathered around an injured man on the street. The climax comes when, on tiptoes, she watches the ambulance surgeon working, and exclaims in delirious delight: "Oh, I do think that his leg is *broken!*"

During the Dry Era, Faysie offered a travesty of "The Face on the Barroom Floor" called "The Face on the Drugstore Floor." In this he played a gum drop fiend unable to kick his habit. When the cost of everything soared, Faysie sang a number about the good old days of low prices.

He usually finished his act with Vincent Youmans and Irving Caesar's "Tea for Two." After each two or three lines, Faysie would stop the house orchestra, interpolate a sarcastic comment, then resume singing. He would start off by singing the first two lines straight:

> *Just picture you upon my knee.**
> *Tea for two and two for tea . . .*

Looking incredulous, he'd stop the music. "Isn't that rich? Here's a guy got it all figured out. He has enough tea for two, so he has two for tea. I suppose if a third person walks

* © 1925 Warner Bros.

in, they'd have to stab him." The orchestra resumes, and
Faysie continues:

> *Just me for you*
> *And you for me alone . . .*

Fay would stop the music again and ask the audience:
"What does he mean—alone? And I've heard of guys asking
dames up to see their etchings, but this is the first time I
heard of a guy inviting a dame up to take a peek at his
tea leaves."

> *Nobody near us*
> *To see or to hear us . . .*

"Nobody near us!" Fay would scoff. "Who the hell wants
to hear two people drinking tea?"

> *We won't have it known, dear*
> *That we own a telephone, dear . . .*

Fay's comment: "All this guy has is a broken-down cup of
tea and a telephone he won't let you use . . ." Then

> *Day will break*
> *And you'll awake*
> *And start to bake*
> *A sugar cake . . .*

A sugar cake? Fay then would demand, shaking his head
sadly, "The poor woman. What a future! She gets out of
bed, washes her teeth and bang—right to the stove! Nobody
up but her. Feeling around in the dark for flour. He probably calls her up too—to remind her. He says, 'Hey, honey,
it's almost light out. What's cookin'?' "

Francis Anthony Fay was born of a theatrical family in
San Francisco on November 17, 1894. Both his parents, Fay
always said, were in show business. Between engagements,

his father occupied his time as an Indian fighter, a conductor on the Union Pacific, and a writer of lyric poetry. Frank made his debut at three in *Quo Vadis?* At five, he appeared in *Babes in Toyland*. He dropped out of school after the third grade. During his boyhood, Fay played small parts in the troupe of Sir Henry Irving, the Shakespearean star.

As a teenager, he knocked around vaudeville for a while with a partner, Johnny Dyer, who played straight man to Fay's low comedy. In that act, Faysie did several things he later said he despised, among them telling illiterate jokes and wearing a fake red nose, oversize brokendown shoes, and baggy pants. This worried Fay so much that eventually he denied ever doing such routines.

Faysie made his first Broadway hit in *Oh! What a Girl!* in 1917. One critic called him "a wild-eyed genius with wild auburn hair and a hot gift for song." In one of his first interviews, Fay managed to insult all other comedians except Harry Kelly, who was in the same show. He praised Kelly as "one who could make me laugh although he resorted to exaggerated makeup. The reason is that he is perfectly natural."

In one early act Faysie had three stooges who kept walking on and off the stage. The best of them, of course, was Patsy Kelly.

Patsy was born Bridget Veronica Kelly and grew up as an incorrigible tomboy on the streets of New York. From the age of seven, she lived dangerously. Veronica's Irish family lived on a street that had both a firehouse and a police station. Most of the police and firefighters were Irish in those days and, loving the frecklefaced little Kelly, they permitted her to clamber all over their equipment. Accident-prone, she was forever falling off the roofs of police wagons and hook and ladder trucks, as well as fire escapes. She was in so many accidents that the men in blue nick-named her Patsy, and Patsy she remained. The doctor in a nearby hospital advised her mother, "Better keep her off the streets, Mrs. Kelly, so she'll at least survive until she reaches the age of puberty."

Patsy became a teenage dance instructor at Jack Blue's Dancing School and brought her earnings home to help her always needy family. "Sometimes I was paid as little as a quarter for a day's work," Patsy recalled.

Her brother Johnny heard one day that Frank Fay, then at the Palace, was looking for a third stooge. The two that Faysie had were George Haggerty and Lew Mann. Johnny was so nervous about asking for the job that he made Patsy go with him. Faysie took one look at Patsy's Irish face and hired her instead of Johnny. He paid her a pittance as he did all who worked in his act, but even so it was a larger pittance than Jack Blue's. In no time, Faysie found out that luck had brought him a treasure, a street kid who could swap wisecracks with him and give funny answers to funny questions. Patsy was shy about everything else but getting laughs with those snappy retorts. He never knew what howler she'd come up with.

Patsy gives Mr. Fay, as she still calls him, full credit for teaching her all she knows about stage comedy. The way she recounts it reveals her innate modesty more than any-thing else: "He would never tell me what to do or what we were going to talk about. So whether it made sense or not, I just had to think fast and feed him the right line or he would tell the audience how stupid I was. He'd say to the audience, 'Isn't that awful? Here I am paying her a big salary and you can see for yourselves how stupid she is.' But what he taught me about timing of comedy, where to pack the punches and other invaluable tricks, will always make me feel that I owe him a debt of gratitude I can never repay."

The greatest achievement in most comedians' eyes is the ability to top the gags or insults of other funny men. Like Frisco, Fay was a champ at this.

One night while he was appearing at the Copacabana, Milton Berle began to heckle him. "This is going to be a battle of wits," challenged Uncle Miltie, who was only Cousin Miltie then.

"If you insist, Milton," retorted Fay, "but I want you to know that it is against my principles to fight an unarmed man." The Peter Rabbit grin quickly faded from Milton's face.

Fay was married three times and divorced by each of his wives. His first was Frances White, an overnight headliner when she became the partner of William Rock, a much older man. Rock was well-known for an Apache dance he'd done with his wife Maud Fulton years before. At Hammerstein's Billy Rock had thrown his missus across the stage with such violence that audiences marveled how she was able to walk afterwards. She divorced Rock, not for attempted mayhem, but for taking on tiny Frankie White—who was in her early teens—as his partner. Frankie was billed at first as vaudeville's "greatest small dancer," but later made her reputation as the singer (or lisper) of "M-i-s-s-i-s-s-i-p-p-i" and "I'd Love to be a Monkey in the Zoo." Nobody in show business was cuter than Frankie with her adorable lisp.

The team had just signed a big-money deal to tour when,

on March 3, 1917, Frankie and Faysie sneaked down to Philadelphia and were married. Her mother and Rock both opposed the match. After six hectic months, Fay was suing Billy Rock for $100,000 for alienation of his bride's affections and she was demanding a divorce. Miss White claimed that Faysie had borrowed $2500 in sums of $100 to $250 and she wanted it back.

Instead of denying the debt, Faysie demanded "Can she prove it?" And when Frankie's process server slipped him the papers in the divorce suit, Fay beat him up. Meanwhile Rock had been divorced by Maud Fulton, who quit dancing and wrote *The Brat,* a Broadway hit that made her rich.

In 1918, Fay married Lee Buchanan, who had worked with him in an act early in his career. That didn't last very long either.

His third bride was Barbara Stanwyck. She started her career as Ruby Stevens, Brooklyn telephone operator and night club showgirl, then became a stage star. The couple went to Hollywood where Barbara triumphed and Fay flopped.

To help him, Barbara returned to New York so they could headline together as a team at the Palace. There Fay suffered a great humiliation: his former wife Frankie White had papers served on him in his dressing room demanding that she be paid back alimony for the past thirteen years. In his agony, Faysie quit the show and disappeared. Barbara, who had to take over his duties as M.C., subsequently divorced him.

There had been an earlier humiliation for Faysie at the Palace which had probably hurt The Great One's pride even more deeply. The revenge-taster that time was little

Bert Wheeler whom Frank had been tormenting for years with his sneers and jibes. At one performance, Bert (whose act went on later than Fay's) persuaded Frank to let him go on first. Wheeler walked out and told every joke and did every routine in Faysie's act. That left Frank, for once, with nothing to say.

In addition to their regular turns, the two appeared together later on the bill and at every show after that memorable one, Fay would tell the audience Bert was so small he had a hard time keeping up with people of normal size. He called attention to Bert's ill-fitting clothes, his lack of intelligence, and other shortcomings. This patter went on for five or six minutes. One night, as usual, Bert didn't answer. He stood looking the picture of stupefaction while the audience howled. "What's the matter, junior," asked Fay when he finished. "Aren't you going to say something to the folks?"

"Oh, yes," Bert said. "I've been waiting for you to finish getting these mild titters and tiny giggles from the good people out front. I'm going to get the biggest laugh anyone ever heard at this theatre."

"Why don't you go ahead and do just that?" asked Fay.

"I will," Bert replied. He walked up to Broadway's Favorite Son, stood on tiptoes, slapped him hard across the face and then ran like a rabbit off the stage. The crowd had been laughing at Fay's remarks about Wheeler, but the slap brought even bigger roars. Fay followed Wheeler offstage, after remarking lamely, "That's what you get mixing with low comedians."

In the dressing room, which they were sharing that week, Fay told Bert, "Mr. Wheeler, Mr. Fay didn't like what you did just now. Never do it again! Do you understand?"

Before Wheeler could reply, there was a knock on the door and the house manager entered. He was beaming. "Boys, that was great. Keep the slap in at every show!"

Big-time vaudeville, we regret to say, cooperated fully in this country's successful efforts to keep the Negro in his place—invisible. Blacks were considered sub-human savages with not much sense. And this was long after students of popular music discovered that blacks had created in jazz America's only original art form. Their other contributions to the musical theatre and vaudeville ranged from the minstrel show to the shimmy.

The minstrel show grew out of the entertainments put on by the Negro workers on Southern plantations. But white minstrels, blacked up, later got the big money and fame. Few of the Uncle Tom troupes that were so popular along with the minstrels after the Civil War let blacks play Uncle Tom or Topsy.

The man who truly broke the Broadway color line was Bert Williams, an unforgettable Octoroon comedian. Another part-Negro comic, Charlie Case, and a few others preceded him, but with no such impact. Bert entered vaudeville as a headliner and stayed on top.

For his stage entrance he used a dazzling device. Before he came on, with the rest of the house dark, a baby spot would focus high on a side of the curtain. In that small circle of light would appear wriggling fingers in a white glove, then the whole hand, an arm, then a shoulder in black cloth. By the time tall, slim, melancholy Bert walked on in tattered black suit, battered top hat, and shoes far too big for him, the audience was his.

There was never a letdown after that hypnotizing start. Williams did not sing or dance well yet he amazed everybody by how resourceful he was at using his thin voice and not very talented feet. He wore bizarre costumes but it was his woebegone manner and matchless timing that helped him put his songs over. He half-sung, half-talked his "Nobody" lyrics:

> *When life seems full of clouds and rain*
> *And I am full of nothin' but pain,*
> *Who soothes my thumpin', bumpin' brain*
>   (pause) *Nobody!*

> *When winter comes with snow and sleet*
> *And me with hunger and cold feet,*
> *Who says "Here's twenty-five cents, go and get*
>   *somethin' to eat?"*
>   (shakes head) *Nobody!*

> *I ain't done nothin' to nobody*
> *I ain't got nothin' from nobody, no time.*
> *Until I get somethin' from somebody, some time,*
> *I'll never do nothin' for nobody, no time*
> *When summer comes, all cool and clear*
> *And my friends see me drawin' near*
> *Who says "Come in and have some beer?*
>   *Hmm—nobody!*

> *When I was in that railroad wreck*
> *And thought I'd cashed my last check,*
> *Who took that engine off my neck*
>   (resentfully) *Hmm—not a soul.*

His jokes were sidesplitting, largely because of his way
of telling them. One small example: "If you have two wives,
that's bigamy. If you have many wives, that's polygamy. If
you have one wife that's monotony."

Bert Williams was at his peak in pantomime. His masterpiece was a portrayal of five poker players done on a dark
stage with a small spot on his head and shoulders. One by
one, he reveals the character and thoughts of the gamblers,
from the reactions of each to the deal, through the hopeful
study of the cards, the raise, the draw, and the climax of
the showdown. It offered the drama of card-playing, complete with craftiness, suspicion, hope, despair, the anguish
of losing and the joy of winning, in a flash.

Williams was born in Antigua, West Indies, on November 12, 1874 (though both place and date have been dis-
puted). He was about ten when his parents moved to River-
side, California, where his father worked for the Central
Pacific Railroad.

Bert started just like the white youngsters seeking a career in show business—doing menial jobs, singing for throw
money, shining shoes. His real career success began when
he was 21 and hooked up with George Walker, a 20-year-
old minstrel out of Kansas. By 1902 they were stars on
Broadway and also had created a sensation in London with
their own black show, *In Dahomey*. Williams was the comic,
Walker, the straight man and cakewalk whiz.

After Walker died, Williams became a star of Ziegfeld
Follies, and the only Negro in a series of those great revues.
Will Rogers, Eddie Cantor, W. C. Fields, and his other co-
stars accepted him as an equal, as artist and man. But Williams never could relax, drank too much, and kept to

himself. One interviewer asked if he'd prefer being a white man. With the offstage dignity that was characteristic, he said, "No. How do I know what I might be if I was a white man? I might be a sandhog, burrowing away and losing my health for $8 a day. I might be a street-car conductor at $12 or $15 a week. There is many a white man less fortunate and well-equipped than I am. In truth I have never been able to discover anything disgraceful in being a colored man. But I have often found it inconvenient in America."

The off-stage Williams, a tall, light-skinned man who had great poise, played on stage a shuffling, bewildered black man. He used black makeup on his face, a kinky wig, and long, ill-fitting white gloves. Invariably his costume consisted of a shabby dress suit, a battered top hat, and oversize shoes that looked suitable only for the junk-heap. Sleeves and trouser were too short and completing the image of a shiftless Negro was the forlorn look on his face.

His voice was thin but his mastery of timing made it effective. His shuffling dances were showpieces of awkwardness. Heywood Broun and other critics marveled that in his pantomimes he seldom moved more than six inches.

Bert Williams's lasting achievement was opening the golden doors of Broadway for other Negro performers. After him the great black performers flourished on the legitimate stage in such dramas as *Porgy* and *The Green Pastures* and in *Shuffle Along* and other all-Negro musicals. And in vaudeville's big time there flashed such talents from Harlem as Bojangles Bill Robinson, Ethel Waters, Buck and Bubbles, Moss and Frye, Sissle and Blake, Miller and Lyles. Ironically, black comics imitated their white imitators by blacking up and using white paint around their mouths to make them look bigger.

Williams, at age 45, died in 1922. W. C. Fields delivered his epitaph: "Bert Williams is the funniest man I ever saw and the saddest man I ever met."

CHAPTER SIX

Minstrels and Musicians

SEVERAL OF VAUDEVILLE's wildest madcaps and zanies came from middle-class or wealthy homes. Ed Wynn's family had a successful hat business in Philadelphia. Walter Catlett's father was a San Francisco banker. Clark and McCullough were from respectable families in Springfield, Ohio. Andrew Tombes's dad, a Chillicothe, Ohio grocer, was wealthy enough to send him to Phillips Exeter Academy, the expensive preparatory school. After a year Andy came back and told his father that higher education was not for him. What he really wanted was to be a circus clown. "He couldn't have been more understanding," recalls Andy, who in time went from circus to success in vaudeville, Broadway musicals, and Hollywood.

Jack Norworth, a deft comedian as well as a singer and writer of song hits, was the always rebellious son of an Episcopalian organ-maker and choir master named Knauff who was intent on teaching him the organ-making trade. Jack was kicked out of one Philadelphia school after another. The climax came when Jack was fourteen and a student at Chester A. Arthur High School. Ordered to the principal's office to receive punishment for raising hell in class, Jack watched the principal pick up a ruler. Before it could be brought down, Jack jumped up, grabbed the educator's long Dundreary whiskers, and pulled them so hard his would-be oppressor screamed in anguish.

His appalled father took what then was considered the last step in disciplining boys headed for the electric chair: he put Jack in the Navy.

But instead of a hard life at sea, Jack was assigned to the *Saratoga,* a Navy training ship for teenagers, where he was put in charge of the ship's entertainment. Instead of scrubbing decks and polishing brass, Jack staged every kind of show and played the leading part in all of them. At 19 he was discharged and ready for his vaudeville career.

Both the Jolson Brothers (Harry and Al) and the Howard Brothers (Willie, Eugene, and Sam) came from fanatically religious Jewish homes. Unlike his brothers, Sam Howard never played vaudeville, but became a burlesque star.

Buster Keaton recalled Harry Jolson as the only black-faced entertainer who sang with a Jewish accent. Al, his younger brother, overshadowed Harry almost from the start.

Al Jolson's success was basically a triumph of his overwhelming personality. Other vaudevillians were funnier, could sing and dance better than Jolson. But none of them captivated audiences as Jolie did.

One observer wrote: "Harry Lauder soothes. Will Rogers amuses. Al Jolson thrills." He hypnotized audiences whether singing Gershwin's "Swanee," sentimental numbers like "My Mammy!" and "Hello, Central! Give Me No Man's Land," or the ribald "Why Do They All Take the Night Boat to Albany?" Whatever Jolie sang, your heart leaped and your backbone seemed to jump and rattle.

Jolson seemed to enjoy entertaining as much as his audiences liked listening to him. When the Shuberts added Sunday performances at the Winter Garden, Jolson was invariably their headliner. He proved tireless. Often, as the curtain was about to come down on a weeknight show, Jolie would tell the audience, "The chorus girls look tired. Let's send them and everybody else backstage home. If you want to hear me sing some more, forget that 11:47 to Larchmont. Just stay and listen to me."

They always stayed—sometimes until three in the morning.

Oscar Levant for a while was the leader of the Winter Garden orchestra. Sometimes Jolie would bawl him out. Levant, usually quick to take umbrage, did not reply to Al's criticism. In his memoirs, Oscar recalled, "I loved being excoriated by Jolson. His voice had such magic, an irresistible baritone beauty, regardless of the words he used."

When Jolie strutted out on stage, he didn't appear to have a doubt that he'd knock the audience dead. His chest would be puffed out, his hands clasped behind him. And as he skipped about, his body would be bent back with the curved rigidity of a taut bow. Audiences were bewitched by his joy and exuberance as well as his eagerness to give everything he had at every performance.

All of the young comics imitated Jolson and put on blackface. He had no rivals but Eddie Cantor came closest. Cantor, who was also Jolie's good friend, never could understand one thing about Al. In the wings before going on, Jolie was the most nervous man in show business. But the moment he was in the spotlight Jolie exploded with self-assurance. A more boastful or more insecure stage star never lived.

Off stage and on his own, Jolson was uncertain about everything: his future, whether he worshipped his current wife (he had four) or wanted to divorce her, what to eat, his health (one doctor commented, "Al has added a new dimension to hypochondria") where to go that day, what to wear, which of his friends could be trusted.

Variety's Frank Scully perhaps said it best when he wrote: "Al blew hot and cold more than anybody else in his time. One day he would say 'Why should I save money? I'm the greatest entertainer in the world.' The next day he would act like a deaf mute with a tin watch and a tin cup."

Jolie remained that way even after he had triumphed as the star of eleven long-run Winter Garden productions and had made millions for Warner Brothers and himself with *The Jazz Singer* and his other immensely popular musical talking pictures. He was so insecure that on meeting strangers, he'd say, "I'm Al Jolson and I have four million dollars." Despite perfect health, he was still taking whole boxes of bromo-seltzer every day.

But the biggest paradox of Jolie's career was his feud with his brother Harry (born Hersh), who was three years older. It lasted almost from the time they started together in vaudeville as kid entertainers until Al died. Yet in boyhood Harry had been Al's defender in street fights against Jew-hating gangs, and was a lifelong admirer of his showmanship.

There were other children—two sisters, Rose and Etta, all born in Shrednike, Lithuania, to Naomi and Moishe Yoelson, a cantor. Asa, as Al was called, was the youngest. When he was born on May 26, 1886, his father, hearing his first cry, said, "With such lusty lungs my son will grow up to be a cantor and will sing with me."

When Asa was four, his father fled to America to escape a pogrom, leaving his family behind. It was four years before the rabbi could send home enough money for them to join him in Washington, D. C., where he was cantor-rabbi of a synagogue.

Three years later Mrs. Yoelson died. Rose, the oldest daughter, had to take over the household.

Like other slum kids who became vaudevillians, Al and Harry began as tiny street entertainers. They fought the tough boys who called them "sheeny" and "kike," sang, danced, and made funny faces on the corners, in backyards, and at saloons. They collected the most nickles singing in front of the Raleigh Hotel where many cabinet members, supreme court justices, senators, and congressmen lived and sat evenings on the front porch.

When their father learned of his sons' unholy street capers, he beat them—again and again. And the brothers ran away again and again. Each time they were found by the police who returned them home.

Losing his mother, who had doted on him as her baby, had been Al's first traumatic experience. A year later he suffered a second shock. One morning he woke up to find Harry gone. Harry had left a note for Al, explaining that he had departed for New York to get a start on the stage and promising to send for him.

After weeks when no letter came, Al hopped a freight train and went to New York on his own. By pure chance, he met Harry on the Bowery. Harry had found no stage job and possessed so little money that they slept in the back of a truck parked in an alley. It was a freezing cold night. When the boys woke up, Al's shoes were gone—they were stolen right off his feet while he was sleeping. Harry had to beg for hours on the street before collecting enough money to buy a second-hand pair for his small brother. Then he sent Al home to Washington aboard a freight car.

Their whole childhood was like that: beatings at home made them run away sometimes alone, sometimes together. In the summer they entertained on excursion boats, shined shoes, sold newspapers. Once when Harry was away, Al ran off to Baltimore where he was picked up by the police. He refused to tell them where he lived, and they took him to a Catholic orphanage. Al made so much trouble there that he was placed in solitary confinement. When he finally gave in and said who he was they sent for his father, who walloped him again. Yet there was an incident revealing Al's attitude toward their father that baffled Harry. He had a job selling candy in the Bijou Theatre, a Washington burlesque house, and one night sneaked Al into the gallery. Usually at such shows, on finishing his most popular number, the featured singer would ask the audience to sing along with him as he repeated the chorus. Whenever Al was there, you could hear his powerful young voice above all others. Vaudeville's popular minstrel Eddie Leonard was the star one week. Jolie's voice so impressed him that Leonard sent for him and he offered Al a job with the show, explaining, "First you'll sing from the gallery, then I'll call you down and you can sing from the stage." Jolie refused—he said his father would never permit him to appear on the stage.

Harry couldn't figure that out. And he was often baffled later on by many other things his kid brother did and said.

Once, without asking his permission, Al used Harry's name on a stage tour and couldn't understand why Harry objected. Al got a second offer at the Bijou while Annie Beeler's Villanova Burlesque troupe was there and this time he jumped at the chance. At age thirteen he worked out the season with Miss Beeler and her beefy, amorous chorus girls.

There followed for the brothers a couple of years of missed meals, nights spent sleeping in the park, and singing for nickles anywhere it was allowed. In New York the boys got their vaudeville start with Joe Palmer as a third partner. An older man and a gifted singer, Palmer was a cripple whom they had to push on stage in a rolling chair. He suggested that the brothers change their names to Al and Harry Jolson. Billed as Jolson, Palmer, and Jolson, the team got bookings. But the brothers quarreled in New Orleans—Harry always claimed that he fell sick there and the others went off without him. The two-man act did all right minus Harry since by that time Jolie was appearing in blackface. The comedian J. Francis Dooley had suggested it on noticing his nervousness when delivering lines.

"You'll relax in blackface, kid," Dooley told Al. "Because you'll know that even if you are nervous, the audience won't know it. Blacking up is like putting on a mask."

Jolie tried it and found that it worked. After splitting with Palmer, Jolie worked as a single on the Sullivan-Considine circuit. Starting at $35 a week, he was making $75 by the end of the tour in San Francisco. There he was booked into a Market Street restaurant with a floor show. The city was trying desperately to recover from the terrible 1906 earthquake and fire. When Al got to the restaurant, he found construction going on all around the place day and night. When he complained, the manager barked, "You've signed a contract with me. You have to make the customers forget the racket."

On the night he was to open, Jolie watched the chorus trying to work. They couldn't keep time with the orchestra because they couldn't hear it, and the people at the tables were ignoring them. When the chorus started to go off, Jolie waved them back. He pushed the piano to the center of the floor. Then he jumped on it and yelled, "We're here to have a good time, folks! Ain't that so?" He gestured to the chorus girls to group themselves around the piano. Finally, he asked the customers to move their tables closer to him.

"I might not sing good, folks," he shouted, "but I sure sing loud." And he did, jumping down and weaving in and around the tables, singing, skipping, telling jokes.

The people loved it. The cafe was jammed every night after that to hear the kid singer yell above the building noises. Al's rise was rapid and steady after that. He worked more vaudeville, then joined the country's best minstrel show: Lew Dockstadter's. Dockstadter was his own star but Jolson, with his boisterous style and rich singing voice, got such wild applause that Lew put the young sensation into the star's next-to-closing spot. It meant demoting himself, but Jolie was that much of a crowd-pleaser even then.

When the season closed, Jolson was submitted to the big time's acid test—a week at Hammerstein's. The toughest performance there came on Sunday night, with professionals all over the house, talking shop like mad, chattering, greeting friends. When Jolie—then 23—came on, they did not quiet down until he gave them his loudest attention-getter, an ear-shattering whistle.

Next the cocky newcomer told the smart, gabby Broadway

crowd, "If you wanted to talk to each other, you could have stayed at home and saved yourselves a bit of change. If you'll let me tell my jokes and sing my songs, I'll go away and leave you alone."

Surprised and amused they gave him his chance. And Jolie, capering, strutting, roaring his songs, knocked them dead. It was the first of ten thousand wonderful Jolson nights on Broadway.

Broadway's musical comedy producers all wanted Jolie. But William Klein, his smart agent, insisted on waiting for a perfect spot. While waiting, he kept Jolie working in the many vaudeville theatres in and around New York.

Klein finally decided that *Vera Violetta*, the show that opened the new Winter Garden Theatre on March 20, 1911, was the best spot for Jolie to make his bow in musical comedy. It was an elegant house, seating 1590, and built on the site of an old horse barn on what was then Upper Broadway, between Forty-ninth and Fiftieth Streets. Though the show on opening night was too long, Jolson was a hit. And the shows he soon starred in there like *The Honeymoon Express, Sinbad,* and *Bombo* made him the world's most popular stage performer.

Jolie was married four times. His first three wives—Henriette Heller, Ethel Delmar, and Ruby Keeler—all divorced him. His fourth wife, Erle Galbraith, was an army X-ray technician whom he met on a tour of World War II service camps. She was 21 and he 57 when they were married on March 23, 1947. Jolie was happy with her until he died on October 23, 1950.

Unfortunately, the most popular entertainer of his time was not always lovable to some of his best pals.

George Jessel was as loyal a friend as Al Jolson ever had. In 1926 Jessel was enjoying the success of his life as the star of the Broadway hit play, *The Jazz Singer*.

Someone tipped him off that Warner Brothers planned to make it into the first talking movie. Jessel figured that the company would try to get either Al Jolson or Eddie Cantor to play the role he had in the play since both were far bigger box office draws. He called up both of them and asked them to turn down the offer and suggest that Warners get him. Both agreed. Jolie exclaimed, "Of course, Georgie. You can depend on me."

Later Georgie explained that when Cantor got the call he said the man who would be great in the part is George Jessel. "Warners must have called Jolie minutes after I talked to him," Jessel then said, "because an hour later when I called him again, his hotel told me he had just left for California."

When Larry Parks played Jolson in *The Singing Fool* (Jolson did the actual singing), he found Al a frightening menace throughout the shooting of the picture. Parks recalls, "Every time I finished a scene, he'd come up behind me and say, 'Parks, do you stink! I'm going to tell the studio to get someone else who won't disgrace the name of Jolson'."

People who had for years heard Jolie phoning huge bets to his bookies were surprised at the size of his estate. They never found out that Al and the bookie used a code. When he said "Five thousand on the nose for Dream Rose" it meant $50. Ten thousand meant $100, and so on. Even on his own telephone Jolie had to put on an astounding performance.

On the other hand there was nothing phoney about the compulsive gambling of Willie Howard, the brilliant little

Jewish comic. He too made millions as a star of Shubert musicals and on the big time, but he squandered every dime of it betting on the horses.

There were certain similarities between his career and Jolson's. Both had beautiful voices, were the sons of cantor-rabbis, and started on the stage working with an older brother. Willie's brother Eugene also had a fine voice and was a capable straight man for Willie's comedy. When Eugene retired as an actor, Willie made him his manager and continued to split the weekly paycheck with him.

Willie was a kind, generous man, greatly loved on Broadway. But other actors made jokes about Willie's weakness for the horses: "Willie is a great man for education. He's sent six young fellows through college—all sons of his bookmakers."

The competition among backstage bookies for Willie's betting business was furious. Willie, they knew, could not possibly have two winning days in a row because he backed horses on every track in the country. One imaginative bookmaker finally sewed up Willie's bet business by offering to give back at the end of each month half of all the money Willie Howard had lost to him. It averaged $7000. But the moment the comedian got back his half, about $3500 a month, he'd wager that away too. Every once in a while—when Willie did win a pile, however, he would change it all into singles, fives and tens and distribute it to the bums on Skid Row.

Willie's first stage experience was a sad one. With Eugene, he won an Amateur Night prize of $5. But the manager refused to give them more than one dollar.

Alistair Cooke, an urbane critic, once described Willie as "one of those little wistful men who came to great fame by keeping up the preposterous pretense of playing the shrewd debonair chap when it was obvious to everybody looking on that this was the last part Nature ever meant them to play." Brooks Atkinson called Willie "one of the essential mountebanks of our day."

The Howards did not look like brothers. Eugene was heavyset, well-dressed, and appeared a typical New York businessman. A connoiseur of food, he was also well-read and a bright conversationalist. Willie was less than five feet tall and weighed ninety-five pounds, with burning black eyes and unruly hair. He was stoop-shouldered as well as scrawny. On the street he resembled a vagrant who had found his wardrobe at the city dump and on stage he managed to look melancholy and audaciously mischievous at the same time.

A master comedian, Willie did hundreds of side-splitting sketches. In one called "French Taught in a Hurry," he talked to pupils in the most garbled language ever heard. The audience quickly gathered that Willie as a teacher was a desperate faker who mispronounced everything substituting tattered scraps of Yiddish and broken English for the French he was supposedly teaching.

Another sketch presented him and Eugene with two buxom lady singers as the spirited quartet from *Rigoletto*. From beginning to end, wee Willie glued his eyes on the cleft in the heaving bosom of the lady at his side. During this operatic number, Willie managed to register amazement, wistful yearning, and finally overpowering lust without moving.

The best of the routines was "Tomorrow Comes the Revolution." In this, a pathetic looking Willie, with his tiny frame, old clothes, and burning eyes, was perfect as a Communist agitator lecturing a crowd from a soapbox. He promises them relief from those bloodsuckers who have always exploited the poor, the greedy capitalists. "Tomorrow, like them, you will eat strawberries and cream." Whereupon one of his listeners pipes up, "But I don't like strawberries and cream." Willie scowls, scarcely believing his ears. Then he thunders, "Tomorrow comes the revolution, you nothing. Tomorrow you will eat strawberries and cream, and you'll like it."

While Eugene ate in the finest French restaurants, Willie remained a lover of Jewish delicatessen food. He said of Eugene's magnificent dining: "My brother doesn't eat like a horse. He eats like a maharajah." Willie enjoyed playing practical jokes on him. One Sunday he invited Eugene and his wife Maude for dinner. When they arrived, they could rouse no one. Going upstairs, they found Willie lying on the bed, apparently stabbed in the chest. Blood was all over his clothes and face. Of course this turned out to be just one of Willie's little gags.

Not surprisingly, when Willie Howard died in 1949 at the age of 63 he left $7000 in assets and more than ten times that in debts. Jolson left over $4 million.

The wholehearted friendship of the partners in some of the two-man headlining teams was quite moving. One thinks of Gus Van and Joe Schenck and of Bobby Clark and Paul McCullough.

Gus Van was a heavy-set, black-haired baritone with a genius for singing dialect songs of every kind. Joe Schenck was younger, slim, blonde and blue-eyed, and had a tenor voice that enabled him to reach higher notes, it was said, than Caruso. When the team harmonized, they always brought down the house, living up to their billing as "the Pennant-Winning Battery of Songland."

The legend was that they first sang together while Van was the motorman and Schenck the conductor on a trolley car in their native Brooklyn. It was almost true. Van was a motorman with ambitions to get into vaudeville. He had won approval singing in the local lodge-halls and barrooms, but felt he would get no further without a first-rate pianist.

Schenck, then only sixteen, heard about this and met Van one day in the carbarns as he was quitting work. They hit it off immediately. At the beginning, Schenck, because his voice was still changing, did not sing in their act; he merely played the piano. But even then, the boys were inseparable and were seen everywhere together.

By the following year, 1911, Joe also was singing and they made the big time. In their act, each sang a song or two alone and several others together. Their harmonizing was superb. Schenck had a round choir boy's face—and voice. When singing alone, he would turn on the stool to face the audience, lean his head back so it rested on his left hand, which was supported by his elbow on the piano, and accompany himself playing with the right hand.

One of his partner's dialect songs was a comic one with a quite suggestive finish for that prissy era. It told of two Italian immigrants bewildered by the machinery they see all around them in New York. They become totally exasperated at the Automat, a restaurant where they get their food by putting nickles in slots in the wall, and the tagline was: "When they start making babies by machinery I go back to Italy."

After triumphing for eight years with the most popular act of its kind on the big time, Van and Schenck went on to star in the Ziegfeld Follies, at the large movie presentation houses, and finally starred in a Hollywood film of their own.

Then in 1930, at the height of their fame, Joe Schenck died suddenly at 35. Gus was inconsolable and couldn't work for a long time without his partner and best friend. When he did, he explained to a reporter, "There is only one reason I am now able to walk on a stage without my lost partner. I am as uncertain as every other mortal about what happens to the soul after death. But if I didn't believe absolutely that Joe Schenck's spirit was listening to my every note—that he is keeping me on pitch, so to speak, as he always did when we were partners—I would never make another stage appearance. I would go back to railroading."

Clark and McCullough met as kids in their home town, Springfield, Ohio. Bobby was 12, Paul 16 and they had had more schooling than most of their fellow artists. Paul McCullough went to both high school and business school. Bobby Clark's father, a railroad conductor, died when he was six but Bobby was provided with a sound education by his grandparents.

Their musical education started when Paul got a bugle for himself after hearing Bobby play the one he had bought with his earnings as a newspaper delivery boy. After that they practiced together and did tumbling and other gymnastics at the "Y." They were determined to get into show business and for five years rehearsed their tumbling tricks and bugle playing together. Meanwhile they had to be content with making appearances at picnics, parades, and Sunday School entertainments.

They got their first job in show business through an ad in *The Billboard,* the theatrical weekly. It was worded exactly like those they had seen:

"Two-act, aged 17 and 21. Can do blackface,
a specialty, and double in brass!"

After some weeks, the boys got a reply from a wandering
troupe: Culhane, Chace and Weston's Minstrels. It offered
them $25 a week plus expenses and instructed them to report
to a small town which they'd never heard of in upper New
York State. Though dubious, Clark's mother gave them $30
for traveling expenses.

The first contract they signed had a number of pretty strict
provisions. Their first six days of salary was to be held back
until the end of the 35-week engagement. A one-dollar fine
was imposed for being late at rehearsal, for causing stage
waits, for having loud arguments or swearing in the hotels or
the theatre, for appearing in muddy shoes during the parade
or dirty shirt fronts, collars, and cuffs. Two dollars was de-
ducted for missing the parade or for playing musical instruments at the hotel instead of in the theatre. The list of
restrictions ended with the warning: "Anyone caught mashing
within two blocks of the theatre or hotel will be fined five
dollars."

The boys from Springfield were fined so often that after
working twelve weeks they had not been paid a penny. One
night the manager ran off and the partners then learned that
no one else in the little troupe had ever been paid anything
either. Clark and McCullough found themselves in a whistle-
stop called Harrington, Delaware, with $3.20 left of Mrs.
Clark's $30 stake. They were lucky enough to be hired by
another troupe for $35 a week, but again they weren't paid—
this time because the show was almost immediately stranded.
Somehow they survived and for the next six years played with

Ringling Brothers and other big outfits that believed in regular paydays. Still, though their circus act became very popular, they never got more than $100 a week.

Hoping to make more money, they left the circus in 1911. Clark told McCullough, "We're getting on. I'm 23 and you're 28. Let's aim for the top. Let's try vaudeville, then go on to burlesque." When he became famous, Bobby Clark, always claimed he had learned more in burlesque where he was allowed to experiment freely with new routines than in either the circus or the two-a-day.

When the team made their vaudeville debut on December 12, 1912, McCullough wore an ancient, moulting dogskin fur coat which he had bought from a department store in Toronto for $6. The salesman told him they had been trying to sell it for thirty years. In their first appearance, Bobby got big laughs by beating this frowsy garment with his cane and raising dust clouds. McCullough—originally the team's comedian—wore a costume that included a straw hat, string tie, and white shoes and carried a college pennant. He later augmented his stage wardrobe with the flashy suits his friend Edward J. Busse, a Cincinnati undertaker, discarded. After a few years Paul also wore the hairline moustache that transformed his bulging baby face into the visage of an idiot.

Bobby Clark, who was a short man, retained the cane, puffed on huge cigars, and wore oversize spectacles dabbed on with burnt cork. In a routine they brought with them from the circus, Clark stood on a table while McCullough tried, with grotesque results, to hand him a chair. After bungling the job again and again, McCullough turned to the audience and confided, "It looks simple but it's really quite complicated!"

Bobby's favorite stage skit was one he and McCullough did in the cage of a circus lion that had just escaped. As substitute lion tamer, Clark talked his partner into putting on a lionskin and playing the part of the missing beast. Clark himself strutted around the cage, snapping his whip to make McCullough stand on his hind legs, lie down, and roll over. Bobby then put his foot on the head of the "beast" and stage whispered, "Paul you're doing great! You even smell like a lion!"

Meanwhile, the real lion entered behind and scared them to death. And true to circus tradition the regular trainer appeared just in the nick of time to save them.

Their comedy was principally physical. Late in his career Clark did a sketch as a doctor examining his overweight patient with a stethoscope. After putting the instrument over various parts of his anatomy, Clark offered the diagnosis: "He's got mice!"

The team often started their act with Clark strutting out, puffing furiously on his cigar, which he then threw into the air and caught in his mouth. McCullough, who always seemed to be in a hurry, would come rushing onstage as Clark began to perform easy tricks that he'd bungle. But Paul, as his simple-minded admirer, went into raptures like a man watching miracles being performed.

After five years in vaudeville, the partners were hired as the chief comedians of *Puss Puss* a Jean Bedini burlesque show. When Bedini brought the show to London the boys from Ohio were acclaimed by audiences there also.

Meanwhile they never stopped devising new skits and improving old ones. When the show returned to Broadway, they were paid $900 a week. Drafted for Irving Berlin's first

"Music Box Revue," they also appeared in its second edition, as well as other musicals. But it was not until 1926—after twenty years in show business—that Clark and McCullough became Broadway stage stars in *The Ramblers.*

They triumphed in other shows, worked in vaudeville whenever free, and starred in 72 movie shorts in Hollywood. But Bobby, who had a most inventive mind, eventually grew tired of being told what was funny and what was not. So the act returned to live entertainment. One of Bobby's comic masterpieces, often repeated, became his delivery with a hick town lady-killer's lascivious gestures of "I'm Robert the Roué from Reading, Pa."

During the middle thirties, however, McCullough was in ill health and often unable to work; Bobby Clark (a careful man with a buck) always sent him half the salary check.

The saddest thing in Bobby's whole life was Paul's suicide in 1936. While in a barbershop, McCullough—who had been in a sanitorium following a motor accident—seized a razor and before he could be stopped slashed his throat and one wrist.

After attending Paul's funeral, Bobby Clark went into seclusion and Broadway never expected to see him clowning on a stage again. But Clark came back to appear in more musicals and crown his career by starring in such classics as Congreve's *Love for Love,* Sheridan's *The Rivals* and Molière's *Le Bourgeois Gentilhomme.* Naturally he didn't stick to the script any more than he had in his vaudeville years with McCullough. In praising him, Brooks Atkinson said, "Clark was so exuberantly comic that he blew the plays right off the stage."

✿   ✿   ✿

Then there were some two-man acts that went their separate ways each night after the show, most notably the big time's gifted eccentric dancers, Doyle and Dixon.

Jimmy Doyle was a high-living sport, always with a new girl, and a racetrack regular. After work he'd head for the drinking spots. His partner Harland Dixon would dine leisurely, then retire to his hotel room to read the books of the world's great scientists and philosophers. He did not smoke, drink, philander, or squander his money.

Doyle, who was an excellent mimic, would often torment him with late telephone calls posing as the hotel manager, saying, "This is a respectable place, Mr. Dixon! Get that young woman out of your room at once or I'll send up the house detective," or "Mr. Dixon, when you were here last year you forgot to pay your bill. Come down to the desk and pay it, besides paying in advance for this week." In the next town, if Harland had cashed a check, he would be called at four in the morning and told it had bounced.

Dixon, who did not have too much humor, usually fell for it and angrily denied the charges. He was a serious-minded man. But the main reason he read the works of wise men was his background in a fanatically religious home. He'd never been able to rid himself completely of the fear of an avenging God that his parents had instilled in him when he was a child. In the books he read he was seeking explanations for the riddles of existence.

Harland's work was highly esteemed by other artists. They didn't mind his reading important books but they did resent his talking about what he'd just discovered. At the Lambs Club in New York and other actors' clubs he would brandish his enlarging vocabulary and startle innocent song-and-dance men and leading juveniles by demanding, "Do you know what acrophobia is?" or "Do you know the real cause of the Second Peloponnesian War?"

His friend Ben Hecht once described him as "the prince of dancers, with Nietzsche dancing in his head . . . the eccentric dancer and even more eccentric reader."

Dixon was a husky, handsome, wistful, blue-eyed Canadian Irishman with a head of curly auburn hair and a jutting chin. He never seemed to get over his astonishment that the amazing dance steps he found so easy to perform were acclaimed everywhere. Yet no classical ballet dancer ever worked harder to keep his body in shape. Harland spent hours every day practicing new routines, boxing with stagehands, and working out in gymnasiums. For years he didn't take a drink, waste time in bars, or have extramarital affairs. He had married his childhood sweetheart Charlotte Jean MacMullen in Toronto and remained married to her until he died in 1969.

With Jack Donahue, his closest rival on Broadway, and Johnny Boyle, who ran a dancing school for professionals, Dixon would spend whole nights in hoofing orgies—the equivalent of musicians' jam sessions. He talked endlessly about how great the others were and considered Boyle the greatest dancer he had ever watched. The reason Boyle never became a star, Dixon thought, was that he lacked showmanship— always half the battle in the theatre. Eddie Foy once told Harland that part of such showmanship was "carrying yourself with pride and confidence. From your waist down, you have to be very good, for there's your money maker. From the waist up is your sales department."

And Harland Dixon always danced like the champion he was.

Harland was born in Toronto in 1885 of Scotch-Irish parents who believed that God severely punished those who enjoyed any sort of good time.

"Between the two of them, my mother and father," he recalled, "I got endless warnings how 'God seest thee!' and big doses of religion at and between all meals. They convinced me that if I whistled on Sunday or picked up a pack of cards, Our Lord would send down a shaft of lightning to destroy our house and the entire neighborhood."

Harland was tortured by the desire to dance even before he knew what dancing was. Full of guilt, he wrestled with this impulse all of the time. At twelve he decided to go in for running and high-jumping and so joined the local "Y." And that's where his sinful impulse to dance got out of his control. It happened during a jogging session. The boys were jogging in step with a dumb-bell in each hand. Harland remembered, "The kid in front of me was making a slap with his foot, a sound I remembered later when I saw my first tap dancer. I imitated the kid. After a while I got so good I could do it with one foot, then the other, finally was able to do a roll. Before long I could do it with both feet, also could hop with the right foot, rattle with the left."

From that day forward, Harland Dixon felt like a lost soul, hounded by a dread of impending doom. Nevertheless, after he met a newsboy who taught him a few steps, they would dance together on street corners. He started working at thirteen but kept losing jobs because of his uncontrollable feet.

The first of these jobs was in a kitchen utensil warehouse where he pushed a hand-truck from the stock room to the delivery department. Every afternoon, as he went along, he would try a few steps. Sometimes, for accompaniment, he would slap a tin pot a few times. The bookkeeping department complained and he was bounced.

Next his father got him taken on as a plumber's assistant. But during the very first week the plumber caught him doing a couple of fast shuffles while he was showing the kid how to join pipe together. Besides being fired, Harland got a clout over the ear. Other jobs were found and quickly lost for the same reason.

His family began to worry about his sanity. What they didn't suspect was that Harland was also dancing every night with Jimmy Malone, who worked at the drug store. Harland would meet him there when Malone took his dinner hour and after hastily eating they would go down a dark street and practice dancing like mad. They were pleased and flattered when passersby stopped to watch them. Harland says, "Malone had no style but he knew more steps than I did. I was glad to dance with him while he taught them to me." Later Jimmy Malone became Dixon's first stage partner.

Curiously, this obsessed young hoofer never danced with a girl at a party then or later when he was famous. "I never could do it," he admitted. "I wouldn't know how."

Ray Bolger who was the next generation's outstanding eccentric dancer didn't doubt this at all. "I'm not surprised," Bolger said. "When I was a young bank teller, I was a wallflower. No girl would dance with me because they never knew what my next step would be and neither did I."

Despite his obsession, Harland never dared go to a theatre until he was fifteen. The first top-drawer hoofer he saw on a stage was Johnny Ford who some years before had been acclaimed as the country's champion buck-and-wing dancer at a contest held at Tammany Hall.

"Johnny," Harland recalled, "was good-looking, had a pleasing personality and was a great stylist." After seeing him, Dixon rushed out to the street and tried to duplicate Ford's buck-and-wing, then the most popular dance routine. "It was an adaptation of the old clog dances and featured hopping, flinging the legs, and clicking the heels."

Johnny was one of the famous "Four Dancing Fords," but at that moment was working alone. The next great dancer Harland saw was Johnny Ford's brother Maxie, who did a routine young Dixon believed was impossible, even as he watched it—managing a wing with one foot and a roll with the other.

A few weeks later Harland entered a dance contest for amateurs and won the $3 second prize. The first prize winner was a brilliant little boy hoofer, Georgie White, the future master of "George White's Scandals."

Harland didn't dare tell his mother about winning the three dollars but he told his father. That was a lot of money in the Dixon home which Mr. Dixon supported on his two dollar a day earnings as a machinist. Mr. Dixon told his wife, who gave Harland a stern lecture. "But she was impressed," Harland remembered. "I heard her boasting about it to a neighbor."

Despite fears for Harland's soul, Mrs. Dixon was proud of her son but she never got over her prejudice against the theatre. Long after Harland was an established and well-paid hoofer, she was afraid to come see him when he appeared once in Toronto. She refused to use the ticket he got for her. Finally she agreed to let him sneak her in through the stage door and watch from the wings.

"It would be terrible if the neighbors heard about this,"

she told him afterwards, "they'd never get done talking about my sinfulness."

When George Primrose and his minstrel show came to town, Dixon and Malone auditioned for him. Becoming one of that troupe was Dixon's greatest dream and it half came true that day. The great George Primrose said that he might be able to use both of them in his new show. They were to watch next summer for his casting announcement in the New York *Morning Telegraph*. If they could get to New York then, he'd try to find a spot for them.

That winter was the toughest Harland ever knew. Hoping to make at least a living wage, he went first to Buffalo, then to Boston. He got jobs as a waiter, freight elevator operator, check room attendant, and paperhanger's assistant. They all paid so little that he was always hungry. The paperhanger, who paid him $4 a week, was so sorry for him that he gave him half of his own lunch every day. While he was a waiter, Dixon was so starved that if a customer left a lamb chop on his plate the famished Canadian would slip it into his pocket on his way to the kitchen, to eat later.

"But all of that time, in Buffalo and Boston, as in Toronto, I never stopped dancing," he remembered. "Every time I had a free moment and was in a place level enough, I practiced. I didn't seem to need music. I had an intuitive sense of rhythm."

Every Sunday he bought the *Morning Telegraph* and on one he went wild with joy on seeing Primrose's ad announcing that he was at his hotel ready to sign up singers, dancers, and musicians for his new show.

After writing Malone the good news, Harland got a ticket to New York on an overnight boat—the cheapest way to go—

and arrived in the Big Town with $1.75. Malone had always been dubious about their ever getting to New York, but he had saved all he could from his earnings as a soda jerk and had $40 with him when he arrived. To Harland, who had never seen that much money before, this seemed a fortune.

Primrose hired the team for $15 a week and sent them to Plainfield, New Jersey, to work with Jimmy Connors, the troupe's dancing master, who drilled Harland, his partner, and the other minstrel men in buck dancing, the Lancashire clog, toe and heel, and soft shoe. The troupe opened in Plainfield and then moved to Brighton Beach, the fashionable New York summer resort. It worried Harland that they were opening on a Sunday. He was lecturing the ten men who dressed with him on how sinful this was and that God might send down a shaft to destroy them all, when he became aware that his boss, George Primrose, was standing in the doorway listening. He shut up.

Harland always felt he owed much to Primrose, a heavily built man who was then about fifty. The master minstrel's soft shoe and other dances were not difficult technically, but when he watched him, Dixon marveled at the accuracy of his stepping and how well he used his body. While imitating Primrose's numbers Dixon made a valuable discovery: "I imitated him as well as I could. But somehow, as I did those same steps, they came out funny." For a year and a half, Harland and Malone did one-week stands, two-night and one-night stands with the Primrose minstrels. Along the way, Harland put in more comic touches. While doing a routine that had eight wing steps which are very difficult to do, he put in first one rest, then two, and finally made them all rest steps. "And that," explained Harland Dixon, "is how I became an eccentric dancer." But by that time the less talented Malone had become discouraged and gone home.

In 1907, Lew Dockstadter, who had a much bigger minstrel show, hired Harland for $20 a week, and later raised him to $35, more than any minstrel show dancer had ever been paid. Harland quit Dockstadter to go into vaudeville with a new partner, Jack Corcoran, who was older and more experienced. Corcoran laid out their whole act—the usual mixture of songs, dances, and funny sayings taken from a joke book. As a finish, they had a song for which Harland, working in blackface, put on a woman's dress over a long pair of drawers with fringe at the bottom.

They had luck at the start: six weeks' booking in and around Denver at $80 a week. After their trial performance, the manager told Harland, "Dixon, you are the best dancer I ever had on the stage of this theatre."

Wherever he traveled, Harland never missed a chance to see other dancers perform. "The good ones all had an effect on my work, because I copied them. But you want to do something original. So you experiment, take a step and try it, forwards and backwards and sideways, then you put the middle in the front, the front at the end, keep shifting and experimenting, and after a while you have an original step."

Despite all of Harland Dixon's dedication and hard work, he never got into the big money until he became Jimmy Doyle's partner. The two met in a New York actors' club and were first seen together in a burlesque show called *Let George Do It*. Then they were booked into a Sunday night show at the Winter Garden. They stopped the show and after that every Broadway producer of musicals and the big time wanted them. They were elegance personified when they danced the most surprising and inventive two-man dance routines New York ever saw.

Dixon felt he was a creative dancer because he could tell a story or offer a complete characterization in his work. One stunning example was the dance number he did as a dental patient, in agonizing pain, seated on a chair in the dentist's waiting room. Doyle was an equally flashy dancer but didn't try to create anything.

"Doyle never had to rehearse," said Dixon. "For two whole years we never even discussed it. He'd just watch me for a minute or two, then do the step with me. We put on some very showy dances without many taps. We put taps in only as you'd put dressing on a salad."

For ten years, they were without a rival. And the breakup, when it came, was not of their doing.

They were rehearsing for Charles Dillingham's 1921 musical "Good Morning, Dearie." As usual, Doyle didn't attend rehearsals except when the producer was expected to be there. On other days he'd go off to the track. But one afternoon Dillingham showed up unexpectedly.

When he saw Harland dancing alone, he went up on the stage demanding, "Where is Jimmy Doyle?" Dixon made all the excuses he could think of, but he was a poor liar and Dillingham finally forced the truth out of him—Doyle had gone to the races.

"Doyle is out of the show," said the producer. "You go on alone."

Two perfect eccentric dancers might be better than one but the public made no uproar over Doyle's absence when the show opened. Perhaps Dillingham would not have been so hasty if he hadn't already seen what Dixon could do alone.

A few months before, Fred Stone, star of Dillingham's hit *Tip Top,* had injured his foot and the producer got Harland, who was touring in Raymond Hitchcock's *Hitchy-Koo,* to replace him. Harland had also played Stone's other roles on the road with great success. It was Harland's proudest moment when he was acclaimed for his ability to substitute for Stone, who could do everything from comedy and eccentric dancing to the wildest acrobatic capers on the Broadway stage.

As a single, Dixon got $1000 a week and worked all the time.

Doyle opened a dance school, but it failed. Broadway never heard of him again.

CHAPTER SEVEN

The Making of Times Square

As NEW YORK GREW, its theatrical and good time center kept moving uptown—from Fourteenth Street to Twenty-third, to Herald Square at Thirty-fourth and finally to Times Square which ran from Forty-second to Forty-seventh between Broadway and Seventh Avenue. Soon its side streets, later called the Roaring Forties, began to fill up with new hotels, restaurants, theatres, and drinking places. So also did Broadway above Forty-seventh right up to Columbus Circle at Fifty-ninth. Eventually the Broadway district came to mean the whole glittering area from Forty-second to Fifty-ninth between Sixth and Eighth Avenues.

Shortly after 1900 visitors from all over the world began acclaiming Broadway as the greatest playground on earth. What helped make it unique were its million lights that "turned night into day." Broadway and Forty-second Street became the crossroads of the world where sooner or later you'd see everyone you knew or had ever heard of.

Meanwhile, vaudeville continued to flourish and grow all

over the country, particularly in large cities. In 1896 the Official Theatre Guide listed ten variety theatres in New York and six in Chicago. By 1910 there were thirty-one in New York and twenty-two in Chicago. Many were neighborhood theatres, but the heart of the two-a-day empire was on Times Square. Almost all of the circuits booked acts out of their Broadway offices and actors' agents also had their offices there. From 1902 until 1913 (when the Palace opened), Oscar Hammerstein's Victoria Theatre and Paradise Roof, on *the* corner—Broadway and Forty-second Street—remained the successor of Tony Pastor's as the showcase for vaudeville's new acts, the make-or-break place. Among the dozens of artists who became famous overnight at Hammerstein's were Al Jolson and Nora Bayes.

The upper half of Times Square was called Longacre Square until 1904. Many New Yorkers thought the square should have been re-named Hammerstein Square because Oscar, the grandfather of Oscar Hammerstein II, had built a theatre there in the nineties when it was lined with livery stables, harness shops, and old brownstones. At night the area was known as "Thieves' Lair" because of the Hell's Kitchen sluggers and crooks who used it as both a promenade and a battlefield. Oscar's Victoria, which opened in 1902, soon became the country's most famous theatre. Oscar himself was also publicized more extensively than any American of his time, except perhaps Theodore Roosevelt.

The city was alive with fascinating personalities then. And all New York, bustling, roaring, throbbing, exploding with life and energy around the clock, was an eye-popping tourist attraction. Nothing like it had ever been seen before. New York was all things to all men. A gateway to a new life, free of hunger and terror, to the millions of immigrants who'd been pouring in from Central and Eastern Europe since the eighties; a different kind of dream come true to the Western robber barons and newly rich industrial tycoons who were building magnificent marble mansions on Fifth Avenue. To their wives and mistresses, New York was a bazaar with its beautiful stores that displayed all of the treasures ever found or fashioned by man. It was Eldorado for adventuresses, swindlers, con-merchants, safecrackers, and crooked gamblers, a glory hole for sailors from every corner of the world.

It was everything other big cities dreamed of becoming with its harbor crowded with ships of all kinds, excursion steamboats and ocean liners to sailing vessels, fishing trawlers, and yachts; with its railroads, El trains and trolley cars; Wall Street, Coney Island, the first skyscrapers; Brooklyn Bridge; Mr. McGraw's pennant-winning Giants; and most of all its Broadway.

The immigrants who settled in New York had splashed new color over the whole city with their foreign clothes, exotic foods, drink, dances, and music. Traveling around the city was like taking a trip around the world. Everywhere there were Little Polands, Hungarys, Austrias, Italys, Irishtowns, Jewtowns. Thousand of these new Americans became vaudeville fans, taking advantage of the low prices. Some sociologists claim the newcomers learned to speak English listening to the artists who entertained them. These immigrants also changed vaudeville since comedians soon began to imitate them. Until then, Irish, German, and Negro characters had provided the laughs with their gaucheries and ludicrous mistakes, but as the melting pot became more mixed audiences were laughing more at routines spoofing comical Jews and

Italians instead of the once surefire Micks and clodhopper Germans.

The Bowery, which cradled so much top drawer vaudeville talent, was crowded every night with busloads of tourists eager for a glimpse of what went on in that notorious Street of Sin.

The Tenderloin lived up to its reputation as Satan's Playground, despite crusades by the town's reformers. Just south of the Gay White Way, it occupied the whole west side between Twenty-third and Forty-second Streets. In the Tenderloin, saloons were on every corner—with others in the middle of the block. Gambling houses and brothels ran wide open. For the sports with short bankrolls, every cigar store had a back room where dimes, nickles, and even pennies could be wagered. Street walkers were on every street. The Tenderloin's most notorious dancehall was the Haymarket, featuring a balcony of enclosed boxes overlooking the dance floor where girls, for the right price, offered sex, straight and kinky, and circuses. Extra business was attracted to the Haymarket by rumors that among its best-looking girls there were Vassar students who had sneaked down from Poughkeepsie for the night to make some extra spending money.

But the million lights and sights of Broadway remained the main allure.

On one illuminated sign a gentleman in evening clothes and top hat could be seen lighting his between-the-acts little cigar. On another, a half-naked nymph, chaste as the morning dew, gazed at a waterfall that magically kept flowing to symbolize the purity of White Rock's sparkling bottled water.

A foreign visitor once described these signs on the Great White Way as "fabulous glow-worms that crawl up and down" while "lightning strikes an acre of signboard . . . a four-story tall Highlander dances a whisky-fling; another pours out a highball with a hundred feet between his bottle and the glass . . . Household words race with invisible pen across a whole city block."

Until the Great War and Prohibition changed everything, the best Broadway restaurants served food that epicures compared to the finest cuisine found in Paris. Gentility had not yet gone out of style in these restaurants and the waiters were deferential and efficient, the decor exhilarating, the prices right. Of course, larceny and deception were found everywhere. In his memoirs George Rector, whose restaurant was considered one of the world's best, confessed that he always cut the whiskey he served.

The beautiful new theatres showed cheerful comedies, melodramas that seem childish today, and musical comedies with meaningless plots. These last were really vaudeville shows with two-a-day stars. The "plot" was thrown in as an excuse to charge more than the $1 top, prevalent at the big-time theatres.

It was a gay and giddy time and the Great White Way epitomized its spirit. The stage door alleys behind those theatres showing musicals were crowded each night with well-heeled college boys and other young sports hoping for a date with a plump chorus girl or soubrette.

Because Broadway was a spenders' paradise, beautiful girls concerned about their futures found it the happiest of hunting grounds. Each of the six girls in the Floradora Chorus who sang "Tell Me, Pretty Maiden" is said to have married a millionaire. One of them, Marie Wilson, who earned $30 a week, then $50, made $750,000 from her admirers' market tips.

Both John Jacob Astor and J. P. Morgan were generous. It is said that when they grew tired of a mistress they gave her $100,000. Morgan would also find a young doctor husband for each light o' love, who could then set up an imposing office on part of that bundle.

The other robber barons in those income-tax free days were also extravagant with their Broadway mistresses, keeping them in luxurious apartments, buying them fine furs and dazzling jewels, and sending them to Paris each spring to buy a new wardrobe. They often appeared with the girl of the moment on their arm at the races or at Rector's. These pampered kept young women observed only one unwritten rule: if their lover walked into a restaurant or theatre with his wife, they never greeted him or signaled they knew him.

Oddly enough, Diamond Jim Brady—the most publicized big Broadway spender—had his cheap side. When he became bored with a girl, he would call on her and get back the jewels he'd given her. "I'll have these put in new settings for you," was his exit line, or he would explain that they needed to be cleaned. But anybody would lay you two to one that he never got a hairpin back from his great love, Lillian Russell. She ran away with his best friend before he had a chance to tire of her.

Sometimes these giddy old millionaires were assigned a table next to one occupied by a party of safecrackers, forgers, professional gamblers, or other underworld aristocrats. They stared at each other with sincere interest but in those days weren't mixing socially as they did later in the Prohibition years. Almost every night you could find some of those high cockalorums, Tammany Hall's Grand Sachems, who did business with both groups. Usually they were accompanied by Al Smith or slim Jimmy Walker, or other promising proteges.

Vaudeville's children, of course, were all over the place when they weren't drinking and laughing it up at their own clubs, the Lambs and the Friars. Dozens of them had their names in lights over the marquees of theatres harboring straight plays and musicals: Nat Goodwin, Eddie Foy, De Wolfe Hopper, Walter C. Kelly, Weber and Fields, Montgomery and Stone. George M. Cohan, the producing-directing-acting genius with his partner, Sam Harris, sometimes had four Broadway shows running at the same time.

Prominent everywhere were the rounders, so-called because they made the rounds every night. The rounder usually started at the Hotel Knickerbocker, where Maxfield Parrish's "Old King Cole" hung over the bar. Unless he was attending a fight or an opening, he would make many of the oases up to Columbus Circle and back, having dinner at Rector's or Shanley's. Some of these bars featured special drinks—Redpath's cafe offered Ramos fizzes and Sazerac cocktails while the Hotel Astor bar had a potent mixture of grape juice and Swedish rum. Rector's, of course, offered every native and exotic drink known to thirsty mankind.

There were dozens of other well-lighted spots which served free lunch to satisfy gourmands great and small. By buying a dime glass of beer, a hungry Broadwayite could fill his plate with pig's feet, shrimp, cold roast beef, pickles, pretzels, and rolls. If he wished hot meat, there were pork, tongue, corned beef, roast beef as well as several sorts of bread plus mountains of potato salad, celery, and hard boiled eggs.

The bartenders were as polished looking as everything else with their shimmering handlebar moustaches and bright eyes. Many also had shining bald heads. They were quick to serve a free drink for each two the patron bought.

One rounder still hitting the Broadway spots every night is Ned Brown, the old New York *World* sports editor, who was ninety-two this year. Once, after listening to Ned describe the enormous quantities of liquor the rounders imbibed, we asked, "Why didn't they get falling down drunk? Was the whiskey better in those days?"

"No," he said, "it was the men who were better."

The artists—famous, famous-to-be, and has-beens—could be found nightly in Hammerstein's lobby. They clustered around the rocking chair in which Oscar's son Willie Hammerstein, who managed the theatre and roof garden for his father, did all his business.

Willie made deals with a handshake, uttered wry wisecracks, and played practical jokes. Many believed Willie was the greatest showman vaudeville ever developed. The proof is that for eleven years Hammerstein's earned $300,000 or more each year for his father. What nobody could understand —including Willie and the Hammerstein family—was why Oscar had nothing but contempt for his vaudeville gold mine. He dumped the millions it made into opera, a form of cultural entertainment that has never paid its own way. And though his obsession to become an opera impresario beggared him again and again, Oscar transformed grand opera in this country forever.

Oscar, eldest of the five children of Abraham and Bertha Hammerstein, was born in Berlin in 1847. His parents, German Jews, were music lovers—his father, a contractor by profession, played the violin, his mother the piano. Their son played the piano at six, the flute and violin shortly afterwards. Almost as early as that Oscar had tutors in Latin, Greek, Hebrew, and religion.

Oscar's father was a stern disciplinarian who thought that all work and no play might make a genius and, of course, in Oscar's case he turned out to be right. Abraham Hammerstein taught Oscar the crafts of plastering and bricklaying which both proved useful later on.

Oscar was like a boy on a treadmill. At eleven he started going to private school. The next year he became a student at the Berlin Conservatory. His father kept him busy the rest of the time in house construction work. After his sympathetic mother died, Oscar began to find his father's tyranny unbearable. The last straw came one winter afternoon two years later when he arrived home late and was beaten unmercifully by his father. He sold his violin for thirty dollars and headed for the promised land, America. He was sixteen years old.

The Civil War was at its height—it was 1863—and the day after he landed, Oscar got a job as an apprentice in a tobacco factory at $2 a week. In no time he became one of the most respected cigarmakers in New York.

During the next seven years, young Hammerstein demonstrated an astonishing versatility. He invented cigar-making machinery; played in and led a theatre orchestra; published, edited, and wrote the *United States Tobacco Journal,* a trade paper. His method of obtaining advertising was simple. If a dealer refused to buy space, Oscar put the fellow's face in a cartoon of a man hanging onto a lamppost, named him in the caption as being plastered *again!* It worked. He also found time to marry Rose Blau—he was 20, she 17—and to father four sons, Harry, Arthur, William, and Abraham Lincoln Hammerstein. His wife died in 1876 and two years later Oscar married Malvina Jacobi of Selma, Alabama, who became the mother of his two daughters, Rose and Stella.

The second Mrs. Hammerstein was a wonderful stepmother to his boys. But Oscar, who had been devoted to his first wife, now seldom came home. Despite his neglect, Malvina and all six children continued to revere him.

Oscar kept inventing mechanical devices. Besides those for the tobacco trade, he got patents for such varied creations as an adjustment for suspenders, a primitive vacuum cleaner, a washstand, a bathtub, and an exhibition hall. In all, he obtained fifty-six patents during his lifetime.

His inventions made millions for the companies who purchased them. And Oscar was paid impressive sums: $110,000 for the first patent he marketed, a machine for making cigars by compressed air; $68,000 for a tobacco stripping and booking machine; $50,000 for an air suction machine, again for making cigars and cigarettes. In one year, he earned $300,000 from his tobacco manufacturing patents alone. Whenever he needed money for his theatrical investments he would sell the patent for another invention.

Curiously enough, it was for the purpose of promoting the sale of real estate and houses he had built that he put up his first theatre, the Harlem Opera House. In 1889 Harlem was sparsely settled and Hammerstein foresaw that the next building boom must come there. A theatre, he believed, would encourage families to move into the area. But his Harlem Opera House, offering opera and other entertainments, had only indifferent success. Undiscouraged, Oscar built another theatre, the Columbus, in East Harlem and made money there with hits that had just finished their runs on Broadway, and later with vaudeville.

Like other imaginative builders and architects, the mistakes Oscar made were whoppers. In his first theatre he forgot to leave space for a box office. In two others he was so eager to open that he did not wait for the paint on the seats to dry. But in all of his theatres the acoustics were remarkable.

Typically, Broadway showmen did not become interested in Hammerstein's operations until 1892 when he built his $350,000 Manhattan Opera House at Thirty-fourth Street and Broadway (where Macy's is now located) and produced opera there. When that lost money he also tried English, French, and American plays, English operettas and comic opera, yet failed to show a profit his first year.

During the second season, Oscar sold a half interest in his Manhattan Opera House for $500,000 to Koster and Bial. These two had begun as saloon keepers, became brewers, and then were owners of a very successful saloon-concert hall on West Twenty-third Street. Observing that the theatrical center was moving uptown, they became Oscar's partners. They tore out the seats on the main floor, installed a huge bar, and opened on August 28, 1893. There was trouble from the beginning.

It started when Oscar became enraged at Koster and Bial's press agent, Carter Clive. Clive had hung a sign in the lobby with his own name on it. Oscar tore it down but Clive replaced it, only to have Oscar tear that one down. The third sign Clive had made of metal and Oscar cut his hand when he tried to remove it.

There were other battles but the big explosion came in the spring over the big billing and salary paid a mediocre French singer, Mlle. de Dio. Manny Kessler, an influential wine agent who was wooing her, tried to get Oscar to sign her, but he refused. However, Adam Bial, who also fell for her busty charms, gave her an engagement.

From a box, Oscar hissed the French charmer while she was singing her first number. Kessler, who was taller and heavier than Hammerstein, reproached him from the adjoining box. They adjourned to battle in the street and Oscar was holding his own when peace-loving ushers dragged them apart.

Mlle. de Dio, in tears over her ruined debut, was told of the fight and immediately flounced to Oscar's office to upbraid him. Before the great impresario had time to reply, the burly Kessler re-appeared and a second fist-fight began. This time the police were summoned and the ferocious pair carted off to the station house. They were given summonses to appear at the West Side Magistrate's Court next morning. Both claimed the other was the aggressor, with Oscar's partners, Koster and Bial, taking Kessler's side. On the stand Oscar insisted that it was his right to hiss an actress in his own theatre if her work displeased him. Both combatants were dismissed with the usual warning of jail terms if they went after each other again.

That ludicrous episode was quickly followed by the dissolution of the partnership. Koster and Bial are believed to have paid a second $500,000 for Oscar's half interest, plus the $125,000 he received as his share of the profits.

It was on this money that Oscar made his biggest gamble, the one that caused people to call him "the creater of Times

Square" for the rest of his life. Oscar told everyone, "This is where the theatrical center is going to be." Some of them thought he was crazy. But with his profits from the Koster and Bial deal Oscar bought the entire block front on the east side of Broadway between Forty-fourth and Forty-fifth Street, as well as the adjacent houses at both ends. He announced that he would build there the world's largest and most beautiful theatre. He had the space for it—a 203-foot front on Broadway, 154 feet on Forty-fifth Street, 101 feet on Forty-fourth. Oscar made all the plans himself. Ground was broken in January, 1895, with the opening scheduled for November 25.

His Olympia, he told reporters, would have three auditoriums: a music hall seating 4000 persons, a theatre for 1400, and a much smaller 600-seat concert hall. In the basement, Oscar planned to install a billiard academy, bowling alley, a café, and a Turkish bath, but these were never finished.

Costs were staggering even though Oscar tried to keep them (and the stealing) down by using three of his sons as aides. Harry ran the construction department, Arthur was in charge of decorating, and Willie booked the talent, getting acts from abroad by the dozen through overseas agents. Oscar made the plans and supervised every detail of the work. Nevertheless the costs kept mounting. When he ran out of money, Oscar obtained a $900,000 loan from the Prudential Life Insurance Company.

The magnificent entertainment palace opened on schedule. This was one of those Hammerstein openings where silk gowns and evening clothes were ruined by the wet paint. And there was frantic tumult outside after the doors opened.

Though the three units had only six thousand seats, Oscar sold ten thousand tickets. The alleys between the theatre's units were so narrow that the crush in them was almost as bad as the one outside. In addition to the ten thousand ticketholders, there were thousands more who had decided to attend at the last moment.

Oscar had hoped to have Yvette Guilbert, the great French chanteuse, as his first headliner. She arrived later and opened a four week engagement on December 15. She was paid $4000 a week and drew a whopping $60,000 in receipts. Oscar renewed Guilbert's booking for four more weeks, then capriciously cut it short because he wanted to put on an opera, *Marguerite,* which he had written himself. This attracted only $4000 a week to the box office. Nevertheless Oscar had a good first season. His second one, however, was ruinous, despite the addition of a roof garden theatre, the first New York had ever seen.

Frivolous New York by then had fallen in love with Oscar as a character. He had tangled twice with Teddy Roosevelt—and won, while getting tremendous publicity for his roof. Roosevelt was then a Police Commissioner working night and day to cleanse New York of its wantonness.

Teddy threatened to raid the Olympia Garden when he heard it was featuring a living statue tableau of famous paintings in which there was a display of near-nudity. But on seeing the show, Teddy became enchanted because one of the paintings in his own home was portrayed. He ignored the suggestive part and told the press he thought the whole entertainment was in excellent taste.

Subsequently though, Teddy ordered the arrest of Arthur Hammerstein—the roof's manager—for "running a dancehall without a permit." Arthur had booked as a freak act, Chuck Connors, the Mayor of Chinatown and Number One Bowery B'hoy, doing an Apache dance with a female billed as "Mag the Rag."

Though it meant publicity that would help business, Arthur must have had mixed emotions about being arrested. Connors rarely showed up for a performance on his own; each night Arthur went down to the Bowery, picked up Mag the Rag and took her along to look for Connors in dives of low character, then sobered him up and hauled him to the roof garden. The papers made a circus of the arrest, kidding Teddy in long stories and caricaturing him for his purity and lofty moral stand. Roosevelt, who in those days knew when he was licked, dropped the case.

There had been many truly memorable shows presented at the Olympia, including satires on current events and the latest scandals plus illustrious acts like the Tiller Girls doing their electrifying precision dancing.

Oscar's audiences had the time of their lives when he brought from the Midwest the Three Cherry Sisters, a terrible singing act which ended with the people out front throwing rotten fruits and vegetables at the girls.

These and other attractions helped, but not enough. The cost of running the huge place bankrupted Oscar. To keep it going, he sold his Harlem theatres and mortgaged the rest of his real estate, including his home. Nevertheless, in that third season Oscar was unable to pay the interest on the $900,000 loan and so the insurance company took over the property and announced an auction. Oscar walked out of his huge entertainment center stone broke. He did not have enough to feed himself, much less support his family.

One night after the auction was announced, he remembered that he had left $400 in the Olympia. It was under the pillow of a bed in a room he had slept in there. But the foreclosure stipulated that he was not to be allowed on the premises until the auction took place. He sneaked in, got the money, but was arrested as he was slipping down a fire-escape. The money was taken from him. In court Oscar made such a heart-breaking speech that the judge not only freed him but ordered the $400 returned to him.

Even then, cynics said Broadway was without a heart . . . especially for losers. However, people in the business who knew Oscar were upset when they heard how despondent he was. One night, meeting a friend on Broadway, he said, "Have a cigar. I have lost all my theatres, my home and everything else. My fortune consists of two cigars. I will share it with you."

On June 28, 1898, the day the Olympia was sold at auction, benefit performances were given for Oscar at three theatres that netted him $8000. Oscar immediately announced he was back in business and would build another theatre soon. Friends shook their heads. They believed that Oscar, then 51, was through despite all of his genius and versatility.

Hammerstein fooled them. He sold another invention for $25,000, managed to borrow some more money, and, with this capital, obtained a lease on the site of the future Victoria, on the west side of Broadway between Forty-second and Forty-third Streets.

Oscar promised he would open his new theatre on March 2, 1899. That gave him less than a year. What followed was probably the wildest, daffiest shoestring building operation

Broadway ever saw. Unlike the Olympia construction, every possible expense was spared. Oscar bought secondhand bricks and used lumber from housewreckers and lights, other equipment, and seats of torn-down theatres from junk dealers. The carpeting came from a retired transatlantic steamship.

Despite all of this desperate economizing, Oscar again ran out of money. His creditors were howling. The roof contractor flatly refused to finish the job without a $2000 payment. Oscar got on a downtown trolley, hoping to find someone on Wall Street he could appeal to. Sunk in his own thoughts, he didn't recognize the pretty girl sitting next to him, even after she said, "I once worked for you in the chorus, Mr. Hammerstein. You were very kind to me. Why are you so gloomy today?"

"I need money," said Oscar.

"How much?"

"A lot. $2000."

"Why, I will lend you $2000, Mr. Hammerstein," she told him. "Or more if you need it." She explained that her father had recently died, leaving her a fortune.

From the trolley car they went straight to her bank and got the money.

Oscar had taught his son Arthur all he knew about building. Now it paid off. At very little expense, Arthur transformed the Cinderella of a theatre into a princess. He painted the plaster white, arranged lights behind gilt fixtures to conceal the supporting beams, and draped the walls of the commodious lounging rooms with regal red plush. And the theatre opened on schedule.

The first bill was headed by the popular Dutch come-

dians, the Rogers Brothers. Others on the bill were Georgia
Caine, the musical comedy favorite, George Marion, Italian
dialectician, and Maud Raymond, a funny, fat jokester.
Oscar made a welcoming speech. He also had written a
march, "Victoria Festival," for the occasion. In his lifetime
Oscar wrote over 200 pieces of music, including at least two
operas. None made much impression.

Again, it was the theatre itself that was the real star of
the opening. Alan Dale, one of the toughest of the New
York critics, wrote, "The Victoria, at a bird's eye view,
looks like a big, tinkling pearl box—all white and gold
with the opals of electricity studding it in profusion, gorgeous carpets, splendid lounges, and all of the ultra-elegance
of an ultra-elegance-loving metropolis was to be seen everywhere."

During its first three seasons, the Victoria offered mostly
plays and musical shows. Oscar used his profits from these
to build another theatre adjoining the Victoria, The Republic, on Forty-second Street, which he rented out. His
real purpose was to have additional space for the roof garden he planned. When it was built, patrons after seeing the
show downstairs, could go to the roof for refreshments and
more casual entertainment.

This was especially appreciated during the year and a
half run of *Resurrection,* the gloomy Russian drama by
Leo Tolstoy. After being depressed by Tolstoy's work, audiences could go upstairs and be cheered by the giddy
goings-on. Later, when the Victoria had become a vaudeville house with Willie doing the booking, there were such
dizzy, unorthodox shows downstairs as well that Broadway
christened it "The Nut House." And for more than a dec-

ade, the nut house upstairs and downstairs made $300,000 or more each year which Oscar spent building opera houses and producing grand operas.

But if the nut house became Number One of the big time, it was because along with his freak acts—champion athletes, snake dancers, and highly publicized murderesses —Willie always put on a particularly good bill of legitimate vaudeville. It usually ran four hours or longer, with as many as fourteen acts doing two shows a day.

Starring champion athletes in melodramas which toured the country often made money, but did not always work out well. John L. Sullivan, the Boston Strong Boy and the first American world heavyweight champion, had wrecked the Uncle Tom show in which he starred as Simon Legree. John L. became indignant because the black man was getting more applause and reveling in it. One night he lost his temper entirely when "Uncle Tom" took his fifth bow. Sullivan chased him off the stage, out of the theatre, and through the streets.

The trouble with Willie's notorious women was lack of talent—for none of them, with one exception, could sing, whistle, or dance. He booked them right after they were freed by sympathetic juries.

Willie paid a young Brooklyn murderess, Florence Burns, $750 a week. She had just shot to death—it was 1902—her 19-year-old lover, Walter Burns, because after "ruining" her he had wearied of her.

The critics were cruel; one wrote that Florence's gait "resembled a sidewheel steamer catching a porpoise." But she drew full houses. One night when she didn't show up,

Willie substituted another young woman and no one knew the difference.

A short while later Florence played—if that's the word—an engagement in Worcester, Massachusetts, that ended when the audience became so menacing that the theatre manager, fearing a riot, called the police. In another theatre the performers walked out in a body, saying they would rather lose their pay than work on a bill with such a gawk. Miss Burns ended her short stage career working as the team-mate of Carry Nation, the hatchet-wielding temperance champion. The audiences were fair: they hissed both.

Willie also booked Nan Patterson, the ex-Floradora girl. She had been acquitted of the charge of killing her lover, Caesar Young, in a hansom cab, for wanting to go back to his wife. She was billed as "the Singing Murderess," though singer she was not. Willie headlined the two girls, Ethel Conrad and Lillian Graham, who together shot W. E. D. Stokes, millionaire hotel owner. They were billed as "the Shooting Stars." When they asked for more work, he suggested they go out and shoot some one else. Willie didn't mind making these freak headliners ridiculous. He booked Florence Carman, the wife of a doctor who shot her rival dead through the window of her husband's office. She suspected that her victim had been coming to her husband for the wrong kind of treatment. Florence might have been a fine markswoman but her voice was awful. Willie had her sing "Baby Shoes," the most sentimental of the current sob ballads, and the people out front howled.

Willie once decided to bring back to New York a famous flamenco singer, Carmencita, who had made a sensation in the city in the nineties until she presumably retired. When his agent in Europe cabled that Carmencita had died, Willie ordered him to find another Carmencita. He presented the counterfeit flamenco queen as the original and fooled everyone.

Other freak acts he put on included Captain Cook, who claimed to have discovered the North Pole but was later exposed as a fake; Jack Johnson, the first Negro heavyweight boxing champion; and Lady Hope, who displayed the fabulous Hope diamond.

Willie would take advantage of any front page happening. A press agent had provoked a reformer into raiding an art store in New York for displaying a painting called *September Morn*. It portrayed an innocent looking girl without clothes entering the ocean. The public rushed to the store to buy copies by the thousands. Willie immediately put a living statue of "September Morn" on his stage. Then he arranged with the art dealer, P. Ortiz, to sue him for infringement of copyright. It got some publicity, though the painting was as chaste as the White Rock girl.

In spite of the Victoria's prosperity, Oscar refused to allow his sons to spend one dollar repairing the big barn. When seats broke down, Oscar ordered them replaced by other secondhand seats. Sometimes they were bolstered up with wooden boxes.

No price was printed on the tickets. They cost a dollar each if nothing outstanding was on the bill, and went up to $1.50 for a real drawing card.

Willie had an arrangement with Morris Gest, who later produced eye-popping stage spectacles like Max Reinhardt's "The Miracle," to peddle tickets in the lobby for whatever he could get. Gest then split the profits with Willie. When business was good Oscar would kick the future impresario out of the lobby. When it was bad, the old man would invite Gest back.

If Oscar did not think highly of his current show and someone asked him about it, he'd say "Phooey!" He once spit on the edge of the box office window to show his contempt. One day a friend on a trolley car asked about the bill and Oscar gave him his trolley car transfer. "You can get in on that," he sneered, "they'll be glad to let you in for nothing. They'll have to shanghai people off the street this week to fill that barn."

The worshipful attitude toward Oscar by his sons was hard to understand. Willie and Arthur, both brilliant showmen themselves, gave papa all the privileges of a king but protected him as though he were a baby.

They seemed to expect nothing from him in return. For years at a time Oscar never saw his wife (their stepmother), his two daughters, or his grandchildren. And Willie seemed to have forgiven and forgotten the cruelty of his father years before. When he was twenty, Willie married a Gentile. Oscar had kicked him out of his life and refused to speak to him for two years.

Oscar's biographer, Vincent Sheean, asserts that Willie never made a move without consulting his father. It may be true. As a young man, Oscar had studied the exhibits of Barnum, the master showman. He certainly emulated that prince of fakers both on his roof and downstairs. On the roof he kept changing the animals in his zoo, which ranged from a troupe of trained fleas to exotic birds and lions. He even exhibited a black girl he billed as "Silent Sue" who never smiled. Willie tricked all of the comics into trying to make

Sue smile. She couldn't—her facial muscles were paralyzed.

It was uncomfortably hot on the roof garden some summer nights. Willie had a gigantic thermometer made, stuck it in a potted plant in the lobby, and hung on it a sign saying, "It's *this* Cool on our Roof!" The thermometer always registered a low temperature since under the potted plant were hidden big cakes of ice. Willie was the only Broadway manager who kept regular hours, arriving at eight-thirty in the morning, leaving at 10:30 at night. He never saw any shows but his own.

During these years, Oscar kept building opera houses in which he offered some of the world's great singers. After he erected one in New York and either had built or was planning to build more in other cities, the Metropolitan Opera Company paid him $1,250,000 for his properties and his promise not to compete with them for ten years. Willie sighed with relief. The next thing he heard was that his father was going to construct an opera house in London where he could compete with Covent Garden.

Despite his age, Oscar kept getting into scandalous fistfights, legal battles, and antics with his opera stars. Once an aide entered an empty theatre and saw Oscar and Luisa Tetrazinni, one of his stars, playing leap-frog on the stage. Mary Garden complained that he treated her like a chorus girl while she worked for him. And he could be very tough on untalented women who were eager for careers. One swore that she would commit suicide if he did not hire her. He handed her a gun and she fled.

Oscar's most embarrassing episode with a singer involved Frances Lee, a married woman, who invaded New York as "Texas Patti." She sang for Oscar. He was enchanted and

offered her all kinds of things, including love. She sued him
for $100,000 when his promises to make her an opera star
came to nothing. Frances had foolish love letters from him
which she threatened to publish.

To newspaper reporters, Oscar didn't deny the love affair,
the silly letters, or his promises to star her. But he did say that
something mysterious had happened to the Texas Patti's
vocal chords after the first time he heard her. He was so
puzzled he took her for an audition to Walter Damrosch, a
leading musical figure of the day, who told him, "You must
be awfully stuck on her, or mad."

Because the letters were published everywhere, Oscar's
lawyers advised him to settle, which he did. The amount was
not made public.

In 1912, saying nothing to his sons, Oscar entered into
secret negotiations with the Shubert Brothers for the sale of
the Victoria. He was about to accept their $675,000 offer,
intending to use the money to build an opera house abroad,
when his sons heard about it. For the first time in their lives,
Willie and Arthur revolted against their father and he called
off the deal.

The following year, after the Palace opened—Hammerstein's potential rival as the showcase of the big time—Willie
offered the freak act that broke the house's all time box office
record and proved to be his masterpiece.

The act was Evelyn Nesbit Thaw, one-time chorus girl and
artist's model, who had been the star witness and heroine at
the trial of her husband "Mad Harry" K. Thaw for the 1906
jealousy murder of Stanford White, America's most famous
architect. Evelyn's testimony had saved Thaw from the electric chair and, after endless legal shenanigans, he had been

adjudged insane, and sent to the State Asylum at Mattewan, in Upstate New York.

For a couple of years Evelyn, often called the most beautiful girl in America, had been a headliner because of the notoriety. She neither sang nor danced like a professional and by 1913 managers refused to book her, telling her frankly that the public had tired of her. She was broke and desperate, she told Willie. Willie advanced Evelyn Nesbit Thaw enough money to go abroad and find a dancing partner to work with. Meanwhile, he had his agents in England book her for a tour of the English provinces. Mrs. Thaw and her new partner, Jack Clifford, a former prizefighter, made no great splash there.

But Willie Hammerstein had foreseen that possibility and took the precaution of concocting rave notices in advance. These he sent to the same agents with instructions to cable them to him no matter what the new act's reception was.

Willie kept feeding these fake rapturous notices to theatrical reporters who printed them and apparently built up enormous public interest in Evelyn all over again. For when Evelyn Nesbit came home, a huge crowd greeted her at the pier. Newspapers lavished space on her photographs and ran long interviews with her. Willie booked her and Clifford into Hammerstein's, but only for two weeks. He doubted whether she could continue attracting large crowds for longer than that.

But during her second week at Hammerstein's, Willie got the biggest publicity break of his career: Mad Harry Thaw, who had threatened to kill Evelyn the moment he got free, escaped from Mattewan. He was reported to be in New York, intent on shooting the beautiful actress who was his wife and

had saved him from the electric chair. The newspapers specu-
lated on whether Thaw would try to kill her while she was on
the stage dancing with Clifford. It seemed quite likely. Mad
Harry had shot Stanford White to death on the roof of Madison Square Garden before hundreds of witnesses.

Hammerstein's began to do a sell-out business at all performances. Crowds of reporters jammed backstage. They demanded of Evelyn: "Have you heard from your husband? Do
you know where he's hiding? If he is in New York do you
think he will try to shoot you here or at your hotel? Do you
think he is really crazy?"

Willie kept the excitement at fever pitch by hiring a small
army of guards to protect Evelyn wherever she went. When
Thaw was found in Canada, Willie had a friend up there
send a wire signed H.K.T. which contained a threat to kill
Evelyn plus a threat to sue the theatre if the name of Thaw
was not instantly removed from the billing.

Thaw did not come to New York. But largely due to the
way Willie Hammerstein ballyhooed the news of his escape
Evelyn remained the box office draw at his theatre for eight
straight weeks, attracting $175,000 during that run. He raised
her salary to $3500 a week then sent her out on tour all the
way to the West Coast.

Willie died the following year, at 42. Soon thereafter the
Victoria was sold, then torn down and replaced by the Rialto,
a movie theatre. Oscar Hammerstein, who did so much for
opera, is remembered today, if at all, as the founding father
of this country's most remarkable theatrical dynasty.

Arthur, the son who survived him, produced several of
Broadway's finest operettas—*Rose Marie, The Firefly, Sweet
Adeline*. Arthur's daughter Elaine, a beautiful woman, was

for years one of the best-loved stars of silent movies. Oscar's grandchildren became prominent in show business, as his great-grandchildren are now.

But the grandchild whom the old man neglected—his namesake Oscar Hammerstein II—came on with Richard Rodgers to write such musical masterpieces as *Oklahoma!, Carousel, South Pacific, The King and I,* and win the love of millions in every corner of the world.

CHAPTER EIGHT

Showcase for Stars

THE DECISIVE YEAR in the history of the big time was 1913. The battle between Martin Beck and Ed Albee was decided then, for the New York Palace opened, and, after a faltering start, it became the glorious shrine of vaudeville and its brightest legend.

It seems curious that neither of the two master showmen, Beck and Albee, realized that the movies sooner or later would supplant vaudeville as the people's favorite entertainment. All the signs were there. The mushrooming film industry could show the world's greatest stars for a fraction of the price asked for vaudeville shows. The first presentation house, the Strand Theatre, was being built on Broadway and would do a fine business with pictures and a full orchestra playing classical music. Both the Keith and Orpheum circuits had many neighborhood theatres that ran newsreels and a feature picture along with four or five vaudeville acts. Beck and Albee had every reason either to start or buy in on established studios but perhaps they were too busy trying to outwit each other. At any rate they let the chance to become movie moguls slip by them.

Their own vaudeville business had grown enormously, along with all theatrical entertainment. Between them, they owned and operated about thirty-five big-time theatres, controlled hundreds of small-time houses, plus booking offices, and collected half the fees paid the agents by artists who worked for them. The average vaudeville theatre's building cost ran from $125,000 to $600,000 and its value usually increased with time. The new Palace was said to have cost $850,000.

That fall The New York *Times* made a study of the whole theatrical field. Its findings showed that the American public was paying for its entertainment between twenty-five and thirty million dollars. And this was at a time when unskilled workers earned less than $500 a year and the average family needed only $800 a year to get along.

There were 2973 regularly booked theatres offering all kinds of entertainment. Brooklyn alone had fifty-three theatres, Cincinnati thirteen, Philadelphia fifty-one, and Boston thirty. There were twelve hundred companies on tour, exclusive of vaudeville. In contrast to the high vaudeville salaries, the average pay for a legitimate actor was $25 a week.

On Broadway—the center of the universe for all show people—hell was popping over the rage for ragtime music and the wild dances that had started two years before with Irving Berlin's popular "Alexander's Ragtime Band" and "Everybody's Doing It Now." Also in 1911 the one-time cornet player Jesse Lasky had introduced cabaret to New York, just as he had earlier produced several beautifully dressed tabloid musical shows for the big time.

But Lasky's "Folies Bergere," patterned on the Paris original failed. By 1913 Lasky had departed for Hollywood where he became a founding father of the movie industry. Meanwhile, his cabaret idea had caught on everywhere with dancing by the patrons of the sexy new dances drawing as much trade as the entertainment. Ranging from the elegant to the gaudy, these cabarets were raided regularly by the police under pressure from the reformers.

Reformers, whose mission, as always, was to stop people from doing what they want to do, were riding high and handsome at the moment. This was because of the murder a year before of Herman Rosenthal, a squealing Tenderloin gambler, by four underworld gunmen. The crime had been ordered and paid for by Police Lieutenant Charles Becker, Tammany Hall's chief graft collector in the Tenderloin, and Rosenthal's secret partner in a gambling house. Public indignation mounted and the reformers made determined efforts to close up the Tenderloin and make Broadway a clean and wholesome place.

Ironically, though the Tenderloin did disappear in the next few years, the reform group had nothing to do with it. Business expansion during the Great War resulted in a takeover by legitimate firms of the whole area once called Satan's Playground.

The reformers also failed to stop the wildest dance craze in American history. Alan Valentine, in his book *1913*, says "the new dances seemed invented to encourage immodesty. To those conservative oldsters to whom the waltz had been the closest and most intimate physical contact on the dance floor, the turkey trot and even the one step seemed inciting and abandoned."

Mayor William J. Gaynor called the turkey trot and such

forays on the city's dance floors "lascivious orgies." The New York *Times* declared the turkey trot a "phenomenon closely analogous to those dancing manias of the Middle Ages . . . to which victims of a neurotic diathasis are susceptible."

The turkey trot was an ungainly dance that suggested the walk of that bird. Other dances named for animals—grizzly bear, bunny hug—also enjoyed a spectacular overnight popularity. Everybody except reformers, the bedridden, those in wheel-chairs, or the permanently disabled were doing the new animal dances. Bowlegged, knockkneed, clumsy men and women who had never dared to dance before could be seen happily hoofing away in cities and towns across the country, along with decrepit old codgers with young ideas.

In Philadelphia, Edward Bok, editor of the *Ladies Home Journal,* fired fifteen girl employees for dancing the turkey trot during their lunch hour. In Millwood, New Jersey, Ogden Bradley, a former Justice of the Peace, had 18-year-old Grace Williams arrested for disorderly conduct. She passed his home singing "Everybody's Doing It Now," while dancing the turkey trot. In court, her lawyer Stuart Baker sang the song and the spectators joined in. When an encore was demanded, Mr. Baker threw in a few steps of the trot. Grace was freed. But in Paterson, New Jersey, a judge sentenced another girl to a $25 fine or fifty days in jail for dancing the turkey trot.

The New York *Sun* demanded "Are we going to the dogs by the rag-time route?" and hurled such harsh phrases as "Decadent drivel, rhythmically attractive degenerator which . . . hypnotizes us into vulgar foot-tapping acquiescence. . . ." Somebody else called the new dances "a substitute for the Turkish bath and the masseuse" while the tango was described as the "dance of the shameless savage and his squaw."

In 1913, Irving Berlin compounded his crime by writing "International Rag" in which he described Britons, Frenchmen, and Germans dancing to a raggedy melody, and dukes and lords, the Russian Czar, and Italian opera singers learning to snap their fingers. The last line was "the world goes round to the sound of the International Rag."

Scandal erupted after George Rector tried to build up his afternoon business with something he called *tea dansants*. The special attraction for ladies were young dancing partners. In no time newspapers were building up Rector's business and those who imitated him by running features almost daily on this new pleasure of the idle rich. The stories were accompanied by artists' drawings, picturing the young men as limp, languid, anemic of character, and shunners of honest toil. Someone nicknamed them "lounge lizards" because they reclined on sofas in Rector's foyer while they awaited the ladies.

Protests tripled when the press discovered that young matrons had gotten in the habit of checking their corsets at the door so they could dance not only cheek to cheek, but everything to everything with their favorite lizards.

While the husbands of the dancing wives were annoyed by the publicity, their tempers exploded when they discovered that their wives were buying their dancing partners expensive suits and other presents. A handful of the lounge lizards went in for blackmail. Whether publicity about this helped shut down the afternoon dansants or not, other factors—the war, the emergence of ragtime and jazz music—shifted the scene.

In complete contrast to all these vulgar forms of hoofing was the popularity of Vernon and Irene Castle, who symbolized refinement and grace in their superb ballroom dancing.

Caroline Caffin described the Castles' "languid energy, drooping strenuousness, a sort of whimsical indifference . . . his long flexible limbs . . . a man so agile, so listless having an impenetrable indifference . . . their floating grace seemed to come without effort . . . they'd not surprise you if they left the solid ground and floated off into space."

Vernon Castle was an Englishman who had been working for six years in Lew Fields' Broadway musicals when he met pretty Irene Foote, a stage-struck society girl from New Rochelle, New York. Castle was 23, Irene 17 when they were introduced in 1910. He got her a job in Fields' show, "The Henpecks," and they were married the following year despite her wealthy father's opposition. Though he was a much admired comedian, Vernon was earning only $75 a week—when he worked. The couple went to Paris not long afterward to appear in the Folies-Bergère from which they soon withdrew.

An agent who had seen them dancing together got them an engagement at the Café de Paris where their dancing made an immediate sensation. They came home and repeated their success in New York at Martin's Café de l'Opéra. In no time they became the most popular dancing team in the United States.

They were so in demand that one week they were booked into both Hammerstein's and its new arch-rival, the Palace. For huge fees they gave private dancing lessons to Mr. and Mrs. William Randolph Hearst, Diamond Jim Brady, and other millionaires. Soon they had a roof restaurant, and Castles-in-the-Air, a night club at the seashore. In a single week of one-night stands the team earned $31,000.

Vernon was killed in an air crash early in World War I. However, long before that Irene, elegant and slender as a reed, had made permanent changes in the shape, looks, and grooming of American women. She created a new industry—beauty shops—when she bobbed her hair. Her slim figure became the ideal of millions of housewives, replacing the big-bottomed, big-busted allure of Lillian Russell.

While Broadway was enjoying this giddy and often graceful time, the men responsible were engaged in more serious business.

Ever since 1905 when Martin Beck moved his headquarters and chief booking office from Chicago to Times Square, Ed Albee had expected him to try to start an Eastern theatre chain there in the heart of the Keith kingdom. The two tycoons had long before signed an agreement to stay out of each other's territory but both had violated it so many times that the pact had come to be meaningless.

Six years later, Beck showed that his fight with Albee was on in earnest by buying a large slice of land on Broadway and announcing that he intended to build a deluxe vaudeville theatre.

Lunching at Rector's one day, Beck saw Felix Isman, a specialist in Broadway real estate. Beck walked over, sat down, and told Isman his plans. He said his project would require a great deal of land since he intended to construct the world's most beautiful theatre—an architectural glory for all time. There would be luxurious dressing rooms, a large backstage area, plus increased office space for him and his staff. Most important of all, he wanted a second smaller theatre on the premises with a unit fully equipped to produce new acts. Beck also intended to install what he called a bank to furnish financing for the acts he and his staff thought were ready for the big time.

Isman said that he knew of a perfect location right on Times Square, a door away from its northeast corner at Forty-seventh Street and Seventh Avenue. Unfortunately, the building on that corner was not available, but the main entrance and lobby could be built next door at 1564 and 1566 Broadway. A stage entrance and dressing rooms would then be constructed just around the West Forty-seventh Street corner. There were ten buildings on the property which would have to be bought and razed.

In January, 1912, backed by Meyerfield and other associates, Beck signed a one-hundred year lease on the property with George Earle representing the owners. It called for a rent of $41,000 the first year, $55,000 for the second and $60,000 a year for the remaining ninety-eight years.

While the ground was being cleared, Beck had a large sign put up facing Broadway. It announced that Martin Beck's New Theatre was to be erected on the site, and would open in September. From the Keith offices in the Putnam Building across Times Square, Ed Albee could see Beck's sign.

Albee was furious but also puzzled. Some years before, the vaudeville managers association had been worried by rumors Oscar Hammerstein was planning to start a chain of theatres in other cities. To prevent this, they had given the Hammersteins an exclusive franchise to book big-time vaudeville shows in the entire Times Square area as far north as Fifty-ninth Street.

Soon Willie Hammerstein was threatening legal action against Beck for violating the agreement. When asked about this, Beck claimed that he was no longer a party to the agree-

ment because he now booked all talent through his own
United Booking Offices. Construction continued. At this time
Beck was also building a Palace in Chicago.

In the midst of the controversy Beck sailed for Europe,
saying he planned to sign up dozens of opera stars and concert
singers for his circuit. What he really hoped to do was to bag
no less an attraction than Mme. Sarah Bernhardt, whom millions considered the world's greatest actress. He'd just read in
a theatrical paper that the Divine One, as many reverently
called the aged French tragedienne, had just scored a triumph
at London's huge Palladium, appearing in scenes from her
repertoire. Though she acted only in French, Beck was convinced that New Yorkers would stampede the box office to see
her as the headliner on his very first bill at the Palace.

Beck's rivals often charged that in addition to his linguistic
abilities helping him to sign foreign acts, he had a habit of
flashing a $100,000 bill of credit as proof of his financial sta-
bility. It's possible. For years unscrupulous American agents
had been luring variety performers to the United States with
promises of high salaries they had no intention of paying. To
keep eating, many of the foreign artists had been forced to
work for less money than they had been getting in Europe.

If Beck used a letter of credit to impress Bernhardt, he
never mentioned it when he announced the great news. Instead he said she burst into tears when he recounted to her
that as a 16-year-old actor in Paris, he had stood in a theatre
line from six in the morning until seven at night to see her
perform. "I told her," the vaudeville king said, "that the
masses in America had never seen her on her previous tours
because they could not afford to pay $7 and $8 for a seat, and
that if she signed with me the whole country would have a

chance to enjoy her art. This seemed to appeal to her, for in a few days she signed for $7000 a week. When I was ready to leave Paris, I looked over the contract and found that I had not included Sundays in her schedule. I was in misery. How could I have made such a blunder? All my houses had Sunday performances; it was often the biggest day of the week, so I decided I would have to explain the situation to her. I expected the worst, however, because extras had walked out on me for less."

"Why all the fuss?" she wanted to know. "I'm in the theatre all of the time, anyway. We play Sundays often in France, too."

Beck came back with a contract signed by Bernhardt calling for her to play twenty-four weeks in theatres on his circuit. Her salary was double that ever paid before to an artist, and it made front page news everywhere. Martin also came back with contracts from forty more concert and opera stars.

He returned full of joy, even though he faced delays in the construction work on both Palaces. Not only was he confident of humiliating Albee, but he had also been dickering with Percy Williams for his eight beautiful theatres. That would be a second staggering blow for his rival. At a San Francisco meeting with his partners a pool of five million dollars was raised for the purchase of the Williams theatres.

Beck, however, was underestimating Albee's cunning. While Beck was abroad, Ed, knowing that old man Hammerstein always needed money, bought back for between $200,000 and $250,000 Hammerstein's exclusive right to produce vaudeville in the Times Square area. This coup put Beck squarely on the spot. Next, on hearing that Beck and his

backers were going to Florida to make an offer to Percy
Williams for his chain, Beck hurried there, hoping to get the
theatres for his own circuit. In the bidding that followed,
Albee did get them for $5,250,000—a quarter-of-a-million
more than the Beck group had put in their pool.

When Beck's men expressed chagrin, Albee said he was
willing to let them in on the deal for a controlling share of
the Palace. Beck almost collapsed in fury before he was finally
forced to agree. He did retain a 49 percent share of the
theatre as well as the lucrative privilege of booking acts
through his office.

And, after all that anguish, the theatre wasn't ready when
Mme. Bernhardt arrived with her entourage to be greeted by
press and public alike as visiting royalty. Her new leading
man and lover was Lou Tellegen, a handsome Dutch professional athlete who was 29, less than half her age. Sarah had
been rehearsing him for weeks in Paris and on the trip across
the Atlantic.

When she heard the news about the Palace—the one in
Chicago was not yet ready either—she cheerfully agreed to
have her schedule changed. She would open on the West
Coast first. This meant more days to prepare her lover for his
stage debut.

When the Chicago Palace opened, it was a fiasco. One
factor was Beck's engagement of Victor Hollander, a classical
German composer and conductor, who directed his orchestra
to play the fast-paced music far too slowly.

Louise F. Brand, Milwaukee *Sentinel* critic, described what
happened in these words:

> The first acts moved slowly. Even the audience, uncon-
> scious of the reason, began to feel nervous tension in the air.

It came to a climax with a display of 'temperament' on the part of Diamond and Nelson, a singing and dancing team. In a fit of disgust over the orchestra's accompaniment, Mr. Diamond left his partner on the stage in the middle of a song. She faltered, stopped singing and followed, leaving the stage empty. The curtain came down.

Mr. Beck rushed from his box and hurried backstage . . . the stage manager, unaware of Mr. Beck's presence on stage, gave the signal to raise the drop for the full-stage act scheduled to go on. As it rose, it revealed Beck in the center of the stage. The excited head of the Orpheum circuit, after giving one enraged look at the rising curtain and the applauding audience, beat an undignified retreat to the wings, where he promptly discharged everyone connected with the incident, and later went to great trouble hiring them back again.

Beck tried to cheer himself up with the thought that the New York opening on March 24, 1913, would compensate for the Chicago disaster. He was convinced that a more beautiful theatre had never been built and everyone who saw the Palace on opening night agreed. Max Gordon, the Broadway producer who years before had produced vaudeville acts, wrote in his memoirs of "the heady excitement of the crowd. The opening was gala, the theatre a jewel. From the curved marble rail in the rear you could hear a whisper from the stage, and wherever you sat in the eighteen-hundred seat theatre—still one of our largest—you could see the stage clearly . . . seats . . . were upholstered in a beautiful flowered cretonne. The two crystal chandeliers suspended from the ceiling bespoke the grandeur of royalty."

The critics also had high praise for the theatre's "palatial lobbies and promenades, the old ivory and bronze decorations and the Siena marble in the inner lobby," and noted that it seated 1800, which made it the largest theatre to open on the Great White Way since the New Amsterdam was built in 1902.

The show was something else. Beck had overestimated the public's enjoyment of arty foreign acts and this time his headline was a Polish dancer. The bill read:

LA NAPIERKOWSKA
Arabian Pantomime "The Captive,"
from the ballet "Les Aisles" (The Wings)
and including "Le Dansse De L'Abeille" (The Dance
of the Bee). Music by Rymski Korsakov and Lewis Lanne

Hy. Mayer		Ota Gygi
Famous Cartoonist	The Four Vannis	Violinist at the Court of Spain

The Eternal Waltz
An operetta in 2 scenes by Leo Fall
With Mabel Berra and Cyril Chadwick

Speaking to Father	The King's Jester	McIntyre and Harty
George Ade's Comedy with Milton Pollock and Company	A Farce by Ed Wynn and Co.	Singing Comedy Duo

THE LONDON PALACE GIRLS

After the first performance, McIntyre and Harty were replaced by Taylor Holmes, a popular monologist. But the headliner, La Napierowska, proved the big mistake. She was described by the *World*'s critic as "a Polish representative of the great horde of wriggle dancers who have swooped down on New York. This lady was supposed to be stung by a bee. She divested herself of her clothing to find it . . . she called herself a classical dancer but no one seemed to notice it."

The *Herald* complained that *The Eternal Waltz* was the only act on the bill that "even slightly resembled a novelty . . . and through a long afternoon the first audience waited . . . and waited . . . and waited."

That week and during the month that followed the Palace lost money. Martin Beck, whose office was doing the booking (temporarily as it turned out) kept putting on bills of headliners and standard acts that had been surefire everywhere else but drew few customers to his gem of a theatre.

When the Palace opened Willie Hammerstein declared, "I give it six months." And to rub it in Willie was just then enjoying his incredible success with Evelyn Nesbit Thaw, the freak act that both Beck and Albee had turned down.

The tide began to turn in the Palace's favor only in its sixth week when the matchless Ethel Barrymore appeared there in *Miss Civilization,* a one-act play by Richard Harding Davis, the famous journalist. Also on the bill were the Courtney Sisters; Bessie Clayton, a much-admired dancer; a surefire comedy team, Dooley and Sales; and Nat Wills, the comedy tramp. Wills had married a circus bareback rider and after she had thrown him out of her dressing room and her life, Wills said, "I should have married the horse."

Booked for the following week with a fortune spent on advance advertising was the one and only Bernhardt. Speaking in French, a language not one out of a hundred vaudeville fans could understand, the Divine One as usual had been smashing box office records in theatres all the way across the country. Sarah was sixty-eight years old and the fire had not gone out of her acting.

Nor had she lost her extraordinary talent for getting publicity. Everything she did made exciting news and she knew how to exploit all of it—her raging fights with directors, the big cigars she smoked, her extravagances, her many men (some very famous indeed), plus the illegitimate baby that the first of her lovers had fathered. Sarah still carried with her an expensive coffin in which she wished to be buried. She told interviewers that she slept in it, wishing to become accustomed to it before she died.

On a previous American tour, Bernhardt had played in tents when there were no theatres large enough to accommodate the crowds that turned out to see her. Though she appealed to the French consul in New Orleans to file a protest in Washington against this "humiliation" of France's greatest actress. This also made good copy.

On this 1913 tour she exploited a small news break. At Los Angeles she was in a car collision and a local newspaper published a story about the accident which said that she had left the scene, unhurt, sitting in a young man's lap and "seemed to enjoy it."

Sarah, the woman who had regaled the world with her many loves and the son born out of wedlock, could not have reacted more violently if she'd been an inhibited old maid. She rented billboards all over Los Angeles to make her reply: "The reporter who wrote this is a liar. I demand an apology for this base canard." Hundreds of newspapers carried the story. The New York *World* ran it on the front page.

And Bernhardt, the star, packed the 1800 seat Palace for almost every performance of her seventeen-day engagement. She grossed $22,000 the first week for a whopping profit. *Variety*, which had been scoffing at the new theatre's $2 top policy as being far too high, reported that the top was now $2.50 and speculators were getting as much as $10 for a pair of tickets. Sarah played excerpts from her repertory in French, the death scene from "Camille," scenes from Phèdre, Tosca, Lucrèce Borgia, and a new playlet "Une Nuit de Noël."

After the Bernhardt engagement, the management closed the Palace and reopened it late in August. From that summer day the Palace never had a losing year until a long time after the empire whose capital and chief ornament it became started to fall apart.

Hammerstein's closed its doors in 1915.

But long before that the elegant Palace had taken its place as vaudeville's show case. Its sidewalk became the place for artists to gather, especially just before the first show of the week, the Monday matinee. Everyone in show business who was in town seldom missed that performance—and that included everyone who could give an artist a job. The biggest of these big shots were the men who produced Broadway's glittering musical shows, Ziegfeld, Charlie Dillingham, John Murray Anderson, George White, the Shuberts. Along with the talent scouts and agents, they were like shoppers visiting some magic-touched bazaar. There they found the bright new faces and unique talent, trained to perfection and ready for stardom, that they needed for their dazzling entertainments. They could also discover every other kind of specialty act— acrobats to magicians, midgets to elephants.

Through its glory-filled years, the Palace was a cornucopia of original and brilliant young musical talent. It was the showcase for stars of the musical theatre who have delighted, charmed, and amused the world through the long years since the twenties: clowns of renown, from Ed Wynn to Bob Hope;

dancers, both delicate and robust, who seemed to have wings for feet; actress-singers, from gentle Elsie Janis to husky, hard-swinging Sophie Tucker. No other American theatre ever offered so many superb shows with so much talent on the genius level.

It soon became Broadway's most enduring legend. Larger and more expensive theatres were built but none of them is recalled with so much affection. To the artist it was Mount Olympus, the shrine of shrines, the make-or-break place, dream's end, the shining Golden Gate to everything in life they wanted—long-term contracts on the two-a-day, fame and great fortune on Broadway, the radio, or in Hollywood.

The late Fred Allen, vaudeville's Voltaire, flopped at the Palace the first time he played there, but later called it "the towering symbol of vaudeville . . . a Palace program with an act's name on it was a diploma of merit . . . an act that played there was booked unseen by any theatre manager in the country."

Performers who appeared at the Palace never wearied of bragging. No vaudeville story was more often told than the one about the small town manager who got sick of his artists' boasting of how they knocked them dead at the Palace. So he hung up a sign that read:

DON'T TELL ME HOW YOU KILLED THEM AT THE PALACE
DO IT HERE

Finding new star talent at the Palace began during its calamitous opening week. Remember that Ed Wynn was on the bill. Florenz Ziegfeld was there to look at him—for a peculiar reason. Zieggy was casting his next production and needed a comic with a hysterical giggle. He'd told agents to be on the lookout and one agent had seen Wynn, whose giggle was a surefire laugh-getter. The agent brought Ziegfeld to the Palace just in time to catch Ed's act. Ed was on and giggling at the moment. Ziegfeld said: "That's the chap I want!"

That was the big break of Wynn's life, after knocking around in vaudeville for ten tough years without getting anywhere. But it was all big money and glory for the owl-faced comic from then on—stardom in the Follies within a couple of seasons, together with shows that he himself produced and starred in. And more and fabulous pay as radio's Texaco "Fire Chief"—with that hysterical giggle still his trademark.

Monday afternoon at the Palace was indeed the place to be seen.

The death of vaudeville was no sudden thing. The big time really began to get smaller in the early twenties, though neither its kings nor its older headliners and standard acts would admit to this. Among the menacing competitors were movies and a new thing called radio which could be heard at home and cost nothing. Even Marcus Loew's small time which ran both feature pictures and live acts was beginning to outgross Keith's. In 1920 Loew bought Metro pictures for three million dollars to insure getting enough good movies for his hundreds of theatres.

He even challenged the Palace in 1921 by opening his Loew's State two blocks south of it on Broadway. The State had almost 3500 seats and although Loew charged lower prices than the Palace he could still outgross it. Albee became so nervous about the State's cutting into the business of his Palace that he had an usher buy a ticket each day when the Loew house opened and another when it closed. Since the tickets were numbered consecutively, by comparing the two Albee could find out how many customers had seen the State's show.

When Marcus Loew learned of this he telephoned Albee, and said, "Ed, you don't have to go to all that trouble. You can call up my house manager and he will give you the box office figures each day."

Albee found his cooperation very discouraging. In the next few years he had to switch the policy of most of his big-time theatres from straight vaudeville to a combination of vaudeville and movies. By 1926 there were only a dozen theatres in America that offered nothing but big-time vaudeville. *Variety,* which had always made vaudeville its main concern, shifted coverage to the back pages and devoted its front section to the movies and their box office grosses. That's where the big money was being made.

Albee insisted that his live entertainment was what drew the crowds and billed the movie picture like an added extra attraction. Unlike Marcus Loew, Albee still held back from the lure of Hollywood. Instead he tried to consolidate his power by acquiring more and more vaudeville theatres as well as whole chains. His biggest deal was a merger of the Keith and Orpheum circuits. Martin Beck, on the other hand, also retained a financial interest in vaudeville but spent most of his time producing legitimate shows at the Martin Beck Theatre which he built in 1924.

However, by the mid-twenties not only movies but also radio was now a huge business stealing away the stars he had developed on the big time. The final blow came when talking pictures were produced and proved an overwhelming success. It was only then that Albee consented to merge his great coast-to-coast theatre chain with David Sarnoff's radio corporation and Joseph Kennedy's Hollywood film studios.

The wheeler-dealer father of the amazing Kennedy clan naturally wanted to run the whole thing. But he might not have been able to gain control of the gigantic entertainment enterprise without the connivance of John Murdock, who since 1913 had been Ed Albee's right hand man and most trusted aide. Murdock had broken strikes for Albee, bought theatres and whole circuits of showhouses, and bulldozed hundreds of Keith artists out of demanding pay raises.

Albee was so impressed by his handling of the purchase of the Kohl and Castle circuit in Chicago that he offered Murdock their own dance studio, a sizable chunk of his corporation's stock. It was this stock that Murdock sold to Kennedy, giving him and his associates majority interest.

Kennedy lost little time in taking over and kicking Albee upstairs. One day in 1928 Albee went to his former office now occupied by Kennedy with a suggestion. Kennedy heard him out, then said coldly, "Ed, don't you know you're all through?"

Edward Albee retired to Florida where he died on March 16, 1930, aged 72. By then vaudeville also was on its way to the grave. Its official death came in November, 1932, when the Palace, which had been running pictures and four acts of vaudeville, announced that it was dropping the acts and would play only movies.

A quarter century after the big time vanished, Richard Maney, Broadway's last literary press agent, wrote, "I mourn the passing of vaudeville along with every theatregoer over fifty. For years it was the amusement manna of the masses.

Vaudeville theatres littered the land from the Rio Grande to Saskatchewan. Their stages supported trained seals and cinnamon bears, tap-dancers, burnt-cork comics and barbershop quartets; jugglers, acrobats and magicians; female impersonators, monologists and harmonica players; xylophonists, dog-and-pony acts and unicyclists."

Vaudeville when it vanished was from every show business point of view the end of an era. It meant the passing of an entertainment that had produced the most gifted dancers, singers, and clowns that ever blessed the world.

But the vaudeville art has never died in the true sense. Just as it flourished under other names the world over since before recorded history, it still continues to enchant when displayed on television or in night clubs or movies.

There will never be another Jolson, a second Nora Bayes, Frank Fay, or Willie Howard. But it is equally true that there never will be another Lucille Ball or Carol Burnett, another Art Carney or Jackie Gleason. They are vaudevillians in heart and spirit.

For as long as there are people in the world who thrill and dazzle us with superb dancing, music, and comedy and there are men and women who enjoy being thrilled and dazzled, vaudeville will always live.

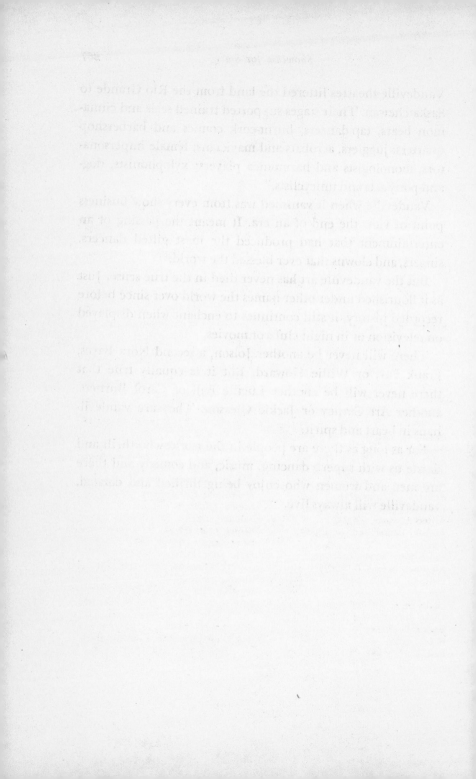

Index

Abrams, Maurice, 99
Actors' Fund, 88
Ails, Roscoe, 66
Albee, Edward Franklin, 34-35, 36-41, 44-45, 46-49, 52, 65, 89, 102-3, 247-48, 253, 254, 256-57, 264-66
Albee, Nathan, 37
"Alexander's Ragtime Band" (song), 248
Alhambra Theatre (New York), 135
Allan, Maud, 63
Allen, Fred, 88, 152-53, 177, 263
Allen, Gracie, 115, 145
Allen, Theodore, 168
Anderson, George, 114
Anderson, John Murray, 262
Arbuckle, Fatty, 29, 142
Arthur, Bedini and (act), 139
Astaire, Fred, 178
Astor, John Jacob, 225
Atkinson, Brooks, 8, 202, 209

Babette (operetta), 113
"Baby Alice," 35-36
"Baby Shoes" (song), 239
Bailey, Pearl, 96
Baker, Belle, 99
Ball, Lucille, 267

Bardeleben, Baron Friedrich von, 114
Barnum, P. T., 12, 106, 241
Barry, Tom, 135
Barrymore, Ethel, 71, 260
Basselin, Olivier, 9
Bayes, Nora, 52, 54, 60, 64, 81-89, 95, 111, 221, 267
Beaverbrook, Lord, 146
Beck, Martin, 25, 29-34, 49, 63, 247-48, 253-59, 265
Becker, Charles, 248
Becker, Ruth, 108. See also Roye, Ruth
Bedini, Jean, 208
Bedini and Arthur (act), 139
Beeler, Annie, 197
Belmont, August, 63
Benny, Jack, 157-58
Berle, Milton, 162-63, 183
Berle, Sandra, 162
Berlin, Irving, 86, 208-9, 248, 251
Bernard, Sam, 20
Bernays, Edward, 55, 147
Bernhardt, Sarah, 32, 255-56, 257, 260-62
Bial, Adam, 230-31
Bierbower, Elizabeth Cockerill (Liz), 67-75

Bierbower, Johnny, 68-69
Bijou Theatre (Boston), 39-40
Billerbeck, Herbert Schussler, *see* Williams, Herb
Birdcage Varieties (Arizona), 129
Blake, Sissle and (act), 189
Blau, Rose, 229
Boag, Gil, 99
Bok, Edward, 250
Bolger, Ray, 213
Bombo (show), 199
Booth, Edwin, 85, 127
Bordoni, Irene, 51
Boyle, Johnny, 211
Bradley, Ogden, 250
Brady, Diamond Jim, 123, 136, 146, 225, 252
Brand, Louise F., 257-58
Brat, The (show), 184
Brice, Fanny, 53, 60, 115, 116
Broun, Heywood, 56, 189
Brown, Jane, 178-79
Brown, Jean, 149
Brown, Martin, 146
Brown, Ned, 101, 227
Buchanan, Lee, 184
Buck and Bubbles (act), 189
Burnett, Carol, 267
Burns, Florence, 238-39
Burns, George, 4, 145
Burnside, R. H., 34-35
Busse, Edward J., 207
"By the Light of the Silvery Moon" (song), 138

Caesar, Irving, 179
Caine, Georgia, 237
Campen, Helen van, 78-79
Cantor, Eddie, 92, 116, 139-40, 156-57, 173, 188, 193, 200
Capitol Theatre (New York), 86
Carman, Florence, 239
Carmencita, 239-40
Carncross Minstrels, 130
Carney, Art, 267
Carus, Emma, 53, 105-7, 111, 112
Caruso, Enrico, 113, 173, 203
Case, Charlie, 186

Castle, Irene, 72, 73, 251-53
Castle, Vernon, 174, 251-52
Catlett, Walter, 191
Cawthorn, Joseph, 71-72
Chapin, Charles, 128
Chaplin, Charlie, 2, 117
Chaplin, Sidney, 141
Chevalier, Maurice, 72
Clark, Bobby, 116, 191, 203, 205-9
Clarke, Harry, 85, 86
Clayton, Bessie, 260
Clement, Helen, 88
Clifford, Jack, 244, 245
Clive, Carter, 230
Cobb, Irvin S., 136
Cockerill, Elizabeth, *see* Bierbower, Elizabeth Cockerill
Cockerill, John, 67
Cockerill, Col. Joseph A., 67
Coffee, Andrew, 174
Cohan, George M., 20, 40, 71, 86, 136, 137, 164, 226
Colisimo, Big Jim, 174
Collyer, Dan, 18-19
Colonial Theatre (Boston), 41
Columbus Theatre (New York), 230, 234
Combs, Marie, 135, 136
"Come Along, My Mandy" (song), 84
Comique Box-House (Seattle), 25-26
Conn (Imhof, Conn and Corinne), 115
Connors, Chuck, 234
Connors, Jimmy, 216
Conrad, Ethel, 239
Considine, George, 26
Considine, John, 23, 25-26, 28, 29
Considine, John, Jr., 29
Cook, Captain, 240
Cooke, Alistair, 201-2
Coolidge, Calvin, 146-47
Cooper, Gary, 175-76
Corcoran, Jack, 217
Corinne (Imhof, Conn and Corinne), 115
Cosmopolitan Beer Hall (Chicago), 126
Courtney, Fay, 145, 260

Courtney, Florence, 145, 260
Cox, Bonnie, 168, 169-70, 171
Cox, Eddie, 175
Crosby, Bing, 176
Crowley, Mother, 168
"Cuddles" (Lila Lee), 138
Culhane, Chace and Weston's Minstrels, 206

Dale, Alan, 237
Damrosch, Walter, 243
"Dark Town Strutters Ball" (song), 173
Darling, Eddie, 65, 89
Davis, Richard Harding, 260
Dean, Mayme, 104
Delmar, Ethel, 199
Dempsey, Jack, 145
Denison, Rev. Frederic, 12-13
Diamond and Nelson (act), 258
Dillingham, Charles, 35, 71-72, 113, 218, 219, 262
Dio, Mlle. de, 231
Dixon, Harland, 2, 210-19
Dockstadter, Lew, 198, 217
Dolly, Jennie (Yansci), 145-47
Dolly, Rosie, (Rozicka), 145-47
Donahue, Jack, 211
Dooley, J. Francis, 197
Dooley, Ray, 115, 116
Dooley and Sales (act), 260
Downey, Martin, 30
"Down Where the Wurzburger Flows" (song), 81, 86
Doyle, Jimmy, 210, 217-19
Dreiser, Theodore, 110
Dresser, Louise, 50, 109-11
Dresser, Paul, 109-10
Dressler, Marie, 111, 115
Duncan Sisters (act), 139, 145
Durant, Will, 9-10
Dyer, Johnny, 181

Earl and the Girl, The (show), 134
Earle, George, 254
Earp, Wyatt, 127
Edison's Unique Theatre, 26
Edwards, Gus, 137-40, 156

Edwards, Lillian, 139, 140
Edwards and Foy (act), 126
Eltinge, Julian, 63, 91
Errol, Leon, 116
Eternal Waltz, The (operetta), 259, 260
"Everybody's Doing It Now" (song), 248

Fallen Star, The (play), 135-36
Fay, Frank (Francis Anthony), 176-86, 267
F. F. Proctor, Vaudeville Pioneer (book), 44
Fields, Lew, 252
Fields, W. C., 15, 20, 40, 67, 116, 153, 156, 188, 190, 226
Fifth Avenue Theatre (New York), 82
Finnegan, Jack, 126
Fisk, Jim, 125
Fitzgerald, Edward, *see* Foy, Eddie
Fitzgerald, John F., 167
Five Columbians, The (act), 141
Floradora Chorus, 224
Folies Bergere, 248-49
Follies, *see* Ziegfeld Follies
Foote, Irene, *see* Castle, Irene
Ford, James, 16
Ford, Johnny, 66, 213-14
Ford, Maxie, 214
Four Cohans, The (act), 20, 40, 137
Fox, Harry, 146
Fox, John, Jr., 114
Fox, Will, 167-68
Foy, Bryan (Lincoln Bryan Fitzgerald), 118, 119, 132-35, 137
Foy, Charlie (Giovanni Vittorio Emmanuel Fitzgerald), 118-19, 137, 175
Foy, Eddie, 58, 71, 117-37, 211, 226
Foy, Eddie, Jr., 118, 119, 136
Foy, Irving, 119, 120-21
Foy, Madeline, 135, 136
Franklin, Irene, 50, 52-53, 75-80
French Twin Sisters (act), 18
Friars Club, 226
Friedland, Ben, 88-89
Friganza, Trixie, 53, 61, 111-12

Frisco, Joe, 4, 23, 99, 172-76, 182
Frye, Moss and (act), 189
Fulton, Maud, 184

Gaiety Museum (Providence, R.I.), 41
Galbraith, Erle, 199
Garden, Mary, 242
Gardner, Jack, 111
Gaynor, William J., 249-50
German Village Hall (New York), 93-94
Gerry Society, 121
Gershwin, Ira, 192
Gest, Morris, 240-41
Giles, Dorothy, 94
Gleason, Jackie, 267
Goettler, Charles, 112
Goldberg, Nora, *see* Bayes, Nora
"Good-by, Little Girl, Good-by" (song), 138
Goodwin, Nat, 20, 226
Gordon, Arthur, 87
Gordon, Max, 258
Graham, Lillian, 239
Grand Theatre (Pittsburgh), 113
Grant, Cary, 105
Gray, Gilda, 99, 104-5
Green, Abel, 164
Green, Burton, 53, 75, 76, 77-80
Green, Helen van Campen, 78-79
Green Pastures, The (show), 189
Green Street Theatre (Albany, N.Y.), 43
Gressing, Otto, 81, 82
Guilbert, Yvette, 233

Haggerty, George, 182
Hallam, Basil, 73
Halperin, Nan, 51
Hamlet (play), 134
Hammerstein, Abraham, 227-28
Hammerstein, Abraham Lincoln, 229
Hammerstein, Arthur, 229, 232, 233-34, 236, 241, 243, 245
Hammerstein, Bertha, 227-28
Hammerstein, Elaine, 245-46
Hammerstein, Harry, 229, 232

Hammerstein, Oscar, 21, 22, 87, 221, 227-46, 254, 256
Hammerstein, Oscar, II, 6, 246
Hammerstein, Rose, 229, 241
Hammerstein, Stella, 229, 241
Hammerstein, William (Willie), 59, 123, 227, 229, 232, 237-45, 254, 260
Hammerstein's Theatre, *see* Victoria Theatre
Hammond, Percy, 55, 91
Harlem Opera House (New York), 229, 230, 234
Harris, Sam, 226
Harty, McIntyre and (act), 259
"Has Anybody Here Seen Kelly?" (song), 86
Havemeyer, "Nunkey," 61
Hayes, Gracie, 174, 175
Hayes, Peter Lind, 173
Haymarket Dancehall (New York), 223
Hearst, William Randolph, 54, 252
Hearts of Oak (play), 76
Heath, Tom, 136
Hecht, Ben, 211
Held, Anna, 51, 59
Heller, Henrietta, 199
"Hello, Central! Give Me No Man's Land" (song), 192
"Hello, My Baby" (song), 92
Herbert, Victor, 113, 122-23
"He's a Devil in His Own Home Town" (song), 108
Hewitt, Abram, 21
Hildegarde, 139
Hippodrome (Cleveland), 35
Hippodrome (New York), 157
Hitchcock, Raymond, 219
Hitchy-Koo (show), 219
Hoffman, Gertrude, 63
Hollander, Victor, 257
Holliday, Doc, 127, 128-29
Holmes, Taylor, 259
Holtz, Lou, 3, 173
"Honey Boy" (song), 84
Honeymoon Express, The (show), 199
Hope, Bob, 262

Hopkins, Arthur, 7
Hopper, De Wolfe, 226
Howard, Eugene, 93, 116, 192, 201, 202-3
Howard, Sam, 192
Howard, Willie, 93, 116, 192, 200-3, 267
Howland, Rose, 129-30
Howland Sisters (act), 129
Huggins (fiddler), 124
Hundred Loves, A (book), 67

"I'd Love to be a Monkey in the Zoo" (song), 183
"I Don't Care!" (song), 56
"I Don't Care What Happens to Me" (song), 79
"If You Don't Like My Peaches Why Do You Shake My Tree?" (song), 103
I'll Cry Tomorrow (book), 145
"I Love My Wife, but Oh You Kid!" (song), 142-43
Imhof, Conn and Corinne (act), 115
In Dahomey (show), 188
"In My Merry Oldsmobile" (song), 138
"International Rag" (song), 251
Iroquois Theatre (Chicago), 132-33
Irving, Sir Henry, 131, 181
Irwin, May, 53, 111, 138
Isman, Felix, 253-54
"It's Moving Day Way Down in Jungle Town" (song), 95
"I Wants My Black Baby Back" (song), 138

Jack in the Box (show), 130-31
Jacobi, Malvina, 229, 241
Jacobs, Henry, 43, 44
Janis, Elsie, 52, 53, 67-75, 263
Janis, Ma, *see* Bierbower, Elizabeth Cockerill
Jardin de Mabille (New York), 168
Jarnigan, Jerry, 80
Jazz Singer, The (movie), 194, 200
Jefferson Theatre (New York), 156
Jenkins, Mamie, 26

Jerome, Billy, 120
Jessel, George, 3, 4, 139, 140, 145, 173, 200
Johnson, Jack, 240
Johnson, Olsen and (act), 116
Jolson, Al (Asa), 146, 173, 192-200, 201, 203, 221, 267
Jolson, Harry (Hersh), 192, 194, 195-97
Jones, Walter, 60
Jordan, Jessie, 59
Joseph, Louis, *see* Frisco, Joe
"Just Break the News to Mother" (song), 92
"Just Tell Them That You Saw Me" (song), 110

Kahn, Otto H., 145
Kahn, Roger Wolfe, 145
Kalish, Sophie, *see* Tucker, Sophie
Kaszkewacz, Chandos, 66
Keaton, Buster, 3, 113-14, 117, 137, 141-42, 192
Keaton, Joe, 141-42
Keeler, Ruby, 199
Keith, B. F. (Benjamin Franklin), 34-36, 38-41, 43-45, 47-48
Keith, Mrs. Benjamin F., 39
Keith Circuit, 21, 25, 97, 174, 247, 265
Keith's Museum, 35-36, 38
Keith Theatre (Atlantic City, N.J.), 97
Kellerman, Annette, 40
Kelly, Gregory, 139
Kelly, Harry, 181
Kelly, Johnny, 182
Kelly, Patsy (Bridget Veronica), 115, 181-83
Kelly, Walter, 165
Kelly, Walter C., 226
Kennedy, Joseph, 266
Kerlin, Billy, 109, 110
Kerlin, Louise, 50, 109-11
Kessler, Manny, 231
"Kid Kabaret" (show), 139
"Kiss Me Again" (song), 50, 113
Klein, William, 199
Klondike Kate, 27, 29

Kohl and Castle, 32, 266
Koster and Bial, 230-31

Lackey, Al, 100
Ladies First (show), 83, 87
Lambs Club, 177, 210, 226
La Napierowska, 259-60
Lardner, Ring, 83
Lasky, Jesse, 248-49
Lauder, Harry, 71, 192
Laurie, Joe, Jr., 34
Laurie, Joe E., 164
Lawler, Charles, 169
Le Bourgeois Gentilhomme (show), 209
Lee, Frances, 242-43
Lee, Lila, 138
Leech, John, 65-66
Leonard, Eddie, 4, 196
Leslie, Amy, 105
Let George Do It (show), 217
Levant, Oscar, 177, 193
Levantine Brothers, 42
Levantine's Novelty Theatre (Albany, N.Y.), 43
Lincoln, Mary Todd, 124-25
Lipton, Sir Thomas, 146, 157
Littlefield, Emma, 115
Livingstone, Mary, 158
Loew, Marcus, 23-24, 264, 265
Loew's State Theatre (New York), 264-65
Loftus, Cissy, 70-71
Lorraine, Lillian, 84
Love for Love (show), 209
Lyles, Miller and (act), 189

McCullough, Paul, 116, 191, 203, 205-9
McDermott, Loretta, 174, 175
McGlynn, Frank, 172-173
McIntyre and Harty (act), 259
McIntyre and Heath (act), 136
McKelvey, Frank, 82
McKinley, William, 69-70
MacMullen, Charlotte Jean, 211
Mlle. Modiste (operetta), 113
Mag the Rag, 234

Majestic Theatre (Chicago), 32
Malone, Jimmy, 213, 215, 216, 217
"Mammy's Little Coal Black Rose" (song), 90
Maney, Richard (Dick), 177, 266-67
Manhattan Opera House (New York), 230
Mann, Lew, 182
Mansfield, Josie, 125
Marguerite (opera), 233
Marion, George, 237
Martha (opera), 113
Martin Beck Theatre (New York), 265
Marx, Edward, 168
Marx, Groucho, 139, 142-45
Marx, Harpo, 142-45
Marx Brothers (act), 142-45
Masterson, Bat, 127, 128-29
Mattson, Sture, 106-7
Mayhew, Stella, 111
Melba, Nellie, 113
Menken, Helen, 139
Meredith, William, 26
Metropolitan Opera (New York), 113, 242
Meyerfield, Morris, 31
Mikado, The (operetta), 38
Miller, Marilyn, 141
Miller, Col. Zach, 148, 152
Miller and Lyles (act), 189
Miss Civilization (play), 260
"M-i-s-s-i-s-s-i-p-p-i" (song), 50, 183
Mr. Bluebeard (show), 132
"Mr. Gallagher, Mr. Shean" (song), 135
Mr. Hamlet of Broadway (show), 134
Mitchell, Dan, 31
Montgomery, Dave, 116, 226
"Mooching Along" (song), 108
Moody, Tessie, 58
Moore, Victor, 115
Morando, Madeline, 132, 134-35
Morehouse, Ward, 73
Morgan, Helen, 172
Morgan, J. P., 225
Morgan, J. Pierpont, 63
Morrell, Ed., 28-29
Morton, James, 165

Moss and Frye (act), 189
"Muldoon's Picnic" (show), 130
Murdock, John, 266
Murray, Mae, 139
"Music Box Revue" (show), 209
"My Gal Sal" (song), 50, 110
"My Mammy!" (song), 192
"My Sweetheart's the Man in the Moon" (song), 169

Nation, Carry, 239
Nazimova, Alla, 60, 71
Nelson, Diamond and (act), 258
Nesbit, Evelyn, 243-45, 260
"Newsboy Quartette" (act), 138
Newsboys Lodging House (Chicago), 124, 125
"Nobody" (song), 187
"Nobody Loves a Fat Girl but How a Fat Girl Can Love!" (song), 92
Norworth, Jack, 64, 82, 83-85, 95, 111, 191-92

O'Callaghan, Brigid, *see* Friganza, Trixie
O'Connor, Donald, 3
Oh! What a Girl! (show), 181
Old Homestead, The (play), 20
Olsen and Johnson (act), 116
Olympia Garden (New York), 232-35
"One Meatball" (song), 154-55
"On the Banks of the Wabash Far Away" (song), 109-10
"On the Benches in the Park" (song), 169
Orchid, The (show), 134
Orpheum Circuit, 29, 31-32, 247, 265
Orpheum Theatre (Brooklyn), 25
Orpheum Theatre (Kansas City), 136
Orpheum Theatre (San Francisco), 31
"Over There" (song), 86

Palace Concert Hall (Denver), 129
Palace Theatre (Chicago), 255, 256, 257
Palace Theatre (New York), 49, 221, 243, 247, 248, 254, 256, 257, 258-64, 266

Nora Bayes at, 86, 89
Jack Benny at, 157
Fanny Brice at, 60
Vernon and Irene Castle at, 252
Frank Fay at, 176, 178, 182, 184-85
Eddie Foy at, 136
Joe Frisco at, 172, 173
Ruth Roye at, 109
Barbara Stanwyck at, 184
Julius Tannen at, 166
James Thornton at, 171
Sophie Tucker at, 97, 98, 101
Mae West at, 103, 104
Palmer, Bee, 105
Palmer, Joe, 197
Pantages Alexander, 25, 27-29
Pantages, Carmen, 29
Parado, Alan, 66
Parks, Larry, 200
Passing Show (show), 142
Pastor, Tony, 15-22, 36, 41, 77
Patterson, Ada, 54-55
Patterson, Nan, 239
Pearl, Jack, 139
Pearl of Pekin (show), 111
Pershing, Gen. John J., 74
Petrova, Olga, 60
Piff! Paff! Pouf! (show), 134
Poli, S. Z., 48-49
Porgy (show), 189
Powell, Eleanor, 139
Power, Tyrone, 122
Pretty Miss Smith (show), 114
Price, Little Georgie, 138-39
Primrose, George, 215, 216
Proctor, Frederick F., 41-44
"Prohibition Blues" (song), 83
Puss Puss (show), 208

"Ragtime Violin" (song), 156
Ramblers, The (show), 209
Rand, Sally, 139
Randall, Carl, 107
Rappe, Virginia, 29
Raymond, Maud, 237
Rector, George, 224, 251
Rector's Restaurant, 224, 226, 253
Redding, Francesca, 58

"Redhead" (song), 50, 78
Redway, Ed, 60
Reinhardt, Max, 240
Reisenweber's Cabaret, 98, 104-5, 174
"Remember Poor Mother at Home" (song), 168
Republic Theatre (New York), 237
Resurrection (drama), 237
Rial, Jay, 81
Richman, Harry, 88, 98-99, 102, 103, 104
Ringling Brothers, 207
Rivals, The (show), 209
"River, Stay Away From My Door" (song), 154
Robins, A., 161
Robinson, Bojangles Bill, 189
Rock, Billy (William), 183-84
Rodgers, Richard, 246
Rogers, Will, 116, 148-52, 156, 165, 188, 192
Rogers Brothers (act), 237
Roosevelt, Theodore, 233-34
Rose, Billy, 162
Rosenthal, Herman, 249
Rosenthal, Morris, 106
Roth, Ann, 145
Roth, Lillian, 145
Royal, John, 36, 97
Roye, Ruth, 50, 107-9
Rugel, Yvette, 51
Russell, Lillian, 18, 20, 136, 225, 253

Sales, Dooley and (act), 260
Salome (opera), 63-64
Sarnoff, David, 266
Savo, Jimmy, 1-2, 153-56
Scheff, Fritzi, 50, 51, 113-14
Scheff, Dr. Gottfried, 113
Schenck, Joe, 203-5
Schiller Vaudeville, 31
"School Days" (song), 138
Schwartz, Jean, 146
Scully, Frank, 194
Sefton, Lola, 130
Seven Little Foys, 132, 134, 135, 136-37. See also *specific actor*
Shapiro, Ted, 98

Shaw, George Bernard, 172
Shea, Mike, 70
Sheean, Vincent, 241
"She May Have Seen Better Days" (song), 169
"Shine On, Harvest Moon" (song), 82, 83, 84
Short, Luke, 127
Shubert Brothers, 243, 262
Shuffle Along (show), 189
"Sidewalks of New York, The" (song), 169
"Silent Sue," 241-42
Silverman, Sime, 103
Silvers, Phil, 139
Sinbad (show), 199
Singing Fool, The (movie), 200
Sissle and Blake (act), 189
"Sister Susie's Sewing Shirts for Soldiers" (song), 84
Smith, Alfred E., 89, 136, 226
"Somebody Ought to Put the Old Man Wise" (song), 79
Some of These Days (book), 94
"Some of These Days" (song), 50
"Sometime" (show), 104
Springer, Ben, 127
Stanwyck, Barbara, 184
Stevens, Ashton, 91
Stokes, Edward, 125
Stokes, W. E. D., 239
Stone, Fred, 15, 116, 219, 226
Strand Theatre (New York), 247
Strauss, Richard, 63
Sullivan, Big Tim, 26
Sullivan, John L., 138, 238
Sullivan-Considine Circuit, 26, 197
"Sunbonnet Sue" (song), 138
Swain, Carrie, 131
"Swanee" (song), 192
Sweet Adeline (show), 80

Tabor, "Silver Dollar," 129
"Take Me Out to the Ball Game" (song), 84
Tammany Hall (New York), 18, 213
Tanguay, Eva, 52, 54-59, 60-67, 95, 96, 102, 103

Tanguay, Dr. Gustave, 57, 58
Tanguay, Mrs. Gustave, 57, 58
Tannen, Julius, 163-66
"Tea for Two" (song), 179-80
Tellegen, Lou, 257
"Tell Me, Pretty Gipsy" (song), 86
"Tell Me, Pretty Maiden" (song), 224
Tetrazinni, Luisa, 242
Texas Patti (Frances Lee), 242-43
That Casey Girl (play), 135
"That Old Black Magic" (song), 154
Thaw, Evelyn Nesbit, 243-45, 260
Thaw, "Mad Harry" K., 243, 244-45
"There's Company in the Parlor, Girls, Come on Down" (song), 90
Thompson, Denman, 20
Thompson, Jim, 127, 129-30
Thompson, Millie, 129-30
Thornton, James, 166-72
Three Allen Sisters (act), 145
Three Cherry Sisters (act), 234
Three Keatons, The (act), 20, 113
Tiller Girls (act), 234
Timoney, Jim, 101
Tinney, Frank, 163-64
Tip Top (show), 219
To a Lonely Boy (book), 7
Tombes, Andrew, 191
Tony Pastor's Minstrels, 21
Tony Pastor's Theatre (New York), 18, 21, 167, 169, 221
Trail of the Lonesome Pine, The (book), 114
Tuck, Burt, 93, 94, 101
Tuck, Louis, 93, 99
Tucker, Sophie, 50, 53, 54, 90-101, 111, 174, 263

Union Square Theatre (New York), 21, 41, 46, 149
United Booking Offices (UBO), 32, 48

Valentine, Alan, 249
Van, Gus, 203-5
Vanderbilt, W. K., 63
Vanderbilt Cup, The (show), 70
Variety, 194, 261-62, 265

Vaudeville Managers Protective Association (VMPA), 45, 46-48, 254
Vera Violetta (show), 199
"Victoria Festival" (march), 237
Victoria Theatre (New York), 21, 22, 221, 235-45, 262
  Nora Bayes at, 221
  Vernon and Irene Castle at, 252
  Eddie Foy at, 122-23
  Gertrude Hoffman at, 63
  Al Jolson at, 198-99, 221
  Billy Rock at, 183
  Will Rogers at, 149-50
  Mae West at, 103
Violinsky, Solly, 161-62
Von Phul, Tony, 65

"Waiting for the Robert E. Lee" (song), 50, 108
Walker, George, 188
Walker, Jimmy, 226
Wallace, Frank, 102
Walters, Gustave, 31
Warner Brothers, 137, 194, 200
Waters, Ethel, 189
Watterson, Henry, 122
Weber and Fields (act), 15, 20, 40, 116, 226
"We Don't Serve Bread With One Meatball" (song), 154-55
Wesner, Ella, 18
West, "Battling Jack," 102
West, Mae, 23, 51, 101-5, 178
West, Matilda Doelger, 102
Western Vaudeville Managers Association (WMVA), 32
Westphal, Frank, 99-100
Wheeler, Bert, 139, 185-86
"When Frances Dances With Me" (song), 162
"When You Were Sweet Sixteen" (song), 169-70
"Which Switch is the Switch, Miss, for Ipswich" (song), 84
White, Frances (Frankie), 50, 51, 183-84
White, George, 214, 262
White, Stanford, 243, 245

White Rats (union), 45, 46-48

"Who Paid the Rent for Mrs. Rip Van Winkle while Rip Van Winkle Was Away?" (song), 97

"Why Do They All Take the Night Boat to Albany?" (song), 193

Wilder, Marshall, 163

Williams, Bert, 116, 186-90

Williams, Grace, 250

Williams, Hannah, 145

Williams, Herb, 158-60

Williams, Percy, 23, 24-25, 256, 257

Williams Sisters (act), 145

Wills, Nat, 260

Wilson, Gilbert, 75

Wilson, Marie, 224-25

Wilson, Woodrow, 53

Winchell, Walter, 140

Winter Garden Theatre (New York), 193, 194, 199, 217

Woolfus, Hilda, 158-60

Woollcott, Alexander, 73-74

Wynn, Ed, 104, 116, 146, 191, 262

Yeager, Anna, 113

"Yiddish Mama" (song), 99

Youmans, Vincent, 179

Young, Caesar, 239

Ziegfeld, Florenz, 59, 64-65, 67, 84, 95, 262, 263-64

Ziegfeld Follies, 116

Nora Bayes in, 82, 83, 84, 86

Dolly Sisters in, 146

W. C. Fields in, 153

Jack Norworth in, 83, 84

Will Rogers in, 152

Eva Tanguay in, 64-65

Sophie Tucker in, 95

Van and Schenck in, 204

Bert Williams in, 188

Ed Wynn in, 264

Zittel, C. F., 64, 66

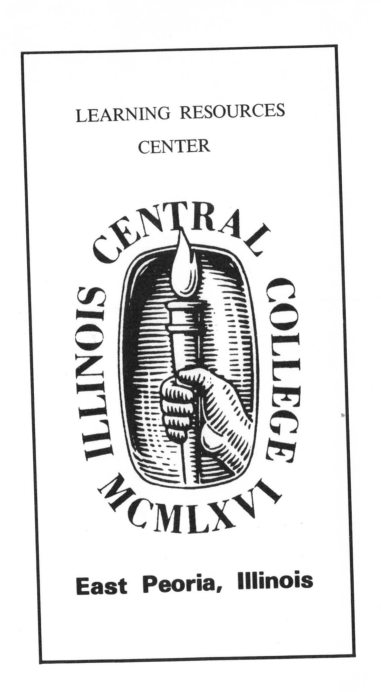

LEARNING RESOURCES
CENTER

ILLINOIS CENTRAL COLLEGE
MCMLXVI

East Peoria, Illinois

LEARNING RESOURCES

CENTER

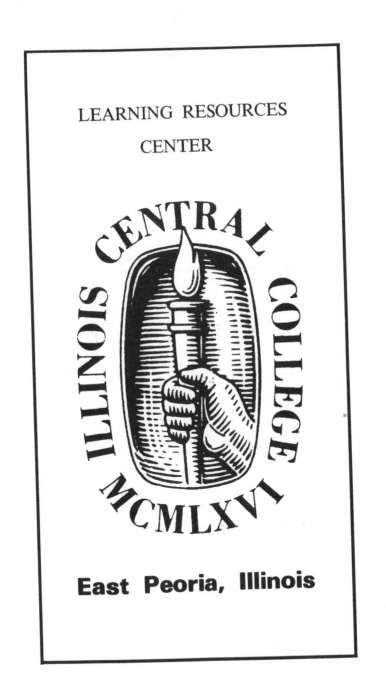

East Peoria, Illinois